TWEEN POP

CHILDREN'S MUSIC AND PUBLIC CULTURE

DUKE UNIVERSITY PRESS DURHAM AND LONDON 2020

© 2020 Duke University Press
All rights reserved
Designed by Aimee C. Harrison
Typeset in Portrait Text and Folio Std by
Westchester Publishing Services

Library of Congress Cataloging-in-Publication Data
Names: Bickford, Tyler, author.
Title: Tween pop : children's music and public culture / Tyler Bickford.
Description: Durham : Duke University Press, 2020. | Includes bibliographical references and index.
Identifiers: LCCN 2019043399 (print) | LCCN 2019043400 (ebook)
ISBN 9781478006855 (hardcover)
ISBN 9781478008194 (paperback)
ISBN 9781478009177 (ebook)
Subjects: LCSH: Preteens. | Music and teenagers. | Music and children. | Popular music—Social aspects. | Identity (Philosophical concept)
Classification: LCC ML3918.P67 T725 2020 (print) | LCC ML3918.P67 (ebook) | DDC 781.64083—dc23
LC record available at https://lccn.loc.gov/2019043399
LC ebook record available at https://lccn.loc.gov/2019043400

Cover art by Aimee C. Harrison

CONTENTS

Acknowledgments ☆ vii

Introduction. The Tween Moment ☼ 1
One. Singing Along ♥ 41
Two. Music Television ★ 56
Three. "Having It All" ☻ 87
Four. The Whiteness of Tween Innocence ✳ 106
Five. The Tween Prodigy at Home and Online ✎ 140
Conclusion. After the Tween Moment ♡ 167

Notes ☆ 187
References ☆ 197
Index ☆ 221

ACKNOWLEDGMENTS

I am able to spend time writing about children's popular music because my position at the University of Pittsburgh includes research leaves and a reduced teaching load, and Pitt can replace my teaching and the tuition it brings in with contingent faculty at inequitably low salaries. Undergraduate student tuition paid for the writing of this book, but other professors did most of the work that brought in those resources. Some people argue that this funding model is justified because research contributes to institutional reputation and rankings, which eventually translate into undergraduate admissions and tuition. This is, at best, astonishingly inefficient, and it is an indefensible way to structure a public institution with a mission to serve the public good. This book, therefore, is the product of a directly exploitative system that extracts value from students and poorly paid teaching-focused faculty and redistributes it upward to better-paid research-focused faculty. I don't quite know how to fit that into an "acknowledgments" section, but it is the single most important fact about the conditions that made the production of this work possible. I would like to hold myself accountable here for continuing to work toward a future in which the work of the professors who bring in the largest sources of unrestricted funds to the University of Pittsburgh is valued fairly. My colleagues on the Pitt Faculty Organizing Committee who are working to transform this institution into a humane, equitable, and democratic community have already transformed my experience of the university from a place of hierarchy and judgment to one of solidarity and mutual support. Without our brain and muscle not a single wheel can turn. Infinite thanks are also due to the organizing staff at the United Steelworkers, especially

Tamara Lefcowitz and Robin Sowards, for making that work so enjoyable and generative.

I have been working on this project in various forms since 2006, and I have accumulated very many debts over that time. Most importantly, this project would not have existed without the kids I cannot name at "Heartsboro Central School," who showed me how weird and interesting all this stuff was and who got me stuck on the question of what it is all about. Sherilyn Saporito, who is my dear partner and the best person I know, showed me the Kidz Bop video that started me on this path. Lorelai Saporito Bickford, who agrees with me about Carly Rae Jepsen and in general has really good taste in music (which happily overlaps very little with what's in this book), inspires me every day. Maria Sonevytsky, Farzaneh Hemmasi, and Lauren Ninoshvili have seen this work at almost every stage for nearly a decade. I can barely express how much I value and appreciate their camaraderie, generosity, and brilliance.

I started thinking about tween music as a graduate student (there is material in here from my comprehensive exams in 2006), and I am grateful to the faculty who supervised and encouraged parts of this project in its early stages, including Aaron Fox, Susan Boynton, Lila Ellen Gray, Ana María Ochoa Gautier, Christopher Washburne, Patricia Shehan Campbell, and Jackie Marsh. I owe even more to the community of supportive peers and friends who offered solidarity, encouragement, and especially practical and penetrating feedback, including Ryan Dohoney, Ryan Skinner, Anna Stirr, Toby King, Niko Higgins, Simon Calle, David Novak, and Amanda Minks. Jenny Woodruff's enthusiasm for thinking about kids and music has been a crucial source of encouragement and insight.

I finished this book at the University of Pittsburgh, where I am grateful to Courtney Weikle-Mills and Jules Gill-Peterson for their feedback and insights, and especially for their shared vision for a critical humanistic childhood studies and a more equitable and humane university. Courtney has been the most generous mentor and friend, reading much of this work in draft form and offering invaluable feedback, and she understands the intersection of childhood studies and public sphere theory like nobody else. Marah Gubar read early drafts and has been an engaging interlocutor and champion to whom I owe an enormous amount. Thanks to Neepa Majumdar and David Pettersen for inviting me to present a version of chapter 2 to the Pittsburgh Film Colloquium; Rachel Maley for teaching me about Caddie Woodlawn syndrome; Jessica Isaac for her insights about kids and the public sphere; Kathleen Davies for introducing me to that Rousseau quote;

Kathleen Murray for helping me figure out what was going on with Bieber digital animation stuff; Clare Withers and Robin Kear for making the library resources so accessible and useful; Gayle Rogers for timely advice and encouragement; and Caroline Lemak Brickman, Kerry Mockler, Ryan Pierson, Don Bialostosky, Mark Lynn Anderson, Adriana Helbig, Rachel Mundy, Brian Beaton, Shawna McDermott, Sreemoyee Dasgupta, Amanda Phillips Chapman, Jordan Hayes, Brittney Knotts, and Mary Gryctko. Kara Boutselis and Alexa Packard undertook a really useful study of *Billboard*'s Kids Albums chart as undergraduate research assistants in 2014. I worked through many of these arguments in undergraduate courses at NYU and Pitt, and I am grateful to the large number of students who responded to these questions enthusiastically and productively, especially Leah Butterfield at NYU, whose critical feedback on an article of mine inspired significant changes in my argument and approach.

Diane Pecknold and Sarah Dougher organized a generative panel on children, music, and the mainstream at the Society for American Music in 2011, and their feedback and conversations at an early stage of this project were vital. I am grateful to Diana Anselmo-Sequeira, who organized and invited me to participate in an incredible symposium on young people, material culture, and media history at Pitt in 2016, and to Meredith Bak, who offered very helpful feedback on an early version of chapter 4 at that symposium. The organizers and participants in a seminar on Childish Forms at the American Comparative Literature Association in 2015 created a community of like-minded scholars for a weekend, including Natalia Cecire, Jules Gill-Peterson, Maria Cecire, Nat Hurley, Mallory Cohn, Anna Mae Duane, Anne Fernald, Devorah Fischler, Samantha Pergadia, Hans Staats, and Marissa Brostoff. Natalia, especially, has been an indispensable interlocutor about the status of childishness in contemporary public culture. Amanda Rossie organized a wonderful panel about postfeminist girlhood at the Society for Cinema and Media Studies in 2013 that clarified and defined my thinking about *Hannah Montana*, and conversation there with Sarah Banet-Weiser helped me sort out how to think about Taylor Swift. Jordan McClain and Amanda McClain organized a really productive panel on the intersections of television and music at the Popular Culture Association in 2013, where Travis Stimeling offered helpful responses to an early version of chapter 5. Meryl Alper was a copanelist at an MIT Communications Forum event about tween media culture that Marah Gubar organized in 2016, and Alper's incisive comments and conversation helped me clarify my own thinking about the tween moment. Thanks also to Luis-Manuel

Garcia, Byron Dueck, Jonathan Toby King, and David Novak for their feedback and participation at panels on music and intimacy at Society for Ethnomusicology and American Anthropological Association conferences in 2016. Thanks to Jennifer Lynn Jones for pointing me to Kathleen Rowe's work on gender and comedy.

I am especially grateful to Torrie Dorell, Moira McCormick, David Pierce, Ted Green, and Regina Kelland for speaking with me about their experiences working in and writing about the children's music industry in the 1990s and early 2000s, which provided the basis for the historical account in chapter 2.

Nicola Dibben, Anna Mae Duane, Sarah Chinn, and Gary McPherson supported early versions of this work as editors. Thanks to Ken Wissoker, Mary Hoch, Olivia Polk, Stephanie Gomez Menzies, and Joshua Tranen at Duke University Press for guiding this work through a complicated process, and thanks to Reader 2 for their generous and generative reading of the manuscript. Thanks also to Toni Willis, Chris Dahlin, and Aimee Harrison at Duke for their work transforming the manuscript into the book you have before you, and to Rachel Lyon for creating the index.

All of this book's failures are my own.

This research was assisted by an ACLS Fellowship from the American Council of Learned Societies. Publication expenses were supported by the Richard D. and Mary Jane Edwards Endowed Publication Fund and the Kenneth P. Dietrich School of Arts and Sciences at the University of Pittsburgh. An early version of chapter 3 appeared as "Tween Intimacy and the Problem of Public Life in Children's Media: 'Having It All' on the Disney Channel's *Hannah Montana*," in *WSQ: Child* 43, no. 1/2 (Spring/Summer 2015), pp. 66–82. An early version of chapter 5 appeared as "Justin Bieber, YouTube, and New Media Celebrity: The Tween Prodigy at Home and Online," in *Musical Prodigies: Interpretations from Psychology, Education, Musicology, and Ethnomusicology*, edited by Gary E. McPherson, pp. 749–67 (Oxford University Press, 2016). Scattered material in the introduction, chapters 1 and 2, and the conclusion appeared in earlier form in "The New 'Tween' Music Industry: The Disney Channel, Kidz Bop, and an Emerging Childhood Counterpublic," in *Popular Music* 31, no. 3 (2012), pp. 417–36.

THE TWEEN MOMENT

INTRODUCTION

In September 2007 I started a yearlong research project about children and music at a small elementary and middle school in rural Vermont. That August, *High School Musical 2*—the massively popular and highly anticipated follow-up to the equally popular Disney Channel movie *High School Musical*—had just premiered on the Disney Channel to much media fanfare and excitement among the students. The timing of the end-of-summer release was almost cruel, as the film focused on the end of the school year and the beginning of summer vacation, just as kids were starting back up at school in the fall. Its first musical number has students rhythmically chanting "summer!" as the clock ticks down to the final bell of the last day of school, when they burst into song:

> What time is it?
> Summertime!
> It's our vacation.[1]

That the release coincided with the start of the school year meant that a lot of kids had *High School Musical* on their minds as they came back to school to spend every day side by side with their friends. A favorite playground game for first- and second-grade girls that September was to play "High School Musical"—which involved a lot of arguing about who got to play the main female character "Gabriella" (including devising a new twin sister role so they could share the character a bit) and a lot of singing of snippets of songs from the movie, but not much actual pretend play or role play as the characters. Some of the first and most intense activity around pop music in my research, then, was around songs written and performed for children.[2]

I started that project hoping to study the everyday experiences of popular music audiences. I had worked with kids in schools before, and I knew that pop music is an important part of the social life and values of schoolchildren. School seemed to be a natural place to uncover talk and action oriented around pop music and media. I expected to find a lot of energy devoted to fine-grained distinctions between popular music genres and formats: rock, hip-hop, country, Top 40. I did not anticipate that music for children would be one of the kids' basic categories of music, comparable to Top 40 or country, because I thought of "children's music" as something for preschool-aged children, in the tradition of Raffi and Barney. In fact "tween" pop—professionally produced recordings targeted to audiences straddling childhood and adolescence—was a central part of the cultural life of the elementary- and middle-school kids that I worked with in 2007 and 2008.

This book is my retrospective attempt to make sense of a cultural phenomenon that, like many parents, teachers, journalists, and even kids, I struggled to fully grapple with at the time. From 2001 to 2011, music for children was one of the rare financial bright spots in a music industry that was otherwise spiraling downward as its business models were made obsolete by changes in information technology. In a decade that I now think of as a "tween moment" in American public culture, a broad swath of the child audience was redefined as be*tween* childhood and adolescence in a precarious terminological balance that teetered between the pleasurable intimacies of children and the defiantly autonomous consumption of teenagers. In this tween moment, children were not just confirmed as the important audience for popular music and other media that they had long been, they were ascendant as a premier audience demographic, to be catered to with mainstream attention and deference.

Children's musical play and performance is a long-standing and well-documented part of children's cultural traditions and social relationships. But the genre of "children's music"—music produced by adults for children's consumption—has not historically been the ground for peer culture and social bonding among children. In North America music composed and performed for children has mostly focused on very young, preschool-aged children, with artists like Raffi, Pete Seeger, and Sharon, Lois, and Bram singing songs with simple arrangements, folk-song and nursery-rhyme structures, and topics conventionally associated with childhood (a lot of animal songs). Such music largely addresses its audience as children in the company of parents, rather than as kids in the company of friends. One widespread narrative among parents, journalists, and media professionals says that kids' tastes have been maturing at ever-younger ages, so eight-year-old elementary-school children who might once have been the audience for traditional children's music now demand the pop music targeted to teenagers. As music to listen to and discuss and then play pretend with friends on the playground, pop music's aspirational associations with adolescence position kids as sophisticated and relatively autonomous listeners and consumers, who relate to one another equally and reciprocally, rather than as dependent and subordinate junior members in their families.

Pop music, though long dismissed as infantile or undeveloped, was not for kids until recently. With its emphasis on romance and sexuality, nightlife, and youth-cultural rebellion, pop does not fit nicely with the vision of innocence, paternal authority, and domestic harmony that continues to structure American ideologies of childhood and the family. Certainly there are abundant examples of pop music marketed to kids prior to 2000s tween pop: children were enthusiastic audiences for the 1960s British invasion, 1970s bubblegum, 1980s glam, and 1990s boy bands. As early as the 1960s children were targeted as audiences through music-based television shows like *The Archies, The Sugar Bears, The Beatles, Josie and the Pussycats*, and later *Jem and the Holograms*, and marketers went so far as to stamp playable records into the cardboard on the back of breakfast cereal boxes (Cafarelli 2001; Sutton 2001). But music-focused toys and cartoon shows separate pop for kids from the rest of the music industry, subordinating it to merchandisable consumer products rather than standing on its own as music. Music-first pop acts like the Osmonds, the Jackson Five, Tiffany, New Kids on the Block, Britney Spears, and many others were certainly happy to include children in their audiences, even making significant efforts to court child listeners (Leeds 2001). Especially during the late 1990s, teen pop acts, including Britney Spears, Christina Aguilera, and boy bands NSYNC and the Backstreet Boys, targeted child audiences and were promoted heavily on children's media. The Disney Channel and Radio Disney, Nickelodeon, and Fox Kids aired concerts, appearances, and music videos daily. Still "teen pop" (like earlier "teen idols") was just that, primarily targeted to and conceptualized around the postwar idea of "teenagers" that remained the dominant lens for understanding young audiences of pop music, despite the actual children included in the audiences for those acts. If anything the construction of teen pop in terms of age categories would ultimately serve to highlight the mismatch between teen pop and child audiences, and eventually cause a breakup between those acts and the children's media networks (Kelland 2001). Over the later decades of the twentieth century, mainstream pop continually assimilated music from subcultures and countercultures with its incorporation of R&B, hip-hop, disco, country, and Latin music, each format valued by the music industry because of its well-defined demographic targets (Weisbard 2014). But it was not until the 2000s that music for child audiences was conceptualized as a pop music format like these others, rather than being mobilized simply as a marketing tool for consumer product sales.

In 2007 adults like me were caught by surprise by the huge popularity and visibility of music for children. In the early 2000s, immediately after the late 1990s peak of teen pop, the children's media industry had begun to openly and enthusiastically restructure itself around producing pop music for kids. In 2001 *Kidz Bop* was released, featuring Top 40 hits rerecorded karaoke-style to include choruses of exuberant children singing along with the hooks, and in 2002 the Disney Channel star Hilary Duff released the first of a series of successful pop albums targeted not to Top 40 radio's teen and young adult audience but to the child audiences already invested in her television show. With the rest of the music industry in freefall, kids' pop grew and grew. In 2005 *Kidz Bop 7* and *Kidz Bop 8* both reached the top ten on *Billboard*'s weekly sales charts and were quickly certified gold. In March 2006 three children's albums—*Kidz Bop 9*, the *High School Musical* soundtrack, and the soundtrack for the movie *Curious George*—held the top three spots on the weekly *Billboard* charts, and the *High School Musical* soundtrack would go on to become the top-selling album of the year (Jenison 2007). In 2007 the Disney Channel sitcom *Hannah Montana* spun off a wildly successful soundtrack and concert tour. It and the *High School Musical 2* soundtrack both held spots in the top ten annual sales charts (*Billboard* 2007). That same year sixteen-year-old country singer-songwriter Taylor Swift released her first album, and in 2009 fourteen-year-old Justin Bieber would rise to fame through YouTube and social media. Eventually a process that had begun as the narrow targeting of children as a previously underserved audience for pop music expanded enough to encroach upon and cross over into the "mainstream" of pop music.

A key term in this development was "tween," a demographic label that became widespread in the 1990s to consolidate an awkward but profitable marketing category of nine- to twelve-year-old kids (though marketers often expanded this range from as low as four to as high as fifteen years old) who might otherwise be called preadolescents (Coulter 2014). Tweens were seen as children, especially girls, who were aging out of children's consumer products but not yet ready to be marketed to as teenagers. Daniel

Cook and Susan Kaiser (2004) argue that the most characteristic trait of the tween consumer industry is ambiguity, in its adoption of multiple and apparently contradictory markers of age and status (both child and teen), so that tween products are simultaneously anticipatory and constraining. While the tween category began as a further segmentation of the children's market into ever more finely graded age categories, it expanded to become a hegemonic frame of the children's culture industries. This expansion makes sense if the tween problematic involves being fully involved in two worlds rather than excluded from either: expanding outward to encompass both childhood and adolescence provides a sort of "both/and" abundance rather than an "either/or" choice, which nonetheless awkwardly asserts that apparent contradictions are not contradictory. This played out visibly in the music industry, as pop music forms associated with teenagers and youth culture were packaged in bright colors and set to childhood themes, in order to address an audience that straddled childhood and adolescence, and whose members ranged from children starting elementary school to young teenagers starting high school.

In the 2000s children's media, with music at its commercial and cultural forefront, grappled loudly and explicitly with the problem of children's relationship to mainstream public culture. The argument of this book is that the culture industries in this period struggled, and eventually succeeded, at converting childhood into a cultural identity "like" race and gender as they are addressed by the consumer industries—which is to say flattened into equivalence and interchangeability as one demographic category among many. This involved the culmination of a generations-long process of reconceptualizing childhood to make it legible as such a demographic category while preserving, and even intensifying, traits identified as authentically childish or essential to the definition of childhood. But like other categories of identity, and in some ways perhaps more intensively for childhood, those authentic or essential traits that mark it off as an intelligible and bounded identity also are in profound tension with the idea of participation in public culture. That is, among the traits that define childhood as an authentic or essential identity that allows individuals to claim membership in a dispersed and distributed group, the definitive ones are dependence, domesticity, and privacy—qualities explicitly opposed to public participation. This form of "identity"—the identity of, for example, "identity politics"—is necessarily public: identities in this sense are "imagined communities," an experience of relationships among strangers produced through the circulation of texts and media (B. Anderson 1983; M. Warner

2002). Therefore the problem that children's media worked through during the 2000s was that to claim childhood as a public consumer identification would require either sacrificing those qualities that make childhood culturally recognizable or finding a way to deny this contradiction even as they promoted it.

The tween music industry addressed this challenge through a novel combination of music and childhood. Moving away from the paternalistic, emotionally evacuated, and didactic kitsch traditionally invoked by "children's music," it invested instead in the heightened emotion and peculiar intimacies to which music and childhood, in different but interestingly parallel ways, both provide access. Music is a medium and childhood is a social status, but both reflect profoundly ideological and intensely felt investments in cultural value, emotional authenticity, and, especially, relational intimacies. While on the one hand pop music's emphasis on romance, nightlife, and affective interiority pushes against ideologies of childhood innocence, those same traits position popular music in terms of intensely felt emotional intimacy and the public display of private feeling, qualities in which childhood, too, is deeply invested. By turning to pop music as the leading edge of this millennial effort to assimilate childhood fully into public consumer culture, the children's media industries did not so much resolve a tension between pop music and childhood as they uncovered their underlying complementarity as cultural symbols. Yoking popular music to consumer childhood amplified their shared investments in intimacy and sentiment and provided a logic for conceiving of childhood as simultaneously an intimate and a public status.

CHILDREN AND COMMERCE IN THE LONG TWENTIETH CENTURY

Tween music developed out of a long history of cultural anxiety about the status of children in public. The history of children in the United States over the course of the twentieth century is a dual narrative of, on the one hand, increasing exclusion from traditional public spaces and confinement within adult-governed shelters and, on the other hand, increasing recognition by media and consumer industries. Their bodies forced further and further out of actual public spaces, children are then asked to sublimate themselves and emerge in an attenuated form as participants in public consumer culture.

In the late nineteenth century, during a period of industrialization and urbanization, children emerged as an important class of wage laborers. As

Viviana Zelizer documents, children's status as economically productive workers peaked in 1910 when nearly two million children aged ten to fifteen, at least one child out of every six, were employed outside of their homes—a number that does not count younger children or children doing productive unwaged labor within their homes (1985: 56). While the numbers of child workers increased dramatically from 1860 to 1910, changes wrought by urbanization and industrialization only formalized and monetized children's long-standing productive contributions to household economics that were informal but no less widespread in pre-industrial agricultural and rural communities. As quickly as the employment of children increased, it later dropped dramatically, and by 1930 with the expansion of compulsory schooling and growing support for child labor restrictions fewer than 700,000 children ten to fifteen were employed, a number that continued to decline. Zelizer's history traces the sentimentalization of childhood in American culture through the intense cultural politics that played out in debates over child labor. Middle-class progressive reformers advocated against poor and immigrant domestic formations by marshaling a moralistic and sentimentalized vision of childhood innocence and selfless parental love threatened by the intrusion of economic self-interest into familial relations. Opponents of reformers deployed equally sentimental accounts of selfless children lovingly contributing to their family's material needs while developing habits of hard work and responsibility. The former vision ultimately won out over the latter, and the idea of children working for wages outside the home has become nearly unthinkable for American adults.

If children were excluded from economic participation in the form of wage labor in the first half of the twentieth century, in the second half of the twentieth century they would be reintegrated into the economy as consumers. The postwar expansion of American consumer culture substantially involved children. The earliest attempts at producing consumer products specifically for children were targeted to mothers, but marketers slowly developed habits of what Cook (2004) calls "pediocularity," in which they tried to see through children's eyes to most successfully market products to them. In the 1950s and 1960s, while the children's media and consumer industries were emerging, "teenagers" were cultivated as a highly visible cultural identity and an independent market demographic, and youth culture, especially rock 'n' roll and pop music, became the focus of the media and consumer industries (Hine 1999; Wartella and Mazzarella 1990). Children were an important and controversial audience in the early period of television's mass expansion (Spigel 1993), but it would not be until the 1970s and 1980s that the establishment of public broadcasting and cable television would create the separate channels for the development of programs like *Sesame Street* and cable networks like Nickelodeon that would provide the basis for a mass children's media industry.

During the same period the ascendant cultural politics of anti-1960s backlash and reactionary white conservatism led to the institutionalization of "family values" discourses. Along with the popularization of psychoanalytic "inner child" discourses and highly publicized debates about child sexual abuse (Beck 2015; Ivy 1995), the cultural politics of this period foregrounded childhood and the family as the site of moral panic and political urgency. As children were increasingly addressed by media and consumer industries created especially for them, they were also increasingly sheltered and worried about by adults who saw threats to children everywhere (Fass 2012). By the end of the twentieth century children were confined to child-focused "islands" of playgrounds, schools, and homes (Gillis 2008). The growing children's consumer industries reinforced this islanding with an intensified emphasis on toys and media that would take place inside the home and that focused on playful and pleasurable activities. Henry Jenkins (1998) has argued that the exclusion of children from public spaces is directly tied to the expansion of children's media products like video games, which provide at least a metaphorical "freedom of movement" within the sheltered family home.[3]

The history of children's exclusion from labor went hand in hand with the exclusion of women from work and mid-century developments like the concept of the "family wage," designed to allow male heads of household to support wives doing unwaged domestic work including caring for children either attending school or innocently playing in the enclosure of their suburban home—a distinctly class- and race-based fantasy of the nuclear family as the foundational social institution. The postwar period saw perhaps the only mass effort in history to implement the vision of sheltered childhood laid out by Jean-Jacques Rousseau in 1762: "It is you that I address myself, tender and foresighted mother, who are capable of keeping the nascent shrub away from the highway and securing it from the impact of human opinions! Cultivate and water the young plant before it dies. Its fruits will one day be your delights. Form an enclosure around your child's soul at an early date. Someone else can draw its circumference, but you alone must build the fence" ([1762] 1979: 37–38). Women—confined to domesticity and then responsible for confining their children—were most strongly affected by the twin ideologies of domesticity and consumerism, as consumption became an increasingly important part of the work of social reproduction (Friedan 1963; Willis [1970] 2014).[4] But as women returned to wage labor in large numbers in the later twentieth century—even as they maintained their responsibilities for unpaid domestic labor (Hochschild and Machung [1989] 2003)—children were the only figures left to stand for the ideology of unproductive, domestic, familial sentiment. As sociologist Allison Pugh puts it, "As mothers' work lives look more and more like fathers', who but the child is left to sacralize as the vessel of all that is dear about domesticity?" (2009: 20).

Just as wage labor was seen to intrude into loving family relationships, media and consumer culture also have long been seen as threatening to the autonomy of the family. If early television brought families together to watch, it also brought information and authority figures from outside the home that could potentially undermine parents (Spigel 1992). Since the 1970s groups like Action for Children's Television (K. Montgomery 2007a) and the Campaign for Commercial Free Childhood have advocated against commercial children's media on the grounds that children are especially susceptible to manipulation and misinformation by advertisements that seek to bypass parental oversight. Pugh's (2009) research in the 2000s suggests that consumer culture binds children most strongly to their peer communities outside the home, as key sources both of social "dignity" in school and friendship contexts and of parental concern and anxiety. Childhood consumerism began as a mid-century rearticulation of childhood to the family and domesticity, and (predictably) wound up as a connection of children to other children and communities beyond the home.

So the long trajectory of children's relationship to the economy from the late 1800s to the early 2000s begins with mass participation in wage labor outside the home, passes through the mid-century nuclear family, and ends with mass participation in consumer culture both inside and outside the home. The tension here, which is a key tension in this book, is that the intensive ideological and historical process of enclosing children fully and pervasively within the home and under the control of their parents made possible the development of a media culture for children that envisions them as participants in a public arena that transcends their local particularity.

THE INFANTILIZATION OF PUBLIC CULTURE

Against this background of children's changing relationship to their families, communities, and the economy, two related discourses emerged to explain and periodize the cultural status of children and childhood at the turn of the century. In the first, anxious narratives of the decline of adulthood and celebrations of grown-ups' "rejuvenilization" (Noxon 2006) urgently diagnosed the infantilization of American culture in recent history. In the second, the rapid expansion of the children's media and entertainment industries over the same period was characterized by anxiety that childhood was disappearing as "kids are getting older younger." That children might be getting more mature even while adults are increasingly infantile suggests at least a surface contradiction between these two discourses. Neither narrative is satisfactory, and both are profoundly ideological, but together they point to a cultural politics of age as an important problem in contemporary culture. While this book is about children's media and child audiences, the thesis that adulthood—especially as it is enacted in entertainment and consumer culture—has been infantilized has significant bearing on my questions about the relationship of children to public culture. If public culture is said to have gone childish, what does that mean for children? I start here with an account of recent discourses about adult infantilization. In the next section I consider the emergence of the age category "tween" and its accompanying discourse about kids getting older younger, a phenomenon termed by marketers as "age compression."

Calling adults childish has a long and dubious history. As scholars including Courtney Weikle-Mills (2013) and Corinne Field (2014) have argued, age and maturity—specifically the capacity of women and people of color to achieve the normatively white and masculine standards of adulthood—were central to early American struggles over racial and gender equality.[5] One longstanding thread in the history of the politics of (im)maturity has emphasized entertainment and consumer culture as especially symptomatic of childishness. For example, Theodor Adorno's foundational critique of commoditized music defined the musical fetish as a "regression." Adorno argued, in a formulation that neatly distills the ideological links among discourses of primitivism, development, and disability, that popular music listeners "are not childlike, as might be expected on the basis of an interpretation of the new type of listener in terms of the introduction to musical life of groups previously unacquainted with music. But they are childish; their primitivism is not that of the undeveloped, but that of the forcibly retarded" ([1938] 1991: 46–47). Importantly, Adorno was not interested in childhood or adulthood as such. Instead those concepts provided him with a usefully loaded shorthand for expressing the value he placed on sophistication, reflection, and rationality. Adorno's target was capitalist culture, and calling adult listeners "childish" provided just one epithet among many to bolster his argument.

Infantilization critiques are not new, but starting with the publication of Neil Postman's *The Disappearance of Childhood* (1982) they began to consolidate as a recognizable genre of criticism concerned especially with age. Taken as a group, these publications outline a trend that highlights age as an especially salient contemporary category of analysis. Moreover they take the "contemporary" as their central topic; that is, the infantilization discourses I consider here are explicitly historical in their efforts to periodize the present through their diagnosis of changing cultures of age. For example, Postman argued that the rise of television disintegrated the boundary between childhood and adulthood that had previously developed through the history of print and literacy.[6] Print spread knowledge through the esoteric skill of reading that even if universalized required years of initiation and training. For Postman, print created the distinction between adulthood and childhood in its distinction between learners and initiates, and that distinction stands for him as the central pillar of modern, enlightenment civilization. Television's orality, accessible to all speakers of a language, eliminated that distinction and therefore threatened civilization as such. Despite his title, Postman was clear that he was much less concerned about the loss of an idyllic Rousseauian childhood, since by his account, before print *everyone* was in a condition of childhood. Instead Postman worried about the re-infantilization of adults by television. Postman followed this argument to its disagreeable conclusion, ending with a note of sympathy for the "family values" of Jerry Falwell's newly ascendant Moral Majority, which had recently emerged as a political force that mobilized religious conservatives and claimed credit for the Reagan Revolution.

In many ways this is a familiarly declensionist argument, but in foregrounding childhood and adulthood Postman inaugurated a genre of criticism that would speed up dramatically toward the turn of the century. In 1997 cultural theorist Lauren Berlant published *The Queen of America Goes to Washington City*. Berlant reads *The Simpsons* and other "silly objects" (1997: 12) from media and entertainment to put forward a "theory of infantile citizenship," which allows for "no vision of sustained individual or collective criticism and agency" (1997: 51). While Postman aligned himself with Falwell's Moral Majority, Berlant targeted the conservative movement and the Reagan presidency for redefining the public sphere as intimate and privatized, and therefore infantile, where the symbolic alignment of the citizen and fetus in anti-abortion rhetoric pointed to the evacuation of political agency and the construction of citizenship as passive and dependent. But while Berlant and Postman claimed different political allies and enemies, their periodizations and diagnoses were broadly parallel: by the late twentieth century the traditionally adult spheres of politics and culture had been infantilized, and for both critics media, entertainment, and consumer culture were key culprits, or at least symptoms.[7]

In the same year the *New Yorker* published an essay by Kurt Anderson titled "Kids Are Us" (1997), which noted a trend of adult women wearing backpacks and worried that "moral sensibilities become juvenilized as well," with the apparently troubling result that a regressive public motivated by "undiscriminating hyper-empathy" was erroneous in celebrating two women, Maya Angelou and Marianne Williamson, as a "great poet" and "philosopher," respectively. Poet Robert Bly's *The Sibling Society* (1997) followed up *Iron John* (1990), his lament for the loss of true manliness, with a lament for the loss of responsible adulthood.[8] And psychologist Frank Pittman's self-help manual *Grow Up!* (1999) exhorted adults to do just that.

In the following decade—at the height of the tween moment—versions of this argument were published again and again in academic books, political jeremiads, and pop culture journalism. University of Toronto semiotician Marcel Danesi published the curmudgeonly *Forever Young: The Teen-aging of Modern Culture* (2003), which argued that psychological theories about adolescent development had spread a pernicious cultural myth that inappropriately prizes youth and in doing so valorizes popular culture (with music coming in for special criticism) while actively undermining the authority of families. Danesi called for "eliminating adolescence" to restore the dignity and authority of the patriarchal family, ironically inverting radical feminist calls to abolish childhood as part of efforts to dismantle the patriarchal family altogether (Firestone 1970). Also in 2003, conservative columnist Robert Samuelson wrote a short piece on the theme in *Newsweek*, and in 2004 the conservative *Weekly Standard* published a long essay by Joseph Epstein diagnosing Americans' "longing for a perpetual adolescence, cut loose, free of responsibility, without the real pressures that life, that messy business, always exerts." In 2006 journalist Christopher Noxon inverted the critical thrust of this argument in his celebratory *Rejuvenile*, which nonetheless ended with a chapter cautioning against too much childishness.

Noted political theorist Benjamin Barber's *Con$umed: How Markets Corrupt Children, Infantilize Adults, and Swallow Citizens Whole* (2007) echoed Adorno with its thesis that infantilizing consumer culture "aims at inducing puerility in adults and preserving what is childish in children trying to grow up, even as children are 'empowered' to consume" (82). In its critique of consumer culture through the lens of age, Barber's jeremiad reiterated Postman's lament of the decline of civilization and Berlant's concerns about the diminution of political agency: "The citizen... is an adult, a public chooser empowered by social freedom to effect the environment of choice and the agendas by which choices are determined and portrayed; the infantilized consumer is the private chooser, whose power to participate in communities or effect changes is diminished and whose public judgment is attenuated. The infantilist ethos, then, does the necessary work of consumer capitalism, but at the expense of the civilization that productivist capitalism helped create" (36). Ironically, while Barber and Postman published these works at the height of their careers as respected and influential scholars and critics, their emphasis on adult sobriety versus consumerist puerility was belied by the sensational tone and packaging of books written for a crossover, and excitable, popular audience. While Postman grudgingly credited the Moral Majority's cultural insights, Barber nostalgically celebrated the moralistic self-denial of early capitalism's "Protestant ethic" (36) and puritanically bemoaned "the new consumer penchant for age without dignity, dress without formality, sex without reproduction, work without discipline, play without spontaneity, acquisition without purpose, certainty without doubt, life without responsibility, and narcissism into old age and unto death without a hint of wisdom or humility. In the epoch in which we now live, civilization is not an ideal or an aspiration, it is a video game" (7).

The late 2000s saw several more such publications.[9] Film critic A. O. Scott wrote a widely read essay in the Sunday *New York Times Magazine* titled "The Post-Man" (2014), mostly about the prior decade of television. The web version was headlined "The Death of Adulthood in American Culture," and the essay recapitulated much of Postman's thesis that adulthood is in decline. But Scott's version of this story is unique for its qualified celebration (rather than lament) of a trend that might dismantle the patriarchal prerogatives of men. Postman, Barber, and the rest were for the most part blithely indifferent to the glaringly obvious gender politics implied by their nostalgia for adult prerogatives and their valorization of children's dependence and active cultivation (by unspecified caregivers). Postman's grandiose comfort with reactionary family values politics and Barber's offhand dismissal of "sex without reproduction" positioned them much closer to right-wing culture warriors than their self-identification as liberals might suggest. Scott, by contrast, foregrounded the status of women and explicitly raised the obvious question that "maturity" might just be a fig leaf for masculine privilege.

Infantilization discourses, especially in their mistrust of consumerism as the opposite of politics, are impossible to disentangle from a parallel genre of "feminization" discourses (see, e.g., Douglas 1977; Gould 1999; Lenz 1985). With the complicated exception of Berlant (who has her own sympathies with but also misgivings about public femininity), infantilization laments almost always express masculinist anxiety about the expansion of the public sphere to include not just women but also working-class people and people of color. Framing this critique in terms of infantilization seems at times like a clever gambit to deflect criticism by rephrasing the same reactionary arguments with the depoliticized language of childhood rather than the highly politicized language of gender, race, or class—as with Postman's awkward attempt to separate out parenthood from patriarchy in his ponderous embrace of the Moral Majority. And the mass cultural objects of infantilization critics—popular television, popular novels, popular music—are historically aligned with women and other nondominant groups (Huyssen 1986). Feminist critics have long argued that because consumerism is coded feminine, critiques of consumerism tend to be implicitly or overtly sexist (Willis [1970] 2014). Insofar as women are also infantilized by a sexist and patriarchal culture, the rejection of consumer culture as childish and immature again lands on women. Thus the most straightforward explanation for the proliferation of infantilization discourses at the turn of the century is that they are just one more in a litany of wealthy white male complaints about identity politics veiled as high-minded concern about the erosion of civil society.[10]

Just as these familiar arguments against mass culture were being reworded using the terminology of childhood and adulthood, the children's media and consumer industries were growing dramatically, and child audiences were increasingly targeted by marketers. Thus, the increasingly widespread claim that consumer culture is childish grew almost perfectly in parallel with the consumer industry for children. Just at the moment that Postman was claiming in the early 1980s that television's erosion of the distinction between children and adults would mean that a separate "children's television" could never be feasible, separate children's television and other mass media began to grow unstoppably, exploding in the late 1990s and peaking in the 2000s. The growth of that industry required defining children as a separate and distinct group from adults and other audiences and consumer demographics. The boundaries and definition of childhood would be intensified and distilled, but with the logic of identity politics and consumer demographics, rather than that of apprenticeship and initiation that Postman admires about print culture. That project required a new concept and a new term: "tween."

WHAT WAS THE TWEEN?

Just as cultural commentators fretted that adults were being infantilized by consumer culture, the discourse of tweens emerged to consolidate a seemingly opposite anxiety: that children were maturing too quickly. This phenomenon was termed "age compression" by marketers and described by the slogan "kids getting older younger," which was ubiquitous enough to circulate among marketing professionals by its acronym, "KGOY" (Brown and Washton 2003: 19; Schor 2004: 55–58). The children's consumer market had long been known for fine-grained subdivisions of age ranges that were seen to be "compressing" into one another as kids graduated earlier to the next range. As Betsy Frank of MTV Networks, which at the time had two cable channels, youth-oriented MTV and child-oriented Nickelodeon, told sociologist Juliet Schor: "If something works for MTV, it will also work for Nickelodeon" (2004: 20). And by extension, the logic of age compression suggests that if something worked on Nickelodeon, it would work on the preschool-oriented programming block (and later standalone channel) Nick Jr. By this view, the age gradations of children's content were continually inflating, such that younger children were presented with more and more mature material, whittling away at the "childishness" of childhood.

What the age-compression narrative misses is that children and children's cultural institutions were not simply being folded or dissolved into mainstream or mature cultural institutions. MTV did not put Nickelodeon out of business—they remained complementary. Instead, part of the logic of age compression entailed a contrary motion, extending childhood rather than abridging it. For example, the expansion of pop music for kids in the 2000s might have supported a "getting-older-young" narrative, since the audience for this music included young children who might otherwise have listened to more traditional children's music in the folk-revival or musical-theater style. If pop music is conventionally associated with teenagers and young adults, then Disney selling kids' pop songs from live-action TV soundtracks instead of musical-theater numbers from animated-film soundtracks can be understood as moving up the age-and-content ladder. On the other hand, we can also see the opposite effect, with kids who might be expected to prefer mainstream pop sticking with Disney acts for a few more years. For example, in 2007 the same kids who were excited about *Hannah Montana* might have instead been excited about the mainstream pop-rock singer Kelly Clarkson, and kids who were excited about Disney's *Cheetah Girls* might instead have been excited about the mainstream girl group the

Pussycat Dolls. What's more, Disney's three prominent mid-decade musical products, *High School Musical*, *Hannah Montana*, and the Jonas Brothers, were somewhat age-graded, so *High School Musical* trended younger and the Jonas Brothers trended older, but all three still overlapped significantly with each other and with other companies' products, like Kidz Bop.[11] This had the real effect, which I witnessed clearly during my research at the time, that fourteen- and fifteen-year-old girls entering high school might still count the Jonas Brothers as their favorite musical act, claiming affinity for musicians who were strongly associated with Disney, definitively a children's media brand, and whose music was just as avidly consumed by much younger kids. If at one time children could be seen to move consistently through age-graded musical tastes—from liking classical music and kiddie music to liking pop music generally to articulating preferences for specific genres of popular music—brands like Disney were now marketing some of the same music to children starting elementary school and others leaving middle school. David Buckingham and Julian Sefton-Green note a similar range of products within the Pokémon brand: "soft toys for the under-fives, TV cartoons for the four- to nine-year-olds, trading cards for the six- to ten-year-olds, computer games for the seven- to twelve-year-olds, and so on. . . . [T]hese overlaps and the connections that cut across the range of products available allow for 'aspirational' consumption, but also for a kind of 'regression'—by which it becomes almost permissible, for instance, for a seven-year-old to possess a Pokémon soft toy, or a twelve-year-old to watch a TV cartoon" (2003: 382). Similarly, in her research about Norwegian children's relationship to Disney's tween products, Ingvild Sørenssen argues that children value "age shifting"—the ability to "be both small and big at the same time" or to be "different ages in different places"—and they see Disney as a "childlike space" that provides access to the pleasures of childhood more than early entry into adolescence (2014: 230–31). Since they merge strictly defined age ranges somewhat, these examples still make sense as age compression. But the directionality is less clear, since the possibility of "regression" is as important as "getting older younger." The category "tween" does a lot of this work, pulling simultaneously downward and upward. Therefore, material marketed to tweens persistently crept outward from a preadolescent center, expanding in both directions to include younger children as well as teenagers.

More than anything, the narrative of age compression as a sociological phenomenon in which empirical changes in the child audience forced the media and consumer industries to react seems to have been the unshakable folk wisdom of the children's marketing industry beginning in the 1990s. My review of the children's media trade press from the 1990s and 2000s finds executives in unanimous agreement that age compression was an urgent and driving force in changing their business. But when I have interviewed music and media executives active in the 1990s they do not provide evidence beyond personal experience—many simply cite their own children. It is not clear that actual children's tastes changed during the rapid process of getting-older-younger that was supposedly catalyzed in the 1990s. For example, a survey and literature review of studies of children's musical tastes in the mid- to late 1980s found a majority of four-year-olds expressing interest in pop music in addition to children's music, and nine- and ten-year-olds' tastes were heavily dominated by pop and rock (Feilitzen and Roe 1990). And, of course, the audience for early 1960s British invasion acts like the Beatles included excited children as well as fawning teenagers. By the early 2000s market researchers Robert Brown and Ruth Washton began to caution marketers that they "run the risk of committing a major error if they miscalculate the maturity and over-emphasize the sophistication of the average middle-schooler" (2003: 19)—this a year before Juliet Schor published her warning about the MTV-ization of Nickelodeon (2004).[12] Perhaps the audience changed, but certainly the industry changed. What we can see overall is the children's consumer industries working hard to define and conceptualize the child audience as an audience. Audiences are not empirical formations in the world; they are ideological constructions that make dispersed and complex groups intelligible.

The "kids getting older younger" view assumes that the direction of influence is always downward, from older to younger. It also carries a suggestion that as children participate more and more in consumer practices, by necessity their activities will be more and more mature; if the public spaces of consumption are characteristically mature rather than childish, then child consumers naturally adapt to more mature content. But the converse argument is compelling: as children's entertainment gains a wider foothold, so do the characteristics and representatives of children's culture filter even more broadly into mainstream popular and consumer culture. It is not just children who adapt to a mature public sphere of consumption; the broader consumer world also adapts itself to the increasing presence of children. Nickelodeon is a case in point, where its presentation of childhood as intrinsically separate through tropes of camp, irony, and grossness had the effect of attracting adult audiences to the children's channel (Banet-Weiser 2007: 5), thus creating opportunities for crossing age boundaries even while defining the categories more distinctly (Hendershot 2004: 184). Another example might include the priority placed on "cuteness" in Japanese popular culture, which filters into the global imagination through brands like Pokémon, *Yu-Gi-Oh!*, and Hello Kitty that are marketed through video games, television shows, websites, toys, and trading cards (Allison 2006; Ito 2007; Lai 2005; Yano 2013). Buckingham and Sefton-Green propose that the global success of Pokémon was part of a trend positioning "children's culture in the forefront of developments in global capitalism" (2003: 396), especially through a (childish) emphasis on active engagement and social interaction. Similarly, we can extrapolate from Kathryn Montgomery's (2007b) history of US policy controversies around children and the internet that childishness is a characteristic feature of "new media": the "Web 2.0" innovations that pushed the internet towards increasing interactivity and connectivity originated in attempts by marketers to adapt digital media to what they explicitly saw as the cultural norms of childhood (the same heightened sociality, immersion, and interactivity that made Pokémon both so childish and so widely successful). Innovative early websites like Bolt.com specifically sought out young people online with interactive games, social networking, and instant messaging services, as well as viral marketing and cross-media brand promotions, which provided rich sources of sensitive marketing data and direct connections to kids' intimate social and personal lives. That configurations of the internet originally understood as characteristically youthful later expanded into ubiquitous adult use of social networking sites like Facebook further suggests that social practices that originate among children are increasingly central to the consumer culture of the new media environment.

This process played out in a unique way in the children's music industry. On the one hand, children increasingly consumed mainstream musical products, sometimes directly and sometimes repackaged by brands like Kidz Bop. On the other hand, children's artists themselves began to play an increasingly prominent role in popular culture. Not simply attracting adult audiences to their niche media, young artists worked to colonize mainstream radio and television forums without shedding key elements of their childish presence. Furthermore, as children's music gained commercial traction during a period of financial retrenchment for the rest of the music industry, long-standing business models from children's media—based on merchandising, product licensing, media mixes and integrated branding, and direct marketing—began to filter into the wider music industry. Thus the bidirectionality of influence is key to the constitution of children's popular music as a successful and growing field.

Disney music executives explicitly aspired to "launch some of its acts into the mainstream, adult audience and all" (Dodd 2007). Tween pop went out of its way not only to be recognizably in pop genres, but also to actively participate in the mainstream of popular music. Artists like Justin Bieber, the Jonas Brothers, Miley Cyrus, and Taylor Swift all had genre identifications beyond simply "tween" (R&B, rock, pop-country, and singer-songwriter country, respectively). Most of the tween music produced in the 2000s by these acts was not marked as childish in terms of musical style or genre. They foregrounded young voices, but otherwise the musical arrangements, production, and style fit neatly in conventional music genres. It was extramusical elements, like the primary-color packaging of Kidz Bop CDs or the depiction of artists in childish settings like schools or surrounded by child fans, that framed these products as being for children. This was one of the key factors distinguishing tween music from earlier children's music: it went out of its way to fit fully within the conventions of mainstream pop, and did as little as possible to clean up those conventions—so while song lyrics downplayed physical sex, they were still full of heterosexual romance, pop music's central subject (Frith and McRobbie 1978/79).

Tween pop was unlike other kids' media with significant adult appeal, like Pixar movies, *Sesame Street*, or even contemporary "kindie" music with its indie-rock sophistication and folk-revival authenticity. The tween acts' model was not the double address, pioneered by *Sesame Street*, of winking jokes for adults hidden within a childish surface, in which material that goes over kids' heads ultimately affirms adults' sophistication and confirms children's media's essential marginality. As A. O. Scott described the 2001 animated feature *Shrek*, "it won over adults (and a good many critics) by pandering to their curious need to feel smarter than the children sitting next to them, conquering the audience by dividing it" (2002: AR11). The tween model also did not seek out adults through nostalgia and sentimentality about "classic" childhood stories as a timeless cultural archive to which Disney's animated musical films aspire. Instead the tween acts made no concessions to adult taste. That is, they made concessions to the forms of mainstream pop music, but they doubled down precisely on those forms of popular music that were seen already as the most childish, feminized, and abject. If anything they fully subjected themselves to adult critiques of pop commercialization, the force of which is magnified by the further charge of infantilism and manipulation. Top 40 pop—itself long associated with youth but also especially with women audiences and performers—is already normatively subject to highly gendered critiques of its authenticity from grown-ups and from authenticity-oriented and generically masculinist genres like rock, hip-hop, and country (Coates 2003; Frith and McRobbie 1978/79; Weisbard 2014). The canonical charge that "she doesn't even write her own songs," which stands in as the metonym for a whole range of inauthenticities (Coates 2003: 66), applies with extra force to kid performers working within the corporate Disney "machine," in which, presumably, they are manipulated into making irresistible music that then manipulates their child audiences.

How is this different from the long history of preadolescent girls' participation as key audiences for pop music—especially the cultural figure of the "teenybopper," which Natalie Coulter identifies as "perhaps the closest precursor to the tween" (2014: 57)? The figure of the tween, and the media and consumer industries that organized around it, is not a radical break with that history, but rather a reinvestment in and transformation of it. My view is that the underlying social structures changed very little. Instead the tween moment was largely an effort to renarrate children's—especially girls'—existing participation in public media culture in ways that would better support corporate efforts to capitalize on it. In particular the tween moment sought to resolve or deflect conceptual challenges that inhered in earlier moments, and it sought to articulate the social role that was central to phenomena like Beatlemania, teenybop, bubblegum, and teen pop as a more stable consumer demographic that could better reward long-term capital investments.

A significant difference between "tween" and "teenybopper" is that teenybopper has associations upward, into full adolescence, while tween has associations that are largely downward, into childhood. Norma Coates notes that the term "teenybopper" was "originally bandied about in entertainment industry trade magazines as shorthand for the pre- and mid-teen adolescent cohort and 'their' music," and it would eventually be applied so broadly that "it doesn't matter whether the teenyboppers in question are 9 or 17" (2003: 68). Other scholars writing about teenyboppers and other instances of girls' leading participation in mass cultural phenomena similarly identify the core age groups as linking preadolescents with full teenagers. Barbara Ehrenreich, Elizabeth Hess, and Gloria Jacobs describe Beatlemania (the mass participation of girls in the enthusiastic reception of the Beatles upon their arrival in the States), as focused on "ten- to fourteen-year-old girls" (1986: 14). That overlaps well with "tween," but they locate Beatlemania entirely in the social and cultural context of 1960s "teenage girl culture"—focusing on a *Life* magazine profile of a seventeen-year-old girl named Jill Dinwiddie (1986: 19) and citing Pat Boone's 1958 book *'Twixt*

Twelve and Twenty, which locates the problem of adolescence centrally in heterosexual contact. Ilana Nash (2003) similarly writes about her own identification as a thirteen-year-old teenybopper in the 1970s, focusing on the compatibility of teenybop culture with second-wave feminist discourse and girls' politicized claims to sexual autonomy—linking teenyboppers not only to teenagers but also to adult women and feminist movements. The category "teenager" is dominant in such accounts, even if the chronological age of the people involved overlaps broadly with those included in the category "tween." That is, while the core group and its practices may have remained largely consistent, prior to the tween moment the discourse around pre-teen girls' musical participation largely centered around terms like "teenager," which, during the middle of the twentieth century, was a rapidly expanding social category that was capacious enough to sometimes include ten-year-olds. The tween moment involved an active effort on the part of media and consumer companies to re-segment their audiences by age: separating what were now called tweens out from the broader categories of teen/youth and rehousing them in spaces marked as childish, such as explicitly child-focused brands like Disney—and then attempting to expand outward again from this new center. Again, that is a more complicated story than growing-older-younger.

THE TWEEN AS CONSUMERIST, WHITE, AND FEMININE

Reframing child audiences in this way required fleshing out the figure of the tween with specific social and cultural markers, especially around gender and race. Like the discourse of infantilization, tween discourse frames the cultural problem it addresses as a problem of age categories, but upon interrogation it also reveals a deep and overriding concern with other identity markers, especially gender, consumption, and race. The tween category's age boundaries, which range widely across childhood and adolescence, are capacious and open-ended, while it is constructed much more rigidly in terms of consumerism, whiteness, and femininity.

A marketing category from its inception, the concept of tweens depends on the notion that consumerism is itself an essential or intrinsic aspect of childhood. But cultural constructions of childhood depend on an ideological opposition of innocence and sheltered domesticity against publicity and commerce, a privileged site as yet unalienated by capitalism (Stephens 1995; Zelizer 1985). The same innocence, naïveté, and credulousness that are supposed to make children unsuited for public roles like working for pay also mark children as particularly susceptible to the pleasures and intrusions of consumer culture. Cook and Kaiser note an "inextricable link between the age category of 'tween-ness' and the marketplace" (2004: 204), and Beryl Langer points out that perhaps the most notable feature of the children's culture industry is "the designation of childhood as a cultural space constituted by consumption" (2004: 260). These claims may be only the correlate of Barber's position that the activities and expectations of consumption are by definition juvenile. But the view of children as natural consumers is a paradoxical and challenging one that the category "tween" treats as settled and easy. That parents, educators, academics, and journalists increasingly used the term as an everyday descriptor of particular children demonstrates that marketers successfully invested their ambitious new subdivision of the consumer market with the authority of a developmental phase. Tween entertainment successes were commonly reported on as business news and described in the media as "marketing phenomena," but almost never simply reviewed by critics like other new music releases. News reports about acts like Hannah Montana / Miley Cyrus or *High School Musical* invariably included comments from "marketing" consultants who gush about Disney's marketing prowess (e.g., S. Armstrong 2009; Farmer 2007; Keveney 2007; Mason 2007; Quemener 2008). Such stories related astonishment at kids' enthusiasm for high-quality media products and suggest a sense of distrust of kids' discernment—a view that kids' commercial activities are necessarily manipulated by commercial interests, and that the whole thing is just commerce, without the possibility of rising to the level of authentic cultural production and participation. Child audiences, from this perspective, are not discerning audiences or connoisseurs with defined tastes; they are simply and definitively consumers.

Furthermore the central focus on age in defining tweens obscures important ways in which the category is racialized and gendered. To the extent that tween discourses emphasize age while backgrounding race and gender, such discourses participate in a wider contemporary ideology of postracial and postfeminist identity. A substantial body of scholarship argues convincingly that cultural efforts to disavow the politics of race and gender ultimately reproduce white supremacist and patriarchal social norms (Bonilla-Silva 2013; McRobbie 2009). In some ways the tween phenomenon has a more complicated relationship to race and ethnicity than to gender, because since at least the 1990s, children's media has been more proactive than adult media about multicultural representations and diverse casting. Angharad Valdivia (2008) notes that in the 2000s Disney Channel shows and films, including *That's So Raven*, *Johnny Tsunami*, *High School Musical*, and *The Cheetah Girls* included actors of color in central roles, even occasionally as leads, and ensemble casts were racially diverse (see also Blassingille 2014). This broke strongly with the established tradition at Disney, whose films had long not only foregrounded white characters but were actively racist in their depictions of nonwhite characters. Valdivia points out that Disney's increasing racial diversity at that time for the most part supported Disney's portrayals of consumerist affluence, with Disney identifying something "spectacular" in mixed-race portrayals to contrast "quotidian" whiteness (2008: 285). Many scholars argue that such efforts ultimately flatten social and cultural difference into a single parameter of consumer "choice" that reifies dominant racial hierarchies even as it appears to undermine them. Sarah Turner argues that despite the multiculturalism on its surface, "the channel's diversity is in fact representative of this new colorblind racism, presenting diversity in such a way as to reify the position and privilege of white culture and the white cast members" (2014: 239). Sarah Banet-Weiser (2007) similarly has argued that Nickelodeon's inclusion of actors and characters of color on its shows was part of a commodification of race and identity that homogenizes social difference and assimilates all racial identifications into an affluent, and presumptively white, cultural norm. By superficially acknowledging racial and ethnic diversity in casting, corporate media institutions implicitly claim to have accounted for social difference and in doing so free themselves to continue their ongoing efforts to target an affluent and culturally normative audience.

Commercial media's implicit claims to have taken race and racism into account through their diverse casting parallel an equivalent phenomenon in "postfeminist" media that, according to Angela McRobbie, "positively draws on and invokes feminism as that which can be taken into account, to suggest that equality is achieved" (2009: 12). In doing so, postfeminist claims to have taken feminism into account provide an ironic foundation for the retrenchment of traditional gender norms. Thus, the construction of tweens as girls is intimately tied up with their status as consumers and their racial coding as white. Children's media companies, with Disney at the forefront, narrated their own projects in the 1990s and 2000s as the pursuit of older and more sophisticated child audiences, largely discussed in terms of age and not gender. But ultimately those efforts were very successful at carving out and defining a new media niche for older *girls*, and by the late 2000s those companies were scrambling to attract boy audiences again (Barnes 2009). Similarly Cook and Kaiser note that early media discourse about tweens was often framed as addressing both boys and girls, though ultimately the primary focus of that discourse was on "the expression of public anxieties about female sexual behavior and mode of self-presentation" (2004: 204). So while the early marketing discourses about tweens were not explicitly gendered, and marketers plainly understood themselves as accounting for both boys and girls when using the term "tween," those same early discourses already revealed a preoccupation with girls and girlhood that would become much more visible by the peak of the tween media and consumer industries in the 2000s.

Childhood and femininity are deeply co-constructed and intersecting categories: women are infantilized and children are feminized (Oakley 1993); female youth and sexual innocence are prized while childhood innocence is eroticized (Kincaid 2004); and women are historically treated as legal and social minors subject to paternal power (Dillon 2004). Moreover, commercial pop music is simultaneously feminized and infantilized (Coates 2003). We can see the intersection of gender and age built into the very concept of "tween." This is because the border of childhood and adolescence represents a fraught and abrupt dividing line specifically constructed in terms of female sexuality and the body that does not apply to boys.[13] Catherine Driscoll argues that the tween girl is defined negatively, "as the gap between the formation of social identity, and thus gender identity, in early childhood and the crescendo of bodily and social change in early adolescence" (2005: 224). This is a long-standing fact in American culture: children's literature scholar Anne Scott MacLeod (1984) coined the phrase "Caddie Woodlawn syndrome" to describe the repeated narration in nineteenth-century children's books of a fraught transition from the free childishness of girlhood to the constrained seriousness and propriety of female adolescence, always framed in terms of preparation for marriage and household maintenance. In these narratives girlhood is not necessarily distinct from boyhood, and outdoor adventure, physical activity, and imaginative play are not seen as improper activities for girls. But upon reaching adolescence, characters like Caddie Woodlawn and *Little Women*'s Jo March are abruptly forced to leave their tomboyish ways behind and dedicate themselves to feminine propriety, in anticipation of marriage. Today the demand that girls begin to police their bodies and sexuality immediately upon puberty remains in force, even as—or because—they are subject to the sexualizing male gaze. Childhood in some ways shelters girls from sexual objectification—or at least, *as children* girls are objectified for their childish innocence rather than their reproductive bodies (Kincaid 1998), even as an objectifying adult gaze anticipates and prepares girls for the objectifying male gaze (Mulvey 1975). But with the end of childhood there is no longer even that bare ideological shelter from the whole apparatus of feminine propriety. The freedoms of childhood have to be relinquished precisely because they suggest a lack of vigilance about policing the body and sexuality.

Boys, on the other hand, are granted all sorts of middle ground. By contrast to the fraught boundaries maintained by "tween" anxiety about girls' maturation, the cultural logic of what Natalia Cecire calls "puerility" (2012a)—"literally not only childish, but boyish, for a particular notion of what a 'boy' is"—provides a masculine scaffold that allows for the easy coexistence of childishness and maturity. In Cecire's telling, puerility "makes everything into a game." An important addition to Cecire's account of puerility's *form*—"detailed, nitpicky, often rulebound, but always in the service of play"—is its conventional subject matter: the gross-out humor, bathroom jokes, and sexual innuendo that Brian Sutton-Smith terms "phantasmagoria" (1997) and Roderick McGillis calls "coprophilia" (2003). In my view, puerility accommodates masculine development precisely because it combines the finicky demand for rulebound precision and Freudian retentive control with exuberantly childish delight in jokes about bodily excretion. It is, by this definition, simultaneously mature and infantile.

Notably, gross-out humor, bathroom jokes, and sexual innuendo are also characteristic of masculine humor traditions associated with young adult and adult men, with audiences for film franchises like *The Hangover* dominated by young men. Because the gross-out humor of puerility is so concerned with genitals and bodily excretions, puerility ends up being something in which boys can embed their sexuality—and Nash points out that behaviors that get dismissed as boyish immaturity are commonly targeted forcefully at girls, frequently taking the form of "violent or humiliating acts of sexual aggression" (2003: 139). While girls are expected to be asexual children and then, all of a sudden, sexual but proper women, with any gray area being grounds for moral panic, boys get to work in the comfortable terrain of puerility for their whole lives. I would suggest that puerility provides an easy scaffold for boys, from childhood to adulthood, where they can build on what they already know. That means that there are fewer moments when boys or the adults around them find themselves worried about being "between" anything, which means that there is less utility in media and consumer products that address the particular situation of tweens.

As much as age, then, tween discourse implicates the body. Kathleen Rowe points out in her discussion of women and humor that "farting, belching, and nose-picking convey a similar failure—or refusal—to restrain the body. While boys and men can make controlled use of such 'uncontrollable' bodily functions to rebel against authority, such an avenue of revolt is generally not available to women" (2011: 64). Rowe goes on to quote Nancy Henley that if such bodily functions "should ever come into women's repertoire, it will carry great power, since it directly undermines the sacredness of women's bodies" (1977: 91). A. O. Scott argues that these forms of humor *have* come into women's repertoires, and he explicitly connects the question of women's humor to the infantilization thesis. Noting the rise of women comedians in television and film over the last decade, he writes, "The real issue, in any case, was never the ability of women to get a laugh but rather their right to be as honest as men. And also to be as rebellious, as obnoxious and as childish. Why should boys be the only ones with the right to revolt? . . . Just as the men passed through the stage of sincere rebellion to arrive at a stage of infantile refusal, so, too, have the women progressed by means of regression. After all, traditional adulthood was always the rawest deal for them" (2014: 41, 60). If this question is at the heart of infantilization discourses, it is also precisely the boundary that "tween" addresses. Female comedians finally beginning to be able to successfully market gross-out and physical comedy in the 2000s were navigating the same terrain of cultural anxiety about women's bodies and feminine propriety that, from the other direction, the tween media and consumer industries navigated. Men and boys alike, of course, never had any problem peddling physical comedy and gross-out humor, because their freedom in and ownership of their bodies is not in question.

If childishness allows for a certain freedom and rebellion long enjoyed by men and increasingly by women, and if freedom is something that is significantly lost in girls' transition from childhood to adolescence, is childhood a space of freedom for children? Or is it only a space of freedom by contrast with the confinements of feminine propriety? Put another way, infantilization discourses and tween discourses both put the same three terms in relation: childhood, femininity, and consumerism. And both discourses make specifically historical claims that the contemporary moment, the period following the 1980s, is characterized by a profound shift in that relationship between childhood, femininity, and consumerism. If our historical period is one in which childishness dominates politics, public culture, and the consumer industries, does that mean that in this era children have attained some new power, status, or freedom in politics, public culture, or consumption? I think the obvious answer is no. Following Daniel Cook (2007), I will not argue here in support of a thesis that children have been "empowered." But reflecting on the compatibility of children's entertainment and consumer culture with the thesis that childishness is uniquely salient in the contemporary moment can provide insights into important questions about the status of identity politics and the changing structures of the public sphere.

Importantly, race is central to all of these questions. Even this basic question of whether childishness offers opportunities for freedom is highly racialized, and ultimately constructs children, and specifically tweens, as white. These questions about girlhood, age, sexuality, and the body have distinctly different implications for girls of color, and Black girls in particular. Ruth Nicole Brown (2009) argues persuasively that discussions of girlhood in media, education, and scholarship exclude Black girls both in the people they focus on and in their underlying goals and values. Robin Bernstein (2011) has influentially argued that the cultural value of childhood innocence has long been constructed in support of white supremacy. Innocence is implicated in many contemporary forms of racial bias and inequity. Contemporary studies suggest that attributions of innocence, and even the status of childhood itself, are frequently denied to Black children. Black girls and boys are both much more likely to be viewed as older than their chronological age, and therefore evaluated by social authorities—police, teachers, and other adults—much more harshly than white peers. Phillip Goff and his colleagues demonstrate that a refusal to acknowledge Black boys as innocent is a distinct form of dehumanization that leads to their increased criminalization (Goff et al. 2014). Similarly, "age compression," the central term in the emergence of tween media, has very different implications for Black girls, as Monique Morris has argued:

> The assignment of more adult like characteristics to the expressions of young Black girls is a form of age compression. Along this truncated age continuum, Black girls are likened more to adults than to children and are treated as if they are willfully engaging in behaviors typically expected of Black women—sexual involvement, parenting or primary caregiving, workforce participation, and other adult behaviors and responsibilities. This compression is both a reflection of deeply entrenched biases that have stripped Black girls of their childhood freedoms and a function of an opportunity-starved social landscape that makes Black girlhood interchangeable with Black womanhood. (2016: 34)

Rebecca Epstein, Jamilia Blake, and Thalia González (2017) term this racialized form of age compression "adultification." Epstein, Blake, and González argue that the adultification of Black girls includes attributing increased culpability for their actions (and concomitantly harsher punishments) and also heightened sexualization—such that the handwringing about the tension between sexualization and childhood innocence that characterizes tween discourses is largely moot for Black girls. And while tween music appeared to amplify children's, and especially girls', voices in public culture, at the peak of the tween moment Black girls' voices were not visible, and the question of voice is itself a highly racialized one. Kyra Gaunt, for example, argues in an analysis of amateur YouTube performances (a genre that figured heavily in the development of tween pop) that Black girls' "bodies speak more powerfully than their voices" (2015: 252). It is important to be clear, then, that the tween category is constructed as white not only through explicit racial presentations, but also precisely through its intensive investments in gender, sexuality, the body, and the voice, which are always already-racialized categories. I explore these questions directly at various points in this book, especially in chapter 4, but it is important to state plainly that race is always a key factor in cultural constructions of childhood.

THE INTIMATE TWEEN PUBLIC

So what was the tween moment? The sustained efforts by major media corporations to articulate childhood as an identity formation structured through media and consumer culture aspired to produce what Berlant calls an "intimate public" (2008). An intimate public should be a contradiction in terms, as the public sphere canonically is defined and structured in opposition to the intimate spaces of, especially, the patriarchal conjugal family (see, e.g., Habermas [1962] 1989: 43–51). And if the public sphere is normatively mature—rational-critical, deliberative, political, worldly, independent—it should be presumptively out of reach to children qua children (Kulynych 2001). Berlant argues, instead, that "publics presume intimacy" (2008: vii) as they circulate claims of shared feeling and social belonging. The insight of the children's consumer industries in the 2000s was to recognize that childhood's status as a private, domestic position outside of politics was not a hindrance to the cultivation of children as a mass audience but rather the very foundation of that project.

Publics—bourgeois publics, counterpublics, intimate publics—are social phenomena produced through the reflexive circulation of media. A public is fundamentally "a relation among strangers" (M. Warner 2002: 74). Publics, therefore, are always a form of "imagined community," to use Benedict

Anderson's (1983) term for the social fictions of nationalism, the classic site of publicness. Insofar as they entail a claim of affinity or co-participation among strangers, publics imagine a community into being, conjuring familiarity where once there were strangers. Hence for Berlant, intimate publics assert the commonality of individual histories and experiences and by doing so speak those experiences into being:

> What makes a public sphere intimate is an expectation that the consumers of its particular stuff already share a worldview and emotional knowledge that they have derived from a broadly common historical experience. A certain circularity structures an intimate public, therefore: its consumer participants are perceived to be marked by a commonly lived history; its narratives and things are deemed expressive of that history while also shaping its conventions of belonging; and, expressing the sensational, embodied experience of living as a certain kind of being in the world, it promises also to provide a better experience of social belonging—partly through participation in the relevant commodity culture, and partly because of its revelations about how people can live. So if, from a theoretical standpoint, an intimate public is a space of mediation in which the personal is refracted through the general, what's salient for its consumers is that it is a place of recognition and reflection. In an intimate public sphere emotional contact, of a sort, is made. (2008: viii)

Public intimacy is furthermore the work of pop music, whose attachments, Simon Frith argues, are constituted through the "interplay between personal absorption into music and the sense that it is, nevertheless, something out there, something public" (1987: 139). Frith notes that pop's characteristic love songs entail a claim of shared affective experience, in which the exceptionality of intense emotions is figured as ordinary, common, and collective, but not boring or banal:

> Love songs are a way of giving emotional intensity to the sorts of intimate things we say to each other (and to ourselves) in words that are, in themselves, quite flat. It is a peculiarity of everyday language that our most fraught and revealing declarations of feeling have to use phrases—"I love/hate you," "Help me!," "I'm angry/scared"—which are boring and banal; and so our culture has a supply of a million pop songs, which say these things for us in numerous interesting and involving ways. These songs do not replace our conversations—pop singers do not do our courting for us—but they make our feelings seem richer and more convincing

than we can make them appear in our own words, even to ourselves. (1987: 141–42)

Thus pop music is already involved in producing public intimacies—the experience of publicness as a claim of shared affective experience, and in which the exceptionality of intense emotions is figured as ordinary, common, and collective.

The "identities" of identity politics take this public form: they are claims of affiliation, identification, and solidarity among strangers that are produced through the circulation of media, texts, and performances. On its own, face-to-face intimacy is contrary to publicness, which is built on stranger intimacy. Face-to-face relationships are insufficient for the construction of an "identity" in this sense, which requires a status that exceeds the local and the personal.[14] For childhood to achieve that status required, in effect, freeing it from its local particularity and its embedding in communities defined by kinship, friendship, and geography. Ironically, then, the increasing privatization of childhood over the course of the twentieth century in the United States, as children were ushered out of public spaces and into the shelter of the patriarchal conjugal family, was the necessary condition for the conception of childhood as a public identity. Children isolated from one another and confined to the interior of their homes, and therefore increasingly consuming media targeted to them in that state, can no longer understand themselves solely as members of families and neighborhoods but are asked to abstract themselves from those local identifications and newly conceive of themselves as members of a community of strangers who share the status of "child." The tween moment needed to be able to ask children to understand themselves in relation to the abstract category "children" in this way. A tween public creates a category to which children might affiliate that transcends the bounds of family, whereas "normally" children's affiliations of religion, community, class, and ethnicity would be authorized through their primary membership in a family. A tween public is a social formation to which a child may belong even though their parents do not.

Ironically, the construction of a public identity for children that transcends their families depends on portrayals of them as subordinate members of families. That is, abstracting childhood out from its particular instances into a collectively shared status required constructing a set of emotional histories and intimate experiences that are claimed to be normal, generic, and common. The generic affective and emotional attachments that are available to be narrated into the public status of childhood center on the patriarchal family, on private spaces like bedrooms, and on intimate dyadic friendships. And therefore the construction of childhood as a public identity mandated further investment in a vision of childhood as the opposite of public: private, domestic, dependent, immature, naïve, and innocent. In this way the tween category in the 2000s imagined childhood as a specifically intimate public, one composed of mutual recognition of shared particularity rather than one based on collective transcendence from particularity.

This attempt at constructing an intimate tween public was part of a sort of trial-and-error effort by the children's media industries over decades, in which music would ultimately play a central role. (Incidentally, this is why bubblegum pop and previous efforts at marketing music to kids were qualitatively different projects: they aspired to merely sell stuff to kids, not to radically reimagine childhood as mode of participation in public culture as part of that consumer marketing project.) The particular stakes of what it means to claim childhood as an intimate public are visible in the contrast between tween media in the 2000s, dominated by the Disney Channel, and tween media in the 1990s, dominated by Nickelodeon. Nickelodeon's approach was to address tweens as what Michael Warner (2002) terms a counterpublic: oppositional, independent, politicized, and anti-adult (see Banet-Weiser 2007). The markers of childishness that Nickelodeon leaned on were grossness and puerility, especially with its iconic green slime and accompanying images of delighted children and disgusted adults—foregrounding opposition to adults more than the shared experience of children. The channel used metaphors of literal politics, branding itself as "Nick Nation," deploying discourses of choice and agency, and hosting public spectacles like "Kids Pick the President." Nickelodeon's vision of counterpublic childhood worked to assimilate childhood to the terms of conventional publicness—rather than, say, figuring out how to redefine publicness according to the terms of childhood. But if childhood and politics are defined in part through opposition to one another, treating kids as all but political threatens to dilute what makes them kids. This is a problem similar to the one Warner poses when he points out that participation in public may necessarily be to "adapt . . . to the performatives of rational-critical discourse" (2002: 124) and thereby lose the distinctiveness that makes counterpublicness attractive and socially powerful in the first place. By involving itself in the existing structures of politics, counterpublicness is always at risk of resolving into regular old publicness.

Nickelodeon's efforts did not so much fail as they were superseded. In the 2000s, tween media was dominated by pop music, with its heightened emotion and emphasis on intimate romance, and by Disney, with its deep investments in the patriarchal family. This formation was much more amenable to a publicness that defined itself not by opposition to a dominant adult culture but through the intimacy of shared affective experience. By putting forward the distinctive view that children "already have something in common and are in need of a conversation that feels intimate, revelatory, and a relief even when it is mediated by commodities" (Berlant 2008: viii–ix), tween media in the 2000s made a claim about belonging that adapted existing models of intimate publicity to childhood. This is not to say that Nickelodeon in the 1990s, with its portrayals of children in terms of literal electoral politics, was "truly" political, while Disney's efforts were depoliticized and feminized. Nickelodeon's campaigns coincided with the peak of an era of political demobilization in the United States in which the child was a central figure of an atrophied and disengaged vision of citizenship (Berlant 1997). That Nickelodeon used politics as a metaphor in its marketing does not mean that it was in fact more political, and it certainly does not mean that it was more successful in its engagements in cultural politics than the modes of public intimacy—and their associations with femininity—that Disney would later put forward. In fact, as I describe in various ways throughout this book, Disney's later approach was almost certainly *more effective* at achieving young people's visible participation in public culture. Many scholars have argued compellingly that girls' media culture is distinctly political: for example, Ehrenreich and her coauthors describe girls' riotous appreciation for the Beatles as "the first and most dramatic uprising of *women's* sexual revolution" (1986: 11), and Nash argues that late 1970s teenybopper culture "gave us the means to participate in a feminist struggle" (2003: 150). My claims in this book are not so strong (I think the jury is still out, and I'm worried especially about how tween media invests in racial hierarchies), but I want to avoid the suggestion that the explosion of tween music in the 2000s reflected a movement away from politicizing childhood, when instead I argue that it sought to reconfigure the cultural politics of childhood.

CHILDREN AND IDENTITY POLITICS

This book, then, is a case study of identity in public and consumer culture. It seeks an understanding of the logic of identity in public life by tracing efforts by corporate and commercial actors to, in effect, add a "new" identity to the mix. By examining childhood specifically from this perspective, this book is also an effort to explore the limits of identity as an analytical, cultural, and historical category. The culture industries clearly see identity as a productive basis for the commercialization of culture and the expansion of consumption and economic relationships into more areas of life (Hochschild 2003; Zelizer 2009). Childhood, in some ways, tests the possibility that the logic of identity can be expanded indefinitely, or if it has some natural limits. That is because in the United States in particular childhood is conventionally defined in opposition to identity—especially insofar as "identity" in the relevant sense implies publicness and politics. Something similar might once have been true about gender as well, and efforts to understand gender as a large-scale social or class relationship rather than a personal, private relationship took generations and are ongoing. Much of that effort was explicitly political: the long task of asserting gender as relevant to politics in the first place involved reconceptualizing the sphere of politics to include personal and intimate relations while reconceiving gendered activities (social reproduction, emotional labor, sex) as public, productive, and political. In parallel the growing consumer industries defined women as a key consumer demographic, treating gender as an abstract national category rather than a particular status of individuals. The identifications that the culture industries appeal to as unique demographics are defined both by politics and by consumption: race and ethnicity, gender, class, and sexuality simultaneously mark out consumer demographics and categories of political conflict. But, as Berlant argues, even where women's culture is ambivalent or skeptical about politics it is "juxtapolitical," a formation that "thrives in *proximity* to the political, occasionally crossing over in political alliance, even more occasionally doing some politics, but most often not, acting as a critical chorus that sees the expression of emotional response and conceptual recalibration as achievement enough" (2008: x). The same is much harder to say for children's culture, which does not have such access to or convertibility into politics. Of course there are all sorts of politics of childhood, as children, reproduction, and the family are central sites of explicit political conflict around government policy and cultural politics. But those are politics of adults about children. There have been brief historical moments in which childhood or youth were identified as a basis for explicit political action, as in "youth liberation" movements of the 1970s (Youth Liberation of Ann Arbor 1972). But there has been no sustained identity politics of childhood. Conceptually, to understand childhood as a political category would entail no longer understanding it as *childhood*, since childhood in the United States has been defined as a status outside of politics (which is not the same as saying it is irrelevant to politics).

The tween moment, then, was an effort to establish childhood as a purely consumer demographic separate from politics.

Such a bright line between consumption and politics is likely too strong, and of course a long-standing body of scholarship addresses precisely the cultural politics of media and consumer culture. Another long-standing body of criticism sees identity politics as an evacuation of the sphere of "real" (that is, economic) political conflict and a move into the atrophied sphere of cultural politics. In this telling there is a tradeoff between a politics of culture and identity and a (presumptively more real or significant) politics of class and economics—a contrast between, in Nancy Fraser's (1998) terms, the politics of "recognition" and of "redistribution." Fraser notes that "identity politics tend to displace struggles for redistribution" (2000: 110), and she argues that that identity-based movements have had the unintended consequence of bolstering the global expansion of neoliberalism and the increasing economic inequality that comes with it (2009). A range of commentators have elaborated on that complaint (Frank 2004; Michaels 2006; Reed 2013a, 2013b). By contrast Judith Butler (1997), Ellen Willis (2006), and many others argue that what critics see as "merely cultural" values are in fact materially salient and socially powerful. As Willis puts it, "To argue that one's 'material interests' have only to do with economic class is to say that sexual satisfaction or frustration, bodily integrity and autonomy or the lack of same in the sexual and reproductive realm, the happiness or misery of our lives as lovers and spouses, parents and children are ethereal matters that have no impact on our physical being" (2006: 10).

I am not interested here in leveling a critique of identity politics. Instead my goal is to ask what identity politics are capable of. Certainly the development of tween media involved the simultaneous cultivation of a cultural identity and a market category, and there is no question of the compatibility of tween identity with capitalist accumulation. It is possible to read this book and conclude that identity politics is clearly pernicious precisely because it is so empty of real political content and so capaciously deferential to the logic of capitalism that it lets even childhood into its impoverished public spheres. But that perspective implies that a robust public sphere should not be open to childhood, and children should be confined to dependence, privacy, and domesticity. If we do not begin with the prior assumption that childhood or childishness should rightly be excluded from serious social participation, the same position can lead to the conclusion that consumer identity politics, unlike conventional politics, is a utopian formation of the public sphere that is radically inclusive enough to contain even children. From this perspective identity politics is the cultural and historical formation that makes possible children's claims to participation in public life, since conventional politics definitionally do not. For marketing consultant Paco Underhill, consumerist inclusion is literally democratizing: the expansion of the children's consumer industry is "just one more example of how capitalism brings about democratization—you no longer need to stay clear of the global marketplace just because you're three and a half feet tall, have no income to speak of, and are not permitted to cross the street without Mom. You're an economic force, now and in the future, and that's what counts" (2009: 152). But affirming a version of identity politics that is so capacious it can contain even apolitical, dependent childhood may be just as untenable, because it posits the sphere of public life as a space with no material or historical implications, a public sphere without politics. Conventional politics is defined by its exclusion of too many valuable forms of human subjectivity (including childhood); and while consumer politics may have the potential for radical inclusivity (clearly it is not fully inclusive), that is achieved only through the commodification of difference and the flattening of cultural life to consumption. If "the political" itself is an attenuated and impoverished space of sociality that constantly limits and circumscribes what realms of human life are open to negotiation or challenge, we can ask what sorts of group solidarity children might claim (or corporate media might claim for them) outside of "the political" that are still based on a politics of distribution (in the form of consumer expenditures) and of recognition (if within entertainment media rather than political discourse).

METHODOLOGICAL NOTE

Popular music was at the core of the tween project in the 2000s, but I consider television, film, advertisements, music videos, merchandise, album artwork, and other texts and objects to be critical to the composition of the tween music industry. Specifically, I argue in chapter 2 that the historical development of the tween music industry was inextricable from the Disney Corporation's broader strategic shift from film to television. Tween pop was centrally *about* music, but that does not mean music was its primary or only medium. It would not make sense to write about tween pop without television, especially, at the forefront.

I also focus in this book on texts and representations, and not on child audiences. My questions are about how the culture industries marshaled a particular logic of identity to reconceptualize children's relationship to entertainment and public culture. How child audiences received the texts that were offered to them is, of course, a fascinating and important topic. But understanding whether kids found the messages offered them persuasive or even legible is a separate project from accounting for the content of those messages themselves. It is also reasonable to imagine that the most receptive audience for the anxious portrayals of kids in public that I trace in these chapters are adults—the people who are inclined to be anxious about kids' consumption and public participation. A number of scholars are producing excellent work about young people's engagement with popular music, including tween pop, especially Sarah Baker (2001, 2003, 2004a, 2004b, 2008, 2013), Diane Pecknold and Sarah Dougher (Dougher 2016; Dougher and Pecknold 2018; Pecknold 2017), Ingvild Sørenssen (2014, 2016), and Rebekah Willet (2011).

My desire to understand how tween pop represented kids was motivated by my own experience talking at length with kids in 2007 and 2008 about popular music (Bickford 2017). From those conversations I learned that the kids I was working with were interested in tween pop for a range of reasons, but their emphasis was decidedly different from mine. For example in 2007 I asked a group of nine- and ten-year-olds (the heart of the "tween" demographic) to watch Kidz Bop's video for Kelly Clarkson's 2004 hit "Since U Been Gone," which I analyze closely in chapter 1. The kids focused on the video's animal drawings and costumes—its particularly "childish" elements. Mary repeatedly pointed out the animals that came onscreen, laughing early on at the drawing labeled "Tiger on guitar." After the video finished and I asked them to tell me about it, Heather said, "I liked it! I liked the tiger, the alligator, and the walrus," and Jesse said, "I liked all the mascots." My own analysis focuses heavily on cuts between a bedroom and stage, but none of the kids voluntarily noted this. I asked, "So first it starts out in her bedroom and then it goes to—?" Several students together said, "A stage," and Mary jumped in, "A stage with the ANIMALS!"

I tried to lead them to a conversation about singing in their bedrooms and fantasies about celebrity, which I assumed they would have a lot to say about, but only finally when I asked, "And do you think that's real?" did Dave comment, "I thought that it was just her imagination."

"What was she imagining?"

"That she was a big rock star in front of all the people."

Here Mary jumped in again, to say, "I thought it was cool how they had all the animals!"

Heather agreed, laughing, "Yeah! And they showed like the tiger dancing!"

So these fourth-graders' excitement about the Kidz Bop video centered much more on the canonically childish tropes of anthropomorphized animals—the animal costumes in the video are very similar to the sort of full-body costumes worn in children's entertainment like *Barney* and *Sesame Street* or at family theme parks, or, as Jesse noted, by sports mascots. They only acknowledged in response to direct questioning, and then without much interest, that the video was centered around images of a child realizing a fantasy of celebrity public performance, and they expressed no personal sympathy with such a fantasy. This book is mostly about those fantasies.

THE BOOK

The chapters that follow explore the boundaries and composition of the intimate childhood public that was the achievement of the tween moment. Chapter 1, "Singing Along," looks at Kidz Bop, one of the earliest and most successful tween music brands. It focuses on Kidz Bop's 2005 video for "Since U Been Gone," which staged a relationship between children's bedroom culture and fantasies of public performance. I trace a history of similar media portrayals of children in fantastic sites of public performance across advertising, television, and music, which culminated with tween music in the 2000s. I argue that at the core of the tween music industry's efforts to legitimate children's participation in pop music performance and consumption was an argument, put forward through the arrangements of adult and child voices in recordings as well as in fictional narratives and visual metaphors, that children's domesticity was complementary, rather than opposed, to their participation in public culture.

Chapter 2, "Music Television," follows the Disney Channel's turn to popular music programming as part of its rise to prominence within Disney's globally integrated children's media empire. Because Disney was such a central player in the development of tween pop music, understanding the particular corporate history that led to its investment in pop music in the 2000s sheds light on the relationships among music, gender, and childhood that structured the tween moment more broadly. This chapter shows how Disney and its competitors saw pop music as a key tool for attracting older children, whom they had identified as the most important demographic to pursue. Pop music's intimate and feminized address allowed Disney to hail children as independent and influential participants in mainstream culture while avoiding the oppositional, anti-adult approach of its competitors. While during the 1990s the tween category was broadly seen by marketers as older children, by the 2000s it had been firmly established as categorically composed of girls. Because Disney's turn to pop music involved adopting a gendered address, it was an important contributor to the feminization of tweens. Pop music, then, provided the foundation for Disney's address to child audiences as an intimate public.

Chapter 3, "'Having It All,'" examines the 2006–11 Disney Channel show *Hannah Montana*, starring Miley Cyrus, which narrated the life of a child pop star as the "situation" for a traditional family sitcom. By focusing on the tensions between its protagonist's public life and intimate relationships, *Hannah Montana* accounted for child celebrity as simply a youthful version of the classic postfeminist problem of "work-life balance," in the tradition of *Murphy Brown* or *Sex and the City*. While the show gently adopted a familiar model, the suggestion that somehow "work" and "life" might be in conflict for the show's affluent white child protagonist demanded a new understanding of the relationship of childhood to the family, the economy, and the public sphere. In this way *Hannah Montana* set up a vision of childhood through direct analogy to femininity, and in doing so staged a struggle to achieve intimacy and affective attachments in a world of public and private contradiction as the sentimental basis for childhood identification.

Chapter 4, "The Whiteness of Tween Innocence," explores the role of whiteness as a central marker of innocence and childishness in tween music, especially as its growing mainstream success exposed age as a cultural and social fault line in the mainstream music industry. It focuses on contrasting strategies taken by Miley Cyrus and Taylor Swift as their careers developed beyond tween music. Cyrus provocatively and controversially adopted Black musical styles as part of a clear effort to distance herself from her past as a child star, while Swift continually reinvested in cultural markers of whiteness in her efforts to claim innocence as an organizing theme in her work, and thus deflect commercial impulses toward sexualization. Race, in this case, worked in part as an avatar for age, making whiteness visible as a foundational value of tween music's investments in innocent femininity.

Chapter 5, "The Tween Prodigy at Home and Online," considers the 2011 concert film *Never Say Never*, which narrates Justin Bieber's rise to fame as an embrace of childhood rather than an escape from it. The film explicitly infantilizes its star, highlighting his immaturity, poor decision making, and dependence on paternalistic handlers who are shown to know his own interests better than he did. Bieber's musical talent is framed as childish and domestic, and early recordings of him performing in his family living room share screen time with shots of him onstage at sold-out auditoriums. This is linked, further, to a specific vision of his audience as similarly confined in their homes. At the climactic moment of his sold-out Madison Square Garden concert, home videos of Bieber performing are paired in a montage with YouTube videos of his fans singing along in their own living rooms and backyards, domesticating the public gathering of a child performer and his young audience as though it were just one more site of childish home performance. Thus, in Bieber's presentation as a child star, domesticity and immaturity are not constraints to be overcome, but instead they are precisely the highly visible traits that authenticate children's public performance and consumption.

The conclusion takes up my periodization of the "tween moment" as the decade from 2001 to 2011, to argue that starting in 2011 tween music entered a new phase. It returns to the peak years of 2008 and 2009 to affirm the tense cultural politics around tween music in this period, noting especially prominent expressions of tween artists' solidarity with one another and in opposition to adults. It then considers developments since 2011 that suggest that the "tween moment" may have ended, and that children's relationships to the media industries and public culture have stabilized. It looks at four examples of changes since 2011: Kidz Bop's shift away from its long-standing emphasis on amateur child voices; Disney's return to animated musical feature films with the success of *Frozen*; changes in the status of Black artists and Black musical forms in tween music; and the mainstreaming of tropes of childishness in broader adult popular music. While not a comprehensive account of recent tween music and media, these examples suggest that many of the considerations that motivated the tween music industry's particular investments during its period of emergence and expansion appear to have become less salient than they were during the "tween moment."

ONE

SINGING ALONG

The first major contribution to the tween music industry was Kidz Bop, which started in 2001 as a series of CDs released by the direct-marketing record label Razor & Tie.[1] Kidz Bop produced compilations of Top 40 hits, rerecorded with groups of children singing along to the choruses and hooks, occasionally interjecting *"yeah!"* and *"woooh!"* They were marketed as the "most popular and most recognized music product in the United States for kids aged 4–11" (Razor & Tie Media 2010). When, in 2005 and 2006, its albums cracked the top ten in the *Billboard* 200 album sales charts, Kidz Bop became a major market force in its own right. In 2015 *Billboard* ranked Kidz Bop fourth on its list of artists with the most top ten albums on the weekly sales chart, ahead of Bob Dylan, Madonna, George Strait, and Bruce Springsteen (Caulfield 2015), and their releases consistently top the Kids Albums charts (*Billboard* 2019b). Kidz Bop also set the stage for the explosion in 2006 and 2007 of tween acts, especially those from Disney, including *High School Musical*, *Hannah Montana*, and the Jonas Brothers.

Kidz Bop presented itself as filling a niche for children who were exposed to hit songs at school, on the radio, on television, or through the internet, but whose parents were uncomfortable purchasing music for their children that includes heightened language or sexuality. A suggestion of danger in popular culture helped Kidz Bop market its brand. One executive stated that Kidz Bop "allows kids to key into more cultural, popular things, but also have it be safe for them, and for parents to be comfortable that it's not as dangerous as everything that's on the radio" (McCarthy 2006). Kidz Bop described its target age group as "kids who have outgrown Elmo but are not quite ready for Eminem" (Pang 2006), citing the saccharine-sweet

Sesame Street Muppet and the rapper who figured prominently in 2000s-era moral panics about popular music's influence on children.

Rhetorics of "safety" were key to entertainment for tweens in the early 2000s, as the apparent contradiction between protected childhoods and public participation was central to the construction of kids as active and engaged consumers. Kidz Bop's intervention in making popular music "safe" involved surface-level packaging more than substantive changes to the content of songs.[2] The compilations avoided songs with overly explicit content, but that is a small category, since those songs already had limited Top 40 radio airplay. Only minor adjustments were made to sanitize the language of the songs they did include. Particular words—"hell," "retarded"—were changed, so in Ciara's 2004 R&B dance single "1, 2 Step," the line "So retarded, top charted, ever since the day I started" was rewritten nonsensically as "credit-carded, top charted . . ." for *Kidz Bop Volume 8* in 2005. But the sexually suggestive line that follows, "Strut my stuff and yes I flaunt it, goodies make the boys jump on it," was included in the Kidz Bop version unchanged (S. Harrison 2006).[3] If the songs were only minimally altered for an audience of children, the legitimacy of Top 40 music for child audiences was accomplished performatively, such that the addition of untrained children's voices to the recordings framed the link between kids and pop music as natural, a settled fact: "If there are already dozens of cute and untroubled kids doing it on the recording, who are we to argue?"

"SINCE U BEEN GONE"

In 2005 Razor & Tie released a DVD of music videos. The standout video on the collection, which was shared widely online at the time, was the music video for *Kidz Bop 8*'s version of "Since U Been Gone," Kelly Clarkson's Grammy-winning 2004 hit. Kidz Bop's video adaptation of the song centers on a girl in her bedroom singing into a hairbrush microphone. With her younger brother's assistance, she performs in front of a home-video camera, backed by a band of stuffed animals (figure 1.1).[4] A portable CD player on the bed plays what is presumably the original Kelly Clarkson track, with which the older sister, the star of the video, sings along. The presence of the CD player next to the sister situates Kelly Clarkson, not Kidz Bop, as the object of musical desire, confirming what is implicit in the recordings: that Kidz Bop inscribes at its center its own secondary relation to "original," "adult" music. As the song builds toward the chorus, the video cuts to drawings of the stuffed animal "band members" made by the

Figure 1.1 Bedroom performance. Still from video for "Since U Been Gone," from *Kidz Bop: The Videos* (Razor & Tie, 2005).

Figure 1.2 Fantasy nightclub. Still from video for "Since U Been Gone," from *Kidz Bop: The Videos* (Razor & Tie, 2005).

younger brother. The drawings animate, and at the chorus the video cuts to a (now-widescreen) fantasy of the sister onstage in a dimly lit nightclub performing for a crowd of children a few years younger than she. The band of stuffed animals are now life-size costumed performers backing up the singing sister. The audience of younger children assumes the role of the Kidz Bop chorus, and the sister fantastically breaks through from play performance to the "real" thing (figure 1.2).

The internet, and webcams or video-sharing websites such as YouTube (which had just been launched in February 2005), is a near-explicit presence here, where the change in aspect ratio articulates a switch from home to fantasy, and presumably from the mundane domesticity caught by the camera to the mediated world of the video's anticipated reception. The video's structure models the song structure, such that the bedroom and nightclub settings correlate with the song's verse and chorus, respectively. Insofar as the nightclub represents unattainable fantasy, the narrative structure of the video provides affective guidance for musical listening: the breakthrough from mundane domesticity into fantastic public performance is correlated with the musical breakthrough into the affective release of a hook.

Marketing literature from Razor & Tie claimed that the Kidz Bop brand was popular with boys as well as girls and also was "geographically diverse throughout the United States" (Razor & Tie Media 2010). By presenting only music from current Top 40 charts, Kidz Bop reproduced the generic naturalness of mainstream Top 40 "pop." As Amanda Minks demonstrates in her study of urban, northeastern fifth-graders (1999), the same Top 40 music provides a shared cultural arena through which an ethnically diverse group of children can claim a collective peer identity, though one that sets up white middle-class American tastes as the comfortable, if exclusive, center. Sarah Baker notes, further, that mainstream pop music specifically provides a "shared marker for pre-teen identity" within girls' peer groups (2013: 18).

The individual musical practices portrayed in the video subtly but clearly articulate gendered roles for popular music production and consumption. While the sister sings and dances for the camera, the brother takes responsibility for the stuffed animal band, animates the toys (like puppets) in the bedroom, and "manages" from backstage in the fantasy performance. Such a division conforms to Lucy Green's (1997) argument that children are taught early to express gendered musical roles along a continuum of uses of technology—where singing and embodied performance are associated with femininity while instrumental performance and digital music production mark musical masculinity. While the brother claims management and planning as his arena, onstage the sister's dancing and singing body is at stake.

The video portrays popular music as a collection of clearly delineated roles. Stuffed animals are cast and named with specific tasks in a conventionalized rock band. The brother/manager confidently sits backstage relishing his (unspecified) accomplishment. Audience members enthusiastically enact caricatured gestures of ecstatic listening: singing along, pumping their fists, and grimacing. The star singer, whose role is in some ways fluid with that of the committed fan in her bedroom, is at the center of this constellation of popular music roles, and she performs the most intricate and subtle repertoire of gestures, expressions, and stances that embody the gendered and sexualized performer's role: shaking her hips, dramatically tossing her hair, and emoting along with the lyrics' emotional meaning. These popular musical roles are reified into limited repertoires of practices, and by isolating these repertoires, the video seems to expose the performativity involved in embodying categories of audience, musician, or star. While gender roles are naturalized, age is represented as complex and contradictory. The video does not depict tween music consumers with age-specific markers of behavior or identity—as teenagers might once have been denoted with cigarettes or letterman jackets. Rather, the fantasy nightclub of the video mixes markers of childhood with adulthood, with stuffed animals as the musicians in a darkened nightclub.

If Kidz Bop triangulated tweens as the negative ground between Elmo and Eminem, as simultaneously both and neither child and adult, the video for "Since U Been Gone" suggests that children need not distance themselves from the trappings of childhood to engage their desire for participation in the public spaces of pop music consumption. Or, more precisely, the very presence of the trappings of childhood—here, the trope of stuffed animals coming alive—transforms the darkened nightclub into a kid-friendly place, just as the presence of kids' voices on the recordings effectively transforms potentially "inappropriate" pop songs into kids' music. In this way, Kidz Bop sold to parents and children a setting for and a vision of children's legitimate participation in popular culture. This was a feat accomplished via elegant contradiction, as the Kidz Bop brand legitimated tween consumption while simultaneously reinforcing anxieties about the effects of capitalist culture on the privileged spaces of childhood.

The video presented models of behavior for children to observe, interrogate, and reproduce in their continuous socialization as participants in public culture. But in practice, those roles would have been inaccessible to them outside of the specific fantasy portrayed in the video. Rather than socializing kids into popular cultural participation, this video might be better understood as constructing children as "tweens," a public group identity clearly and structurally separate from teenagers, from adults, and from a mainstream popular center. The fantasy of celebrity performance separates tween marginality from mainstream youth and adult culture while situating desire for the images and experience of that culture at the core of tween popular music consumption. This video presented tweens to themselves, as an audience of outsiders looking into a (partially imagined) world of older practices. This marginal tween gaze is canonically situated in the bedroom, performing in front of a mirror, even as it narrates that trope's shift to the video camera or webcam. The home-video camera here, and the imagined, mediated, and displaced environment of reception via the internet, provides a nice twist that encourages the narrative conceit of the fantasy nightclub, but in the end the result is the same: in the privacy and domesticity of the bedroom, tweens present themselves to themselves as publicly constituted persons.

The performance of public, commercial personhood in private settings was the central trope of tween practice as it was constructed in the rapidly expanding children's music market in the 2000s. As such it highlighted the contradictions of marginality—simultaneous separation from and dependence on the adult center—as preadolescents were inducted into public popular consumption. In this, the tween market existed on the same periphery in the culture industries as children themselves do in homes, schools, and communities—one in which children constantly make use of adult practices from the vantage of their own marginal position in public culture, in the peripheral spaces of bedrooms, playgrounds, and schools. Despite Razor & Tie's claims to address both boys and girls, the slippage between age and gender in the structure of tween marginalization is pronounced. As Diane Pecknold has argued, "Because the tween market is so gendered, . . . the marginalization of children becomes a kind of metaphor for female marginalization" (2011).

In 2007, shortly after the DVD of music videos came out, Kidz Bop rolled out a Web 2.0 version of their website, KidzBop.com. They refigured the site as a video and social-networking location for children to upload videos of themselves singing along to favorite recordings (thus distributing their own private performances in a public forum). The home-movie theme of the "Since U Been Gone" video, then, was contextualized within the growing popularity of video websites like YouTube, so the change in aspect ratio, which articulates a switch from home to fantasy in the video, also suggests a shift from the mundane domesticity caught by the camera to the digitally mediated world of the video's anticipated reception. This focus on domestic performance and media production calls to mind Mary Celeste Kearney's (2007) emphasis on kids' bedrooms as "productive spaces," though Kidz Bop was clearly trying to appropriate the trope of domestic production to elicit even more consumption.

FANTASIES OF CHILDREN AND MUSIC IN PUBLIC

The images in "Since U Been Gone" continued a tradition of commercial representations going back at least to the 1980s that was especially common in television advertising, which depicted fantasy spaces in which children

Figure 1.3 Still from 1980s television commercial for Teddy Grahams.

participate in exuberant musical spectacles modeled on teen or youth culture. As Ellen Seiter (1993) noted, in the 1980s television commercials for children's snack foods used rock 'n' roll as an important trope in a wider genre of advertising that depicted fantastic and utopian spaces as the setting for children's consumption. Nabisco's Teddy Grahams cookies were advertised by a band of life-sized bears performing a version of Elvis Presley's "Teddy Bear" as "I Want to Be Your Teddy Graham." In a later commercial, it was a version of "Rock 'n' Roll Is Here to Stay" (figure 1.3). These commercials specifically refer to 1950s and 1960s rock 'n' roll and teen culture in their music, costuming, and set design. One commercial showed the Teddy Grahams bears descending an airplane staircase with a crowd of excited child fans screaming on the tarmac, in a clear allusion to the Beatles' 1964 greeting by crowds of emotional teenagers upon arrival in the United States. Seiter points to other commercials, like one for Surf's Up Fruit Snacks, that imitated 1960s rock 'n' roll beach movies. Rock 'n' roll is an easily legible symbol of adolescent youth cultural freedom and pleasure, while nostalgia for 1960s teen culture perhaps dulled the sharp edges that might be implied by more contemporary pop.

Natalie Coulter (2014) has noted that the tween consumer industries regularly modeled themselves directly on teen culture. While Daniel Cook and Susan Kaiser (2004) argue that the tween market originated with the apparel industry, Coulter points to musical offerings, like *Jem and the Holograms*, that adapted teen music genres to children's cartoons as some of the earliest tween products. While phenomena like Beatlemania were distinctly gendered—teenage girls were widely acknowledged as their core participants (Ehrenreich, Hess, and Jacobs 1986)—the Teddy Grahams ad campaign framed its reworking of 1960s youth culture as a clever downward shift in age, foregrounding boys and girls together. The Teddy Grahams campaign was built on an almost simplistic adaptation, the one-to-one substitution of kids for teenagers in the familiar cultural territory of rock 'n' roll. But in fact that seemingly obvious gag performed a complicated ideological task, reworking the history of music and youth culture to highlight the centrality of age in a way that was ahistorical, if appealing from the perspective of many popular narratives. Importantly, the participants in phenomena like Beatlemania already included the nine- and ten-year-olds who are so prominent in the Teddy Grahams commercials. The unexpected inclusion of children in popular musical spectacles in nightclubs and on tarmacs seems to be a cute gag that frames the commercials as aspirational and impossible fantasies. But precisely those cultural touchstones of teen musical culture were already understood to express a gendered logic of privacy and publicness. Simon Frith and Angela McRobbie, for example, argued that teenybopper music offered a venue for girls' public participation:

> Unlike their brothers, girls have little chance to travel about together. As groups of girls they don't go to football matches, relax in pubs, get publicly drunk. Teenage girls' lives are usually confined to the locality of their homes; they have less money than boys, less free time, less independence of parental control. A live pop concert is, then, a landmark among their leisure activities. The Bay City Rollers' shows, for instance, used to give girls a rare opportunity to dress up in a noisy uniform, to enjoy their own version of football hooligan aggression. (1978/79: 12)

This is precisely the logic of pop music offering relief from domestic confinement that Teddy Grahams presented as a pleasurable fantasy for children. Of course 1960s popular culture was widely narrated in terms of age, with "youth culture," "teenagers," and generational conflict as central tropes, and the Teddy Grahams campaign took that literally, simply extending that age-based logic further downward. But age never was an isolatable or even necessarily highly important category in the cultural phenomena that the Teddy Grahams adapted—especially by comparison to race, class, and gender. If pop music was already widely seen as expressing particular social dynamics, especially around gender, the Teddy Grahams campaign

Figure 1.4 Still from "Nickelodeon Nation House Party," television commercial, aired 1999–2000.

could be seen to be actively suppressing that narrative, to reassert the centrality of age to the history of US popular music. This, in turn, helped lay the groundwork for efforts at developing a children's media culture over the next two decades. I argue in chapter 2 that the corporate pursuit of "tweens" in the 1990s was explicitly framed in gender-neutral terms, even though it ultimately targeted audiences by gender. We can see here how the logic of reframing gendered phenomena as age-based phenomena, specifically with reference to music, worked during a very early period in the development of tween media.

This trope of children's fantastical public music consumption reappeared in another ad campaign in the late 1990, when the cable television channel Nickelodeon rebranded itself around the tagline "Nickelodeon Nation." The campaign was based on a literal reading of "nation" as an imagined community of strangers who share essential (biological/cultural) traits and political institutions (e.g., B. Anderson 1983). It included a waving, patriotic Nickelodeon flag, and it primarily used images of children of varying races, genders, and ages dancing and playing at locations around the country, interpellated as sharing membership in the Nickelodeon Nation (Banet-Weiser 2007). Central to the campaign was a version of the song "Iko Iko"—another 1960s throwback that was a hit by the Dixie Cups in 1965—with Nickelodeon-focused lyrics. While most of the Nickelodeon Nation spots showed individual and small groups of children, one depicted a large crowd of children in a brightly sunlit warehouse space dancing to a live band with an adult woman singer and child musicians (figure 1.4). Diluting the 1960s references, this ad suggested a more contemporary venue

Singing Along ♥ 49

for children enjoying music performances (with metal catwalks common in 1990s depictions of music venues), though one that clearly takes place in the daytime. Unlike the explicit fantasy of the food commercials from a decade earlier, this commercial was realist, even if its portrayal of a kids-only rock concert was unlikely. For Nickelodeon the "nation" trope was a literal claim that kids around the United States were in fact members of a community organized by their media habits.

The Kidz Bop video for "Since U Been Gone," in its own way, is also committed to realism, even with its costumed animal musicians that recall the Teddy Grahams commercials. That is because it explicitly depicts the fantasy performance as a fantasy based in children's imaginative pretend play as part of their media consumption practices at home. The fantasy nightclub, in Kidz Bop's telling, is simply imaginary. The earlier television ads did not depict children at home, and when one did, as in the Surf's Up Fruit Snacks commercial, the real world was portrayed as dreary and unpleasant, dominated by adults who lack humor and enjoyment. The Nickelodeon Nation commercials showed kids in outdoor spaces rather than at home, and the "house party" commercial provided no context or explanation for the implausible scenario. The "nation" of kids was portrayed as actually real, a description of Nickelodeon's audience rather than an aspirational fantasy, except that nations are always already imagined. Kidz Bop, by contrast, went out of its way to provide a "realistic" explanation for the by-then-conventional image of children in fantasy pop music spaces: they are shown to take place in children's imaginations. In doing so it also located children not just as the audience, as in earlier examples of this trope, but as the central celebrity performer (for the girl character) and the controlling manager (for the brother). Musically it shifted from 1960s rock 'n' roll nostalgia to immediately relevant contemporary pop hits.

So from 1980s snack-food commercials, to 1990s cable TV campaigns, to 2000s tween music videos, we can see a repeated image of children in fantastical spaces as exuberant participants in popular music spectacle. That image is contextualized differently in different periods, but by the 2000s it had almost been made literal, except that it in doing so it was framed as simply the product of a childish imagination. By 2005 pop music was no longer simply a fantasy allegory for some other pleasure—junk food, television viewing—but instead itself now the topic. Thus the image of children consuming pop music was charged with newfound relevance, since the emergence of the tween music industry meant that the fantasy of pop music participation would no longer be just an allegory.

Figure 1.5 Still from *Never Say Never* (Paramount Pictures, 2011, dir. Jon Chu).

This image was finally, fully literalized in the 2011 concert film *Never Say Never*, about Justin Bieber's first national tour, which I analyze in detail in chapter 5. In the film Bieber, at fifteen still explicitly identified as a child rather than a teenager by audiences and critics, is shown onstage at night in darkened music venues—no longer a commercial fantasy or imagined scenario but real documentary footage. At a crucial moment in the film, his audience is depicted simultaneously as fully present at the venue (like the kids in the fantasy nightclub in the Kidz Bop video, but real this time), but also online, which is to say in their homes (like the kids pretending at home in the Kidz Bop video), in videos posted to YouTube that show them singing along to Bieber's hits, which are assembled into a single shot using computer-generated 3D effects (figure 1.5). Again we have the same impossible fantasy presented in the Kidz Bop video of child audiences at home somehow transported to a major music venue. This time the fantasy is real on both ends: a child performer and child audiences fill the actual venue, and real children consume and record themselves performing Bieber's music at home. The internet here provides a sort of magic portal between the two, framing the space of home and concert as essentially the same.

Proceeding deeper into the interior of the family home, into the child's bedroom, these representations come out the other end at exuberant public participation. We see something similar in the Disney Channel show *Hannah Montana* (discussed in chapter 3), in which the protagonist's secret identity as a celebrity pop star is hidden in the depths of her bedroom when her closet is suddenly much bigger than it should be and contains an unending selection of clothes and costumes. Previous depictions of children and pop music were simply fantasies, and if anything the incongruous juxtaposition of children with pop music contexts made the fantasy spectacle that much more pleasurable. But now that same imagery was combined with the parallel image of the child consumer in a bedroom to literalize the fantasy and justify rather than reject as utopian the idea of children as actively participating pop music audiences.[5]

The kids-only "house party," a fantasy in the Nickelodeon Nation campaign, became the standard image for tween and children's music videos, as in videos by aspiring amateur performers like Rebecca Black, Sophia Grace, Johnny Orlando, and many others, which would repurpose and domesticate the hip-hop video trope of the house party or pool party to show kids performing and consuming music at parties in and around their affluent suburban homes. As the commercial music industry for children grew, an image of fantasy performance that was once utopian in its vision of children's pleasurable independence and often explicitly opposed to paternal authority was, quite literally, domesticated. This move toward depictions of children within the family home and under the care and authority of parents ironically but necessarily was also a key part of the expansion of a music industry that asked adults and children to think of children as legitimate members of the audience for a show at a darkened music venue at night.[6]

KIDS' VOICES

With the bright colors and solid shapes on Kidz Bop albums' cover art, the immature humor and childhood settings of shows like *Hannah Montana*, and media discourses that constantly noted the age of popular performers like Justin Bieber and Taylor Swift, the images and discourses that surrounded 2000s tween music marked it as childish. But sonically and musically (rather than visually and discursively), the general rule with tween music was that the recordings were actively scrubbed of markers of childishness in an effort to link them as closely as possible to mainstream pop. With the Kidz Bop recordings, for example, the songs were rerecorded to sound as much like the original as possible, and changes to make the lyrics kid-friendly were kept to a minimum. Unlike the Teddy Grahams and Nickelodeon ads, which changed the words to existing songs to make them directly about children, none of the lyrics on Kidz Bop recordings were changed to be more explicitly about childish topics. The same was true of other tween music recordings as well, which went out of their way to conform to the songwriting and production norms of mainstream contemporary pop.

The exception was the prominent role these recordings gave to children's voices. The distinctive sonic feature of Kidz Bop's recordings was the inclusion of amateur children's voices singing along to the choruses, along with the absence of the identifiable voice of the pop celebrity from the original recording. Kidz Bop's early recordings pointed to a different logic of popular music than the now-conventional account that follows Simon Frith's emphasis on the "grain" of the particular embodied voice of the pop celebrity (1998; following Barthes [1972] 1990). By contrast Kidz Bop was perhaps more like karaoke in emphasizing, as Karen Tongson puts it, "how close pop prowess is to amateur recreation" (2015: 86). By foregrounding a crowd of young voices in the mix, Kidz Bop staged a particular vision not only of child audiences but also of popular music itself as a mass medium. To my (admittedly idiosyncratic) ears, Kidz Bop's early recordings sometimes transcended their originals.[7] In "Since U Been Gone" the urgently full-voiced choruses of child singers overflowed from the crooning verses with an energy unmatched even by Clarkson's own high-powered performance. Kidz Bop's recordings reflected an insightful reading of pop music as a social and sonic phenomenon in which space for a crowd of voices singing along is perhaps already implied in pop recordings. Unlike similar contemporary phenomena like televised reality singing competitions (e.g., *American Idol*) that traded on an ideology of the "diamond in the rough," in which supremely talented individual performers wait to be discovered among an otherwise astonishingly unmusical population, Kidz Bop envisioned a mass audience that was already fully present, or at least hailed by the hooks of pop songs. Kidz Bop's recordings treated the celebrity voice as a mere commodity, easily replaced by professional studio singers on hourly contracts.[8] Rather than intently focusing on the fine-grained details of the celebrity voice, Kidz Bop suggested that audiences might fold themselves in among an already constituted mass of voices singing along, drowning out the lead vocal. In a review of the soundtrack album for the Jonas Brothers' 2009 concert movie, *Billboard* described this as "another kind of spectacle: the screams and squeals of an arena full of freaked-out tweens" (Wood 2009). And in a way Kidz Bop was finally including *in the mix* the "screaming fans" that had so long been central to pop music, but had long been dismissed as a symptom of pop's abjection rather than a core feature of its business and culture (Coates 2003; Nash 2003). Although again doing so involved re-presenting those screaming fans not as girls but as children.

The logic of Kidz Bop, and of tween music more generally, was at least initially to distance itself from the construction of mass culture as feminine (Huyssen 1986), only to double down on a construction of mass culture as childish. Counterintuitively, the lengthy exclusion of tween acts from mainstream radio airplay helps illustrate this logic. For years Hilary Duff, Miley Cyrus, Justin Bieber, and Taylor Swift all struggled to get their hit records played on the radio, where programmers were concerned that they and their voices were "too young" (Stern 2013).[9] Diane Pecknold has argued that tween music is based on an ideology and aesthetics of "ordinariness," in which "girls inhabit a subject position predicated on ordinariness, on equality and equality of feeling, while the adult world is predicated on individual expression, autonomy, and uniqueness" (2011). Performative ordinariness is a long-standing trope in popular music targeting girls and women (Dibben 1999; Pecknold 2017; Warwick 2007). But Pecknold notes that the "new teen girl sound" that dominated popular music in the 2000s and 2010s was invested not just in an ideology of vocal ordinariness but even more strongly in performances of vocal limitation or even failure, deploying "evident vocal techniques and technological manipulations that not only retained adolescent vocal failings but performatively emphasized them" (2016: 84). Pecknold argues compellingly that the new teen girl sound seemingly contradictorily framed girls' voices as both authentically embodied (emphasizing laryngeal tension, breathy voice, etc.) and artificially technological (with transparent autotuning and other manipulations), so the foregrounding of teen girls' voices in popular culture staged even broader questions about the relationship of the body and voice to language, communication, and public culture. All the tween acts were operating in this context, but Kidz Bop especially, with its anonymous choruses of kids singing along, pushed this vocal ideology even further in the direction of literal ordinariness and interchangeability. The "too young" voices of the individual artists suggested a problematic exchangeability of one voice for another, and the Kidz Bop Kids' voices were quite literally untrained and undeveloped. The recorded voices of tween pop, then, did not highlight the "non-verbal ... devices," the "emphasis, sighs, hesitations, changes of tone" (Frith 1988: 90), that would conventionally emphasize the grain of the celebrity voice in pop recordings. Being "too young" partly means these artists' voices sounded objectively different from older voices, but perhaps it also explicitly staged a juvenile subject position that cuts a little too close to home in historic critiques of pop's immaturity.

The mass voice of the Kidz Bop chorus emphasized not just ordinariness and equality, but quite literally equivalence, exchangeability, and sameness, with no time whatsoever for celebrity particularity. Perhaps a chorus of enthusiastic children singing along to every pop song is what pop songs *already sound like*, the negative space implied by the celebrity subject. In this telling Kidz Bop's unabashed foregrounding of amateur children's voices and Cyrus's and Bieber's and Swift's excessively childlike voices announced a return of the repressed, where what had been repressed was the shameful massness of pop musical experience (rather than the masterful particularity of celebrity virtuosity), with the grain of the voice as the covering fig leaf. Kidz Bop's insight was to reveal (and revel in) the looming presence of the mass audience, normally hidden in the mix, standing ready to drown out the celebrity voice.

TWO — MUSIC TELEVISION

This chapter traces Disney's dramatic entry into the pop music industry in the early 2000s, a move that provided a center of gravity and institutional heft to what was an otherwise scattered or diffuse trend. This move represented a dramatic departure from the previous folk revival, bubblegum pop, and musical-theater traditions of children's music. In 1999 Alice Cahn of the Children's Television Workshop (now Sesame Workshop) told the *New York Times*, "It's harder to get away with doing schlock television for kids now" (Mifflin 1999). A similar shift was happening in children's music. Disney Channel executive Rich Ross pointed out that kids had been "looking for more sophisticated content" (Mayo 2007). Steven Pritchard of EMI, who represented Disney's catalogue in the United Kingdom, noted that music for children had long been "a market where there is an absence of pop music" (Dodd 2007). By the mid-2000s, Disney's popular music offerings stood out for their high production values, sophisticated songwriting, and contemporary sound, such that the recordings themselves were not readily distinguishable from standard radio fare.

Disney has been a key figure in children's music since the success of its earliest animated musicals. But it was not until its cable television channel began pursuing tween audiences that Disney would fully move into the world of pop music. Music was central to a process that would see the Disney Channel overtake Disney's film studio as a driver of corporate profits and creative energy at the media giant, and tweens shift from an aspirational audience to the core constituency.[1] Disney's revival of its animated films, with new classics like *The Little Mermaid, Beauty and the Beast, Aladdin*, and *The Lion King*, had profoundly impacted the children's music, film, and home-video industries, even as the Disney Channel mostly languished as a premium subscription channel through the 1990s, with limited original content and disappointing viewership. In the 1990s Walt Disney Studio's films almost completely drove Disney's strategic decisions, such that the TV and music companies were forced to passively follow. But by the late 2000s, the balance had shifted, with the TV and music arms overshadowing the films. In 2006 the soundtrack to the made-for-TV movie *High School Musical* (HSM) was the top-selling music album of the year in any category, and that same year the Disney Channel had another top ten album with the soundtrack to the sitcom *Hannah Montana*, about an eighth-grade girl who lives a double life as a pop star. In 2007 Disney released popular follow-ups to both of these albums, and also introduced the Jonas Brothers, a pop-rock group of three real-life brothers, with film and TV tie-ins to follow. The film studio now followed the Disney Channel, producing concert films and movie adaptations of TV shows in search of hits, directly inverting the 1990s situation where the Disney Channel would air Walt Disney Studios films every evening. In perhaps the clearest expression of the larger company's direction, in 2009 Rich Ross, who ran the Disney Channel during its ascendancy, was put in charge of Walt Disney Studios in order to rebuild the company's film business on the model of its TV successes (Graser 2009).

The ascendance of the tween-focused Disney Channel in Disney's media ecology has only recently begun to receive attention in cultural studies or media scholarship, though that is changing (Blue 2017; Hentges and Case 2013; Hogan 2013; Mjøs 2010). So it is worth stressing that this Disney is very different from the animated movies and theme parks that have traditionally received scholarly attention (e.g., Drotner 2002; Giroux 1999; Götz et al. 2005; Hunt and Frankenberg 1990; Sammond 2005; Telotte 2004; Wasko, Phillips, and Meehan 2001). Those Disney products frame child consumers as innocent and familial—"child" much more than tween. But though the Disney Channel in the 2000s did support other Disney products (through show tie-ins and constant advertising), its content attended more directly to the ambiguity that characterizes tween audiences. And pop music was central to Disney's strategy for negotiating the core tween problematic of age compression without losing its family-friendly brand identity.

While it would not be correct to say that pop music alone drove the success of the Disney Channel, it is hard to overstate its importance. Pop music allowed Disney to appeal to older children, as well as young children increasingly interested in more sophisticated content, without adopting the politicized, oppositional, and anti-adult rhetorics of its competitor Nickelodeon (Banet-Weiser 2007). Nickelodeon's gross-out humor and explicit language of child empowerment was the established model for attracting tween viewers, but its adoption would have risked alienating the adults whose nostalgic investment in the Disney brand remained a major part of its market. Pop music was not so much a watered-down compromise or a middle ground between Disney's traditionally family-oriented themes and newer mature materials. Rather, pop music allowed Disney to sidestep the presumption that there is a necessary trade-off between those values, in favor of a way of thinking about "age compression" or "kids getting older younger" as a "both/and" rather than "either/or" phenomenon. The Disney Channel's turn to pop music represented a significant move toward older audiences and more mature content. But it simultaneously allowed the network to retain both cultural markers of childhood and commercial marketing strategies for children. That is, pop music allowed Disney to double down on elements of childishness even as it offered a vision of sophistication and maturity. This double motion—moving simultaneously toward maturity *and* childishness—is a distinctive dialectic of tween media, and it is not just a representational phenomenon but also a commercial one: just as pop music programming would bring a traditionally more mature medium to younger children, it simultaneously facilitated the incorporation of business models from the children's television and consumer industries into tween media in a way that had previously been a struggle. This contradictory double motion, as I argue throughout this book, is the central logic that makes possible the conceptualization of childhood as a public identity and as an identity politics.

POP MUSIC AND DISNEY, 1990–2007

In this section I trace out a history of Disney's changing relationship to pop music starting with a series of instructive failures during the 1990s and culminating in the 2006 release of *High School Musical* and *Hannah Montana*, which together redefined the kids' media business and reoriented Disney toward TV and away from film. Attempts to attract older audiences with pop music in the 1990s floundered due to concerns over age appropriateness and the poor fit of existing music business models. In the 2000s, developing pop music acts in-house as integrated parts of larger televisual properties allowed Disney not only to finely calibrate the "appropriateness" of its content but also to build on established children's media business models (especially around product licensing and media mixes) that made use of its corporate strengths. A key contribution here is to recognize business models as themselves meaningfully linked to age categories, and therefore to recognize elements of "childishness" as much in the horizontal integration of Disney's pop music marketing strategy as in the content of lyrics or scripts. Furthermore, identifying how Disney targeted audiences based on age categories sheds light on the pervasive gendering of tweens, and the slippage between categories of age and gender. Disney's turn to pop music was framed as an effort to attract older, more sophisticated child audiences, with little mention of gender. But because music formats are already saturated with cultural logics of gender, race, and class, the effect of Disney's turn toward Top 40 pop was at the same time a turn toward girls. Thus the history of the Disney Channel's development of pop music is partly a history of the gendering of the concept of tweens.[2]

Walt Disney Records, 1990–1993:
A First Attempt at Original Pop Music for Kids

In the early 1990s Disney's Walt Disney Records was focused almost entirely on producing audio products supporting Disney's film and animation arms. In particular this meant "book-and-tape" read-alongs—audio recordings of an actor reading the text of a book that narrates a story from a successful video product. In that model the record label played an almost entirely supporting role. Disney was in the midst of its "renaissance" of enormously successful animated musicals, which included audio products: the soundtrack to *The Little Mermaid* quickly went platinum, and in 1994 the *Lion King* soundtrack was the best-selling album in the United States (*Billboard* 1995). In 1990, Walt Disney Records brought in Mark Jaffe to run the label, building on his success at A&M signing the superstar children's music artist Raffi. Jaffe tasked Torrie Dorrell, a journalist and publishing executive who had also just been brought to Disney to oversee production and development in the read-along business, to "start a children's music label that acted like any other mainstream music label" (Dorrell, interview, May 23, 2014). Dorrell signed several successful (adult) children's music acts, including Norman Foote, Craig Taubman, and the trio Parachute Express, as part of the newly created Music Box Artists Series. Disney was not alone in pursuing adult acts in the early 1990s; other major labels like Sony Wonder and Warner Bros' Kid Rhino also signed many new acts (McCormick, LaFollette, and Stasi 1991). But by 1994 major labels had stopped signing new acts and turned their focus to multimedia cross-merchandising of their existing acts, while artists returned to the smaller-scale independent model they had developed in the 1980s, and which had supported long-lived acts like Bill Harley and Trout Fishing in America (McCormick 1994).[3]

Dorrell worked to connect her original music products with brands across Disney. Radio airplay was always a problem for children's music, but Dorrell produced music videos for her artists, despite the lack of a consistent outlet (she says she "was convinced that a kids' version of MTV was right around the corner"), and she convinced the Disney Channel and Disney Home Video to run them as interstitials (in place of breaks for commercials, which the network never aired) or at the beginning and end of home videos. But it was a struggle to put the full force of Disney's brand awareness and marketing power behind the children's music acts, especially since the model of a "mainstream music label," unlike Disney's traditional emphasis on corporate-developed "characters," involved signing already established artists and taking responsibility for only a limited portion of their business—especially promotion and distribution, but not, necessarily, songwriting, production, or touring. Unlike multimedia products like *The Little Mermaid* in which the characters, and even the overarching Disney brand, are centrally featured, with live music acts "it was really the artist that we are featuring." Dorrell notes that "Disney had never had human beings on a record label before, and human beings can do all sorts of things they know characters won't. They can tarnish the Disney name in any number of ways and so the company was nervous at the outset of having human beings representing the Disney banner. And so my artists had strong moral compasses and were all family people who had kids themselves and were very good stewards of the brand."

Despite the good stewardship, when it came to branding the Music Box Artists Series recordings for retail sales, Dorrell recalls that it was difficult to use the Disney logo prominently: "I wanted [the word 'Disney'] in forty-eight-point type at the top, then a little '[Music Box] Artists Series,' and then the name of the artist. . . . And because these were human beings, and it was new still, and this was a dangerous territory, I had this tiny little bug that said 'Disney's [Music Box] Artist Series' at the top—you could barely see it—then the artist name. So I barely got to even visually leverage the Disney name" (interview, May 23, 2014).[4] For example, the cover to Norman Foote's 1992 album, *If the Shoe Fits*, was dominated by the artist and album title and photographs of a shoe and children's toys (figure 2.1). The only references to Disney were in very small print at the

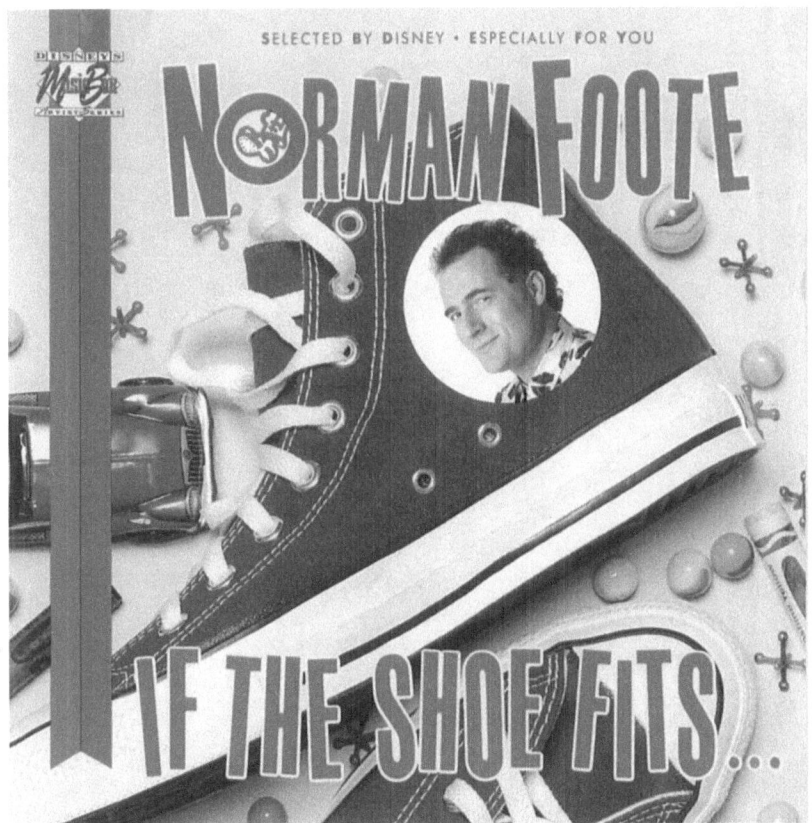

Figure 2.1 Cover of *If the Shoe Fits* by Norman Foote (Walt Disney Records, 1992), with minimized references to Disney at the top.

top: the phrase "SELECTED BY DISNEY • ESPECIALLY FOR YOU" and the tiny "Disney's Music Box Artist Series" logo in the top left. Notably the word "Disney" never appears in the distinctive looping handwritten logo that brands the vast majority of the company's products. Trying to build a mainstream music label meant producing content that did not fit neatly within Disney's existing models, which made it difficult to leverage Disney's brand to promote those acts.

In addition to signing established adult children's musicians, during this period Walt Disney Records also developed music acts based around child performers, significantly prefiguring the success of its child pop stars a decade later. In 1990, *Entertainment Weekly* wrote in a profile of ten-year-old recording artist Christa Larson that "Walt Disney Records, after years as a low-profile Disney subsidiary that subsisted on soundtracks, nursery

Figure 2.2 Cover of *Minnie 'n Me: Songs Just for Girls*, featuring Christa Larson (Walt Disney Records, 1990), with dominant Disney logo.

rhymes, and assorted novelty records, is embarking on the production of original contemporary music especially for kids" (Rhodes 1990). Walt Disney Records signed Larson and attached her to the classic Disney character Minnie Mouse to record a pop music album titled *Minnie 'n Me*. Unlike the Artist's Series releases, *Minnie 'n Me* strongly foregrounded the Disney branding, with the Disney logo dominating the album cover, and Larson's name minimized in small lettering toward the bottom (figure 2.2). Notably, Minnie 'n Me was already a consumer products program at Disney focused on using the Minnie Mouse character to develop products geared toward younger girls, in a period before the company had developed the Disney Princesses brand (Orenstein 2011). Unlike the difficulties they had tying their adult artists to the Disney brand, here they developed an act with the express purpose of, as Dorrell puts it, "drafting off" the Minnie 'n Me program, which allowed them significantly more access to cross-marketing with Disney's consumer products and other divisions: "not just an album but a 'lifestyle campaign,'" as the *Los Angeles Times* put it (Heffley 1990). Walt Disney Records arranged a national tour to promote the *Minnie 'n Me* album, and the company was geared up to really pursue popular music for children performed by children. At the time Dorrell told *Entertainment Weekly*, "Our objective is to have Christa become a singing star.... But this [*Minnie 'n Me*] is a great vehicle for her to get started. If we just released a Christa Larson album, people would look at it and say, 'Who's Christa?' But doing an album with Minnie on it heightens her exposure and gets her immediate sales before she's even known" (Rhodes 1990). Jaffe argued for a vision of children's music that looks very much like what would eventually dominate Disney's approach a decade later, using rhetoric that anticipated discourses about age compression and tweens: "I think we are really on the threshold of a brand-new era in children's music.... Children are so sophisticated now, the time is right to expose them to all sorts of musical genres on a level that is relevant to them" (Rhodes 1990). And while Jaffe's prior success was primarily around adult singer-songwriter Raffi, he argued that "there's a need ... for a child who can communicate with kids, rather than having adults singing to children" (Rhodes 1990). But the experiment was cut short when Larson's mother died in a traffic accident during the *Minnie 'n Me* tour in Australia, after which Larson left the entertainment industry for several years (Rackl 2011).

Another act was based around *The All-New Mickey Mouse Club*, a revival of the popular television show from the 1950s (which had already had a brief revival in 1977–79). Called MMC, this act used talent from the show including Keri Russell and JC Chasez. (Russell later starred in the television shows *Felicity* and *The Americans*, and Chasez went on to perform in the boy band NSYNC.) In 1993 they released an album of pop songs titled MMC and also developed a twelve-song choreographed concert that toured nationally. According to Dorrell the other future stars from that era of the Mickey Mouse Club—Britney Spears, Christina Aguilera, and Justin Timberlake—were too young to participate in the national tour. Even more than Christa Larson, MMC was a pop music act that aspired to transcend the children's music market. Despite the group name's reference to the Disney Channel show (which was also sometimes abbreviated to MMC), the Disney ties were deemphasized. The album cover, for instance, included only the letters MMC and a photograph of the band members—conspicuously lacking the words "Mickey Mouse" or the Disney logo and name that Dorrell

Figure 2.3 Cover of MMC (Walt Disney Records, 1993), with no explicit references to Disney on the cover.

had struggled to feature prominently on the Music Box Artists Series records (figure 2.3). Dorrell commented: "The absence of Disney on the MMC album was indeed intentional. This was my teen pop album, as [New Kids on the Block] were going strong and there was certainly a market, and I was pushing the songs to mainstream radio. So while the album was certainly appropriate for Disney, Disney and the Mickey Mouse Club were essentially persona non grata on mainstream radio. And yes, the album cover was the subtle but distinct tie back to the show and would be recognizable to the show's fans" (email communication, June 27, 2014).

Walt Disney Records promoted MMC beyond the Disney Channel to Top 40 pop radio. Dorrell told me,

> We pushed it at pop radio and we managed to get some play. The primary problem was if you heard the songs without knowing who you were

listening to they all sounded like straight-up pop. Then the minute we said who was singing the song the attitude would change because it was kids' music instead. It was difficult for me to break out of the kids' music genre with MMC because we were ensconced in it to begin with. So had I to do it over again I would have separated out the effort more outside of Walt Disney Records because that ended up actually hurting MMC from a pop standpoint. (interview, May 23, 2014)

Referring to the future success of Disney's Hollywood Records label in representing both conventional adult artists and Disney Channel artists, Dorrell comments that "had MMC been founded as part of Hollywood Records and had Hollywood Records worked MMC as a pop album and pop singles, I think they would have had more mainstream success as a sort of New Kids on the Block–type of music because it's straight up in that vein." In fact mainstream gatekeepers' bias against tween artists' youthful voices would remain a barrier to radio airplay for years, even after tween music's meteoric rise. So these early 1990s Disney pop acts point to an important tension between pop music, child audiences, and traditional forms of children's media. This tension would not necessarily be resolved in later years, but it would be transformed into a productive tension, rather than an inhibiting one.

Disney Channel, 1996–2001: Top 40 Teen Pop on Kids' TV

In the later 1990s Top 40 radio was increasingly dominated by youthful "teen queens and boy bands" (McCormick 2001), like Britney Spears, Christina Aguilera, the Backstreet Boys, and NSYNC (many of whom started their careers on *The All-New Mickey Mouse Club*), who were taking over the music industry, setting album and ticket sales records, and attracting large child audiences in addition to their teenage and adult listeners. Like many kids' media companies, Disney recognized these acts' appeal to older child audiences, and strongly pursued them. In 1996, Disney introduced Radio Disney, a network of child- and family-oriented FM radio stations that a decade later would be credited along with the Disney Channel for the dramatic success of *High School Musical* (Sisario 2006). Most of Radio Disney's programming was not original Disney music, however, but a mix of current Top 40 pop like Britney Spears and the Backstreet Boys that appealed to children, novelty songs, and kid-friendly "oldies."

In 1999 Walt Disney Records released the first of a series of Radio Disney Jams CDs that packaged the Radio Disney format of pop, novelty, and oldies songs (with few or no Disney acts) for retail sale, which topped the new *Billboard* Top Kid Audio chart. At the same time, record labels including Disney were declining to sign even successful independent children's artists, turning instead to pop music as a strategy to address "age compression." Carol Lee, an executive at Kid Rhino, told *Billboard* that "eight- to 11-year-olds and younger—the 'pre-tweens'—are listening to pop music that teens and even adults are listening to. It's affecting the children's music business" (McCormick 2001). Walt Disney Records' Mike Bessolo described the Radio Disney Jams compilations as the label's effort to "keep the label contemporized, keep it in tune with the tastes of the kids.... We want to continue to appeal to kids whose tastes are increasingly sophisticated" (McCormick 2001). *Radio Disney Jams 2* was the top-selling album on the *Billboard* Top Kid Audio chart for 2000, mirroring Radio Disney's programming by including "a canny mix of top 40 hitmakers (Britney Spears, Christina Aguilera, Backstreet Boys, Will Smith, 98° [with Stevie Wonder]), kid-beloved novelty acts ('Weird Al' Yankovic, Lou Bega doing a customized 'Disney Mambo No. 5'), kid-beloved oldie acts (KC & the Sunshine Band, Queen, the Village People), and prepubescent newcomers like Aaron Carter" (McCormick 2000). The Radio Disney Jams compilations anticipated the success of Kidz Bop in repackaging Top 40 pop for the children's market only a few years later. The Radio Disney CD art emphasized the Disney brand and "childish" coloring and lettering, using the visual design to fold the Top 40 pop recordings into the child-friendly Disney brand (figure 2.4).

The Disney Channel also responded to this trend. In 1997 new management was brought in to revamp and rebrand the network, which was limited by its status as a subscription-based premium cable channel with a lack of original programming, and it had long failed to compete with basic cable channels Nickelodeon and Fox Family, especially among older children (Sterngold 1997). New executive Anne Sweeney told *Condé Nast Portfolio*, "We wanted tweens, but there was no formula out there for how to get them. We tried animal shows, game shows. We put Mad Libs on the air" (Greenfeld 2008). Pop music programming would turn out to be the thing that succeeded. While Dorrell had convinced the Disney Channel to air music videos by Walt Disney Records artists as interstitial programming in the early 1990s, under Sweeney the channel had deals with outside record labels to air videos and live concert events by the same pop acts who were being programmed on Radio Disney and the Radio Disney Jams CDs. In 1997 the channel aired a high-profile concert by the young country singer LeAnn Rimes, and over the next four years it would daily air music

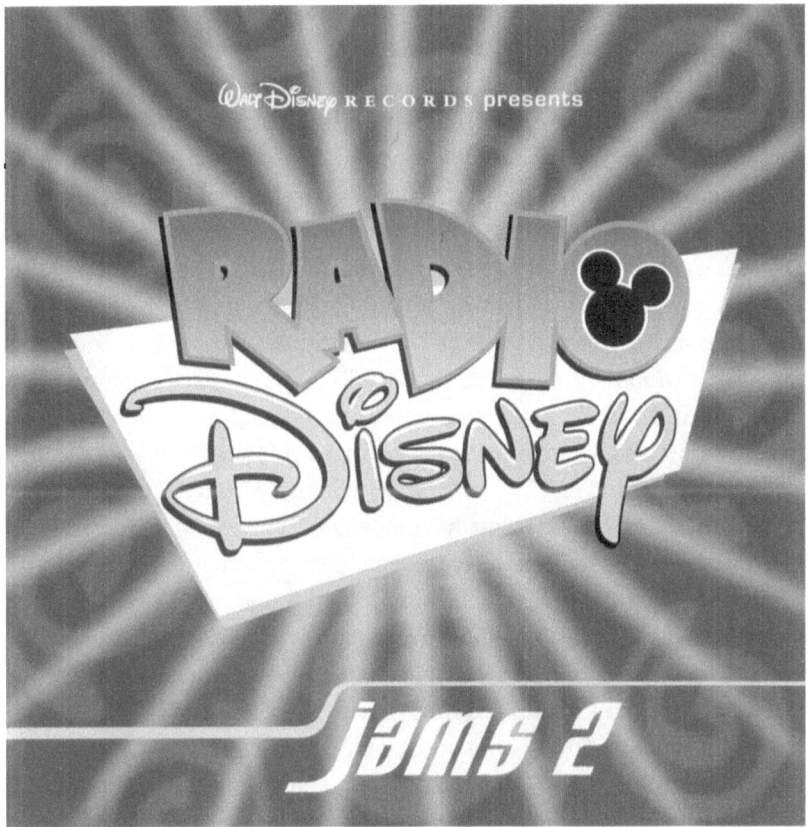

Figure 2.4 Cover of *Radio Disney Jams 2* (Walt Disney Records, 2000), emphasizing child-friendly design and Disney branding.

videos and concert footage from the same young artists collected on the Jams recordings: Spears, Aguilera, the Backstreet Boys, NSYNC, and others. From the start, children had been a key audience for the late 1990s wave of teen pop, so outlets like Radio Disney and the Disney Channel were central to those artists' business strategies (Leeds 2001). Disney's goal was to use pop music to attract tween audiences and distinguish itself from Nickelodeon and Fox Family, but those networks quickly followed suit. Music was seen by all the networks as a key source of interest for and access to the older kids they were all pursuing. As one Nickelodeon executive put it, "Music is important to kids lives and it allows us to stay knowledgeable with their lives" (Umstead 2001).

By 2001, however, the Disney Channel ended its arrangement with outside record labels to air their artists' videos, in large part because of concerns about how "family friendly" the Top 40 pop videos really were. Rich Ross related parental concerns that the sexual themes and provocative performance style of Britney Spears's music were inappropriate: "We were getting into a dangerous area, particularly with the parents, to a point where we had to take a stand," he said (Umstead 2001). Echoing Dorrell's difficulties in the early 1990s associating the Disney brand with live children's artists, Ross elaborated to the *Los Angeles Times* that live artists threatened Disney's carefully controlled brand: "If you attach your name to a pop star and that pop star does something potentially inappropriate in the world of their lives or the world of their music, you've taken your brand and put it together with something you can't control. . . . It's a really dangerous place to go" (Leeds 2001). This reflected a core tension in Disney's pursuit of the tween market and its attempts to address age compression in its audience's tastes and preferences. It also pointed to a financial problem that age compression raised for children's media companies: if children were increasingly interested in content intended for older audiences, it may cut out the companies that once served them. Umstead reported that the "Disney Channel was also dismayed by its inability to reap any tangible benefit from the free promotion it provides labels through music videos. The network did not receive a split from CD sales and almost none of the videos aired were exclusive to the network" (Umstead 2001). Subsequently, Disney Channel star Hilary Duff would have major success as a Hollywood Records recording artist, inaugurating a model of developing pop music acts internally that would address both the cultural and commercial tensions.

Disney Channel, 2000–2007:
A Second Attempt at Original Pop Music for Kids

Age compression arguably affected Disney more intensively than other children's media companies. The contrast with Nickelodeon is instructive. Through the 1990s Nickelodeon built its audience around oppositional and anti-adult themes. Disney was much more conservative, emphasizing the family sentiment and nostalgic parental goodwill that were especially important during a period when animated films that explicitly recalled a previous era of children's media were central to the company's success. During the 1997 rebranding, executives at Disney stressed that they were not trying simply to imitate Nickelodeon's approach, though they did hope to compete with its success (Richmond 1996). On the one hand, Disney's existing brand and goodwill from adults were too important to give up, and Disney-branded programming needed to be central to the channel. As Sweeney told *Variety*, "Disney is Disney. I work for a very big company with a very big legacy around the world, and it would be unfair to the consumer to deliver anything but Disney to them" (Richmond 1996). On the other hand, Disney Channel executives admitted to the *New York Times* that "the channel was thought of as being for babies," with too much programming like "Winnie the Pooh" focused on young children (Sterngold 1997)—an obvious problem in an era of age compression. Nickelodeon's president—reflecting his network's generational us-versus-them mentality—commented bitingly that the Disney Channel had "missed a generation. The brand name is more relevant to parents than kids" (Sterngold 1997). The Disney Channel hoped to thread this needle by emphasizing "families" and by focusing on programming that parents and children could watch together (J. Graham 1997). Rich Ross told the *New York Times*, "Our humor cannot just arise from dissing parents. What I think we're doing is providing situations where kids and families see themselves in a positive way" (Sterngold 1997). The goal, then, was to "create original programs that cut across age groups and that projected a reassuringly positive view of life . . . very different from the 'kids rule' irreverence that Disney's competitors have found so successful" (Sterngold 1997). Nickelodeon also cultivated audiences other than children as viewers for its edgy and irreverent shows like *Ren and Stimpy* and *SpongeBob SquarePants*, but through double-coding and divisive rhetoric that attracted teenagers and young adults, as well as irony and camp that borrowed directly from queer media (Banet-Weiser 2007: 178–210). Such cross-generational appeal specifically excluded *family* audiences, and the idea of children's commercial relationship or affiliation with nonreproductive adults is a frequent object of moral panic around children's consumer culture (e.g., Ito 2007).

The tension here is clear: the Disney Channel was under pressure to change with its audience, but it was also under pressure to maintain its existing brand identity and parental goodwill. Nickelodeon provided a model for attracting tween audiences, but it required alienating adults, which Disney was unwilling to do. Pop music attracted kids, and the network *was* able to find some youthful artists like LeAnn Rimes who "appeals to both kids and their parents" (J. Graham 1997). But music was also a problem, in that the same music that appealed to kids also frequently exceeded the bounds of "appropriateness," and Disney drew those lines strictly. Nonetheless music would turn out to be key to developing an alternative model to Nickelodeon.

In 2000 the Disney Channel's live-action show *Lizzie McGuire*, starring the teenaged Hilary Duff, became a hit. After the show's successful first season, Duff—now an important star for the network—reportedly expressed a desire to sing, so she was put in touch with Hollywood Records. It was Disney's more traditional record label, and had been distinctly unsuccessful during the 1990s, signing a distribution deal for Queen's catalogue and not much else. Unlike Walt Disney Records, Hollywood Records was not focused on secondary audio products based on traditional Disney films, so it lacked even that derivative business model. But with Duff, Hollywood Records put out *Lizzie McGuire* soundtracks and then five solo albums under her own name, which together sold over ten million copies (Chmielewski 2007), inaugurating the model of tightly integrated music, film, and television products all gravitating around a Disney Channel brand. The two Disney record labels, Hollywood Records and Walt Disney Records, now consolidated under the leadership of Bob Cavallo, would release records by Miley Cyrus (as herself and as Hannah Montana), the Jonas Brothers, Demi Lovato, and Selena Gomez, among others.[5] With the exception of Gomez's *Wizards of Waverly Place*, the television tie-ins for all of these artists revolved around music and performance: Cyrus's *Hannah Montana* was about a child pop star; a rock band from the start, the Jonas Brothers quickly starred in the TV movie *Camp Rock*, about a music summer camp; Lovato starred opposite the Jonas Brothers in *Camp Rock* and then got her own show, *Sonny with a Chance*, about a child actor on a television show. At least for several years, none of these shows presented problems of "appropriateness," since the acts were all developed and controlled by Disney, which could calibrate their content. Then from this base of success with TV-related tween pop acts, Hollywood Records began signing nontween artists like Grace Potter and the Nocturnals and Plain White T's (whose hit "Hey There Delilah" reached number 1 on the *Billboard* Hot 100 in 2007), and it started developing into a successful pop record label in a more traditional model.

POP MUSIC AND THE BUSINESS OF CHILDREN'S TELEVISION

Disney's earlier efforts to use pop music to attract older audiences failed repeatedly, but then, starting with *Lizzie McGuire* and peaking dramatically after 2006, they succeeded. What changed? The part of the story most commonly told involves careful calibration of age-appropriate content, balancing the pop appeal of a figure like Britney Spears with the imperative of age appropriateness. But another, equally important, factor is that they changed their business strategy. The 1990s attempts were largely based around the model of established record labels, in which the primary goal is album sales, and the means to achieve that is promotion through radio airplay and touring. Instead, starting in the 2000s, rather than trying to reproduce music industry models that had never succeeded for kids' music, Disney moved to integrate pop music into an established approach to kids' *television*. By doing that, they resolved a long-standing problem in children's television, in which the imperative to emphasize animated programming that supports consumer merchandising clashed with the growing need to appeal to older children with live-action shows.

Since the 1980s, toy-based cartoon shows oriented around merchandising, licensing, and cross-marketing had been a key source of profitability and financial stability for TV networks. But live-action shows, which provided fewer opportunities for merchandising, were more attractive to tween audiences. In the later 1990s especially, TV networks urgently pursued tween audiences—both chronologically older children and their traditional audiences who were widely perceived to desire more mature programming. Pop music provided some unique tools for live-action TV shows to extensively merchandise, cross-market, and license products ranging from musical toys to celebrity-branded clothing, concert tours, and films. Moreover, popular music, especially with its strong cultural connections to adolescence and youth culture, was precisely the sort of "mature" content that tween audiences were understood to desire. Pop music–based television, then, had the double effect of appealing to children seeking more mature programming while also supporting a business model associated with media for younger children. Which might be to say: culturally, pop music for kids was a phenomenon of age compression and children's advancing tastes, while commercially, it was a strategy for salvaging and renewing an established children's entertainment business model.

In the 1970s and 1980s the Federal Trade Commission had significantly loosened regulations of advertising in children's television (K. Montgomery 1989; Pecora 1998), leading to an explosion of toy-based cartoons on TV like *The Smurfs, He-Man and the Masters of the Universe, G.I. Joe, Thunder Cats, My Little Pony, Care Bears,* and *Teenage Mutant Ninja Turtles*. These shows were all developed in partnership with toy producers like Hasbro and Mattel, to the extent that the intellectual property for many of them was created and owned by the toy companies themselves. Norma Pecora (1998) argues that this model allowed broadcast television networks to minimize the cost of developing new programs while ensuring advertising commitments for the shows when they aired. Importantly, the cartoon format uniquely facilitates merchandising. Plastic and plush toys, dolls, or action figures work better when based on a drawing than a realistic live-action character. And the specific format of shows like *Thunder Cats* and *Care Bears*—and later "media mixes" like *Pokémon* and *Yu-Gi-Oh!* that combined television, video games, trading cards, and toys (Buckingham and Sefton-Green 2003; Ito 2006)—allowed for unlimited casts of characters and therefore unlimited possibilities for new products to sell. Notably, music fit neatly into the toy-based Saturday morning cartoon model. *Jem and the Holograms* was an animated show in the style of *He-Man* and *My Little Pony* about an all-girl band, complete with villains, science fiction techno-magic, and origination by toy company Hasbro, while Mattel competed with *Barbie and the Rockers* (Coulter 2014). And kid-oriented boy band New Kids on the Block spun off a heavily merchandised Saturday morning cartoon in 1990.

The commercial pressure to produce cartoons is visible in the history of Nickelodeon. Nickelodeon had started out as an explicitly noncommercial channel that did not sell advertising for its first four years. Nickelodeon's successes were based on a core lineup of live-action shows like the variety show *You Can't Do That on Television*, the game show *Double Dare*, and the sitcom *Clarissa Explains It All*. In fact Nickelodeon's Geraldine Laybourne said of "animated toy-related programming" that her goal as a children's media executive was "to put that kind of programming out of business" (Brennan 1988). This was part of a stated view of children as more sophisticated than traditional media companies and adults credited them for. Laybourne continued: "My notion was that kids only liked what they were only exposed to and that if you exposed them to other things you could elevate their tastes and move them along" (Brennan 1988; for further discussion, see Banet-Weiser 2007: 57). Here turning away from toy-based animation and toward live-action shows was a move toward more "elevated" tastes, while, later, Disney record executives had described their use of pop music as an acknowledgment of kids' increasingly "sophisticated" tastes (McCormick 2001). That is to say, live-action shows were part of a story about age compression in which children's media sought out more mature or sophisticated audiences. Laybourne's comment reframed conventionally anxious rhetorics of age compression in a more optimistic direction. Her implication of children's "uplift" appealed to the paternalism of her adult interlocutors, while the suggestion of children's sophistication and even rights fit neatly in Nickelodeon's larger rhetoric of politicized childhood. But that rhetoric was belied by the commercial realities. By the mid-1990s Nickelodeon shifted nearly half of its programming to cartoons, putting heavily merchandised animated shows like *Ren and Stimpy*, *Doug*, *Rugrats*, and *SpongeBob SquarePants* at the front of its lineup, signing licensing deals with Mattel, and even developing an in-house merchandising division (Pecora 1998: 93–99). Despite its explicit ideological opposition to animated toy-based shows and access to alternative revenue sources from advertisements (which the Disney Channel continued not to sell), Nickelodeon eventually gave in to the strong financial pressure to create the merchandising opportunities made possible by animated shows.

During the same period, the kids' TV networks were identifying tweens as an untapped market and a key site for growth. But the pressure to merchandise militated in favor of animation and toy-based programming, running counter to the simultaneous pressure to attract older children outgrowing cartoons and toys. Both motives were very clearly present for children's media professionals during the 1990s, as Pecora shows for PBS, which chased *both* merchandising dollars and older children. After 1990 PBS developed heavily merchandised programs like *Barney* and *Lamb Chop's Play-Along*, but before that only *Sesame Street* (with its easily merchandised Muppets) had been tied to toys and character licensing (Pecora 1998: 105). But at the same time PBS actively began to pursue older children. As PBS president Ervin Duggan explained to *Variety* in 1994, "Public television has never been quite as strong with the older child. . . . Nickelodeon and MTV have been enormously successful in attracting that audience in the commercial media. Now we are involved in an effort to become attractive and arresting to that age group, to be fresh and hip but also high-minded and enlightening" (Zimmerman 1994; quoted in Pecora 1998: 106).

In my reading of the industry press from the 1990s the pursuit of older children was largely defensive—based on a sense that the younger child audience was shrinking due to age compression—and business models for tween television were not yet well defined. Nickelodeon, at least, sold advertising, so its successful live-action shows could draw older viewers to commercial spots for toys, food, or other products not necessarily linked to the programs. The Disney Channel had long depended on premium cable subscriptions, but in order to grow its audience it aggressively pushed to be included in basic cable packages (Richmond 1996, 1997). But it was unique among basic cable channels in not selling advertisements (J. Graham 1997), raising questions about its business model and sources of revenue (S. Levine 2003). The channel had always functioned to promote and raise awareness about other Disney products like theme parks, cruises, DVD releases, and live events. But that model was in tension with the Disney Channel's efforts to move away from established Disney brands targeting younger children to produce more original programming that would attract their desired older audience.

Live-action television for tweens also pursued merchandising opportunities. For example, the iconic green slime on *Double Dare* and *You Can't Do That on Television* was quickly merchandised as green slime shampoo and slime toys like Gak. The central conceit of *Lizzie McGuire*, even before Duff began her recording career, was that an animated version of the title character alternated with the live shots to provide internal commentary on the action—and having an animated version of the main character allowed for the sale of dolls based on that character. Even without such clear merchandising hooks, companies still did their best to sell school supplies, stickers, charm bracelets, books, and videos linked to their television brands. Shows like *Lizzie McGuire* may have already resembled the previous era's cartoons in that "the line separating content from commercials is admittedly fuzzy" (S. Levine 2003).

Music-based shows amplified this trend. If shows like *Jem and the Holograms* and *New Kids on the Block* demonstrated the compatibility of pop music and merchandise-focused TV animation in the 1980s and 1990s, in the 2000s music-based shows created new opportunities for merchandising and cross-marketing of live-action media brands. Just as the purchase of an action figure is implied as a natural accompaniment to watching a cartoon—to the extent that it is not clear which activity is primary—purchasing a soundtrack album or concert ticket naturally follows from following a television show about pop music. The tie-in between television viewing and purchasing was much less directly implied for green slime shampoo or *Lizzie McGuire* dolls, or even for cartoons like *SpongeBob SquarePants* that lack the expansive cataloguelike casts of characters and teams of good guys and bad guys that point to new purchases and scripts for play. With music shows, to be a fan of the show implies being a fan of the music. And while most of the franchises appear first on television, once they are established, there is a sort of chicken/egg question of whether the music or TV show "comes first" in their public reception, or even conceptually. After the release of her first album and wildly successful summer tour in 2007, did it make more sense to call Hannah Montana a pop act with a TV show, or a TV show with a pop act?

In 2006 the first season of *Hannah Montana* was a hit, but since the Disney Channel did not sell advertising the show itself would not have directly brought in much money. But the soundtrack debuted at number 1 on the *Billboard* 200 chart, where it would spend seventy-eight weeks—a pop album success by any measure, not just for kids' music. A concert film then sold out theaters nationally (Bowles 2008), setting winter sales records, and as of 2018 its $65 million gross domestic sales still wildly outpaced any concert film other than Bieber's *Never Say Never* and Michael Jackson's posthumous *This Is It* (*Box Office Mojo* 2018). Further albums and films followed. Like the self-proliferating cartoon toys, music allowed for the continual production of new recordings, new versions, new tour dates, and new concert videos. Then, in addition to this core music-related business, Disney sold Hannah Montana novels, video games, and an extensive line of retail merchandise, "including clothes, watches, bedding, luggage, shoes, makeup, spa kits, and toys" (Tirella 2008). A singing Hannah Montana doll strongly competed with Barbie and Bratz dolls during the 2007 Christmas shopping season (Pesce 2007). Despite being a live-action show, the performativity of pop stardom and the profoundly fantastical quality of child celebrity provided natural scripts for doll- or action figure–based toy play. A Hannah Montana doll fit naturally among fashion and dress-up dolls like Barbie and Bratz, but it also scripted an additional mode of concert performance play and karaoke-style singing-along that fed back into further music listening and purchases. (The previous generation of shows like *Lizzie McGuire* and *That's So Raven* had fantastical magic or supernatural elements that similarly gestured toward pretend play and merchandising, just not with the same scope.) While Disney has always had more integration among its film, music, television, and consumer products arms than its competitors, Cyrus pushed this integration farther, centering the different divisions around her own celebrity, as the first artist to have simultaneous deals with each of the Disney TV, film, consumer products, and recording areas (McNamara 2007a)—revealing the unique affordance of music to expand the commercial possibilities for narrative visual media.

Clearly *Hannah Montana* is markedly different from toy-based shows like *Care Bears* or *Teenage Mutant Ninja Turtles*. It most noticeably differs in being based around a live individual celebrity who performs pop music, linking it to a very different, significantly more "grown-up" world of media and popular culture. But at the same time precisely this fact, that it is based around pop musical celebrity, creates possibilities for merchandising and cross-marketing that would not be available were it just a conventional high school sitcom, which makes its business model closer to the toy-based cartoon shows than, say, *Clarissa Explains It All*. Disney was uniquely positioned to capitalize on the potential for horizontal integration of pop music and television precisely because Disney is a children's media giant, and merchandising and cross-marketing have been central to children's media for decades.

By the 2010s it would be more or less standard for live-action shows on the Disney Channel to include a music tie-in, and even stars of nonmusical shows like Selena Gomez of *Wizards of Waverly Place* were making successful pop records. While Nickelodeon dominated the tween television market in the 1990s, it fell behind in the 2000s and also turned to musical programming in an effort to catch up. The Nickelodeon shows in the mid-2000s did not incorporate music directly, but *Drake and Josh*'s Drake Bell released a moderately successful rock album in 2007, and *iCarly*'s Miranda Cosgrove eventually began a recording career. Nickelodeon had one musical show already in 2007, the *Naked Brothers Band*, though as also with Drake Bell the music was conventional guitar-driven rock rather than contemporary-sounding Top 40 pop. Self-serious guitar rock's investments in musical authenticity and interiority may not encourage the same sort of performative play and spectacle as pop music does. But starting quickly in 2009 and 2010 Nickelodeon's next generation of shows clearly followed the Disney Channel model of incorporating pop music performance into their narrative core: *Big Time Rush*, about a boy band of hockey players, and *Victorious*, about an aspiring singer at a performing arts high school, from which several soundtracks and Ariana Grande's music career were spun off. Recalling broadcast TV deals with toy manufacturers in the development of cartoon shows, Nickelodeon partnered with Sony Music early in the development of *Big Time Rush* to release the band's music (Idelson 2010).[6]

The mainstream music industry adopted similar strategies in pursuit of alternative sources of revenue, as the traditional model of album sales promoted by radio airplay was dramatically undermined by the internet and digital media (Knopper 2009). Ticket sales became increasingly important, and so did merchandising, with stars putting their names and likenesses on lines of clothing and fragrances. And television became a major outlet for popular music. *Variety* pointed out that musical tween television connected to a trend of successful prime-time network shows like *Glee* and *American Idol* and their competition and jukebox musical imitators, which contributed licensing fees and promoted songs to a broad audience (Idelson 2010). Labels also turned to licensing songs for TV advertisements as an important source of revenue and promotion (Klein 2008). Large media corporations increasingly capitalized on their horizontal integration, using their television shows to promote new music from their record labels (Anderman 2007), effectively reproducing a business model that children's media had organized around decades earlier.

In important ways, then, it is clear that a turn to music involved a recommitment to a children's media business model, and not simply the abandonment of traditionally childish things in favor of increased maturity and sophistication. In fact, if we can see mainstream popular music increasingly adopting similar strategies developed by children's media—strategies that have been criticized precisely for taking advantage of particular developmental traits of child audiences (K. Montgomery 2007b; Schor 2004)—then we might argue the inverse: consumer industries were increasingly targeting adults like they did children. Rather than kids getting older younger, age compression was as much a phenomenon of adult media increasingly resembling children's media.

MAKING KIDS' MUSIC POP

In addition to these marketing strategies, Disney had to deal with the problem of making pop music that was both "safe" and appealing to kids. In 2006, while three children's albums, including Disney's *High School Musical* soundtrack, were at the top of the overall record sales charts, Walt Disney Records executive Damon Whiteside told the *New York Times* that Disney was developing music that is "still safe, but it's got a little bit of an edge" (R. Levine 2006). Pop music appealed to tweens and created opportunities for merchandising and sales, but as the Disney Channel's experience airing Britney Spears videos showed, certain videos and lyrics were seen by many adults to be inappropriate and threatening to child audiences. The trick for the Disney Channel was to make music that appealed to kids the same way the teen pop acts did, while somehow subtracting the objectionable content or recontextualizing the music to deemphasize those themes. But that created a new problem: when you scrub the objectionable stuff, the music gets coded as childish and you cannot get it played on the radio, which removes the key promotional tool for traditional pop music. Successful mainstream pop was too problematic for adults to permit for child audiences, but then child-friendly pop was too childish to succeed outside of the children's market. Despite, on the one hand, their clear appeal to each other (pop music desires child audiences, and children desire pop music), pop music and children seemed to be constitutively incompatible. This section explores how Disney resolved that tension.

Not Very Childish

So how did Disney make original pop music "safe" for kids, without losing that "little bit of an edge" that makes it desirable as pop music? In part writers and producers very carefully negotiated different elements of pop music, treating lyrics, sound, costume, dance, and genre independently. Even as they scrubbed away potentially inappropriate elements, they were thorough about retaining explicit and implicit signifiers of contemporary mainstream pop. A good example of this negotiation comes from the Cheetah Girls, who were an early musical act that fit the model of integrated music, film, and television being developed at the Disney Channel. The Cheetah Girls were an all-girl singing group that spun off from a Disney Channel original movie that was itself adapted from a series of young adult novels. Their membership at times included established Disney Channel personality Raven-Symoné, who starred in the hit sitcom *That's So Raven* and had recorded both soundtracks and solo albums with Walt Disney and Hollywood Records. The Cheetah Girls' first record was released in 2006, around the time the pop group the Pussycat Dolls were popular. The similarities between the Cheetah Girls and the Pussycat Dolls are readily apparent. Both were girl groups with "cat" references in their names. The Pussycat Dolls' 2005 debut album was titled *PCD*; the Cheetah Girls' 2007 debut studio album was *TCG*. Like a conventional adult girl group, the Cheetah Girls danced and sang R&B pop songs. Like the Pussycat Dolls, the group was multiethnic, with an "urban" style that sonically and visually emphasized nonwhite ethnicity (Valdivia 2008). Much of their music had a Latin sound, as in their single "Fuego." This linked them to the early-decade popularity in the United States of music with occasional Spanish-language lyrics by Latinx artists like Shakira, Jennifer Lopez, and Ricky Martin. In contrast to the insistently sexual Pussycat Dolls, the Cheetah Girls' sexuality was thoroughly backgrounded. Their dance moves were never very suggestive, and their costumes, though sometimes tight-fitting, were not very revealing. In the video for "Fuego," for instance, all three Cheetah Girls wear multiple layers and cover their legs below the knees in most shots. Most of the similarities to the Pussycat Dolls were likely not direct imitation. The initial concept came from a series of novels first published in 1999, and the first Disney Channel original movie was aired in 2003, when the Pussycat Dolls had only just signed with a record label after years as a live burlesque troupe, so they would have been in development simultaneously. But their similarities suggest that Disney was attuned to the popular music market in the early 2000s and made decisions about developing musical acts that reflected compatible views on contemporary trends as the Pussycat Dolls' label Interscope Records, the edgy label whose 1990s successes were based on bringing gangsta rap to mainstream prominence.

In some clear ways the Cheetah Girls had "a little bit of an edge," especially compared to traditional forms of children's music. Their music was driving and energetic, and it had clear connections to contemporary, sexually assertive pop music. And though it went out of its way to minimize explicit tropes of sexuality such as exposed skin, certainly the display of its female performers' vigorously dancing bodies was a core element. Similarly, topics for lyrics included crowded parties with dancing "all night long" ("Fuego") and romantic love ("Uh Oh," about a breakup, or "Crash," in which "love happened so fast"). Perhaps not least, for this act in particular, the emphasis on nonwhite ethnicity—both in the group membership and the musical style—may also have contributed "an edge" to the music, especially in a cultural context where childhood innocence as well as tween consumerism have strong racial codings as white. By 2003 ethnically diverse casting was a dominant convention in children's television, but this usually involved a homogenization of race and ethnicity into simplistic consumerist "diversity" that reasserted the priority of whiteness, as Sarah Banet-Weiser argues persuasively about Nickelodeon (2007). This perspective can apply to the Cheetah Girls as well, whose style very clearly domesticated ethnicity into Disney's bland consumerism. But the Cheetah Girls' cast was entirely Black and Latina, and the absence of Anglo performers highlighted ethnicity in ways that exceeded the normal conventions of diverse casting in children's television at the time.

To the extent that the Cheetah Girls may have been coded as "children's music," it would largely have been through the absence of strong language or explicit sexuality; the age of the performers, who were all under twenty years old at the time of their signing; and, perhaps most importantly, the Disney Channel's sponsorship. Otherwise they did not present explicit markers of childishness. The same was largely true of acts like Miley Cyrus, the Jonas Brothers, and the stars of *High School Musical*, all of whom were fourteen to seventeen years old during their heyday in 2007. The music of all of these acts was stylistically connected to contemporary trends in mainstream pop, country, hip-hop, and rock, and the lyrics commonly addressed romantic love and parties—the most conventional topics of Top 40 pop songs. The records were not readily distinguishable from conventional Top 40 pop. Rich Davis, program director at the "mainstream top 40" radio station KDWB in Minneapolis, described acts like Cyrus, Gomez, Lovato, and the Jonas Brothers as "putting out mainstream, right-down-the-middle pop music... really good pop records, really well-produced" (Stern 2013: 25).

That said, there were certain references to childhood in these acts. The show *Hannah Montana* directly addressed issues of childhood and public participation. It was structured around the conceit of a "normal" girl with friends and a social life focused on school who leads a double life as a pop star. The motivating "situation" of the episodes involved the question of maintaining traditionally childish family and friendship intimacies despite Miley/Hannah's public double life. The *High School Musical* movies included themes relevant to children with songs about school ("What Time Is It? Summertime") and school-based athletics ("Get'cha Head in the Game"). And the Jonas Brothers, who in 2007 might have been the most mature of Disney's offerings, still released explicitly kid-related singles like "Kids of the Future," along with standard pop-radio fare like "S.O.S." and "Hold On," and serious love songs like "Hello Beautiful." The clearest connections to childhood occurred not in the music but in the visual and narrative aspects of the television shows and films. In *Hannah Montana*, for example, the show included jokes at the expense of the adult music world, as Miley/Hannah and her friends frequently act ridiculously, wearing costumes or disguises and covering themselves in food, to the chagrin of uptight adults, reaching a level of silliness that is unusual in more serious (and more grown-up) music. These three acts were also somewhat age-graded, with the musical-theater camp of *HSM* geared toward the youngest audiences, while the Jonas Brothers cultivated young teenagers, with Hannah Montana / Miley Cyrus in the middle. But there was so much overlap that the effect of this age grading was to provide a scaffold to bring younger music to older kids and older music to younger kids, as opposed to the marked division between age groups characteristic of traditional children's marketing.

Beyond these explicit references to childhood, the basic move of including a strong musical component in television for children situated these shows in a long tradition of children's television. Children's media has long been unique in its emphasis on integrating music: as early as 1913 publishers were packaging books with musical recordings (Tillson 1995), while film and television from Disney's animated films to *Howdy Doody* to *Mr. Rogers' Neighborhood*, *Sesame Street*, *Barney*, and *The Wiggles* all put music front and center. In fact, one of the reasons efforts to develop a children's recording industry fell flat during the 1990s was that the burgeoning home-video market was so musically saturated it effectively crowded out CDs—both in shelf space at big-box retailers who invested heavily in home-video sales and in parents' budgets.[7] Narrative musical television—not music videos specifically developed around a song, but scripted shows with music fully integrated into them—are so specific to and dominant in children's media that the format itself might be seen as a strong marker of childhood. Just as incorporating music into its television shows supported Disney's existing children's media-based business models, it also would signify children's media even in shows for aspirational tween audiences. In subsequent years shows like *Glee* and *Smash* would incorporate music into scripted shows for older audiences, reflecting the logic of mainstream media adopting models from children's media. If there was something new here it was the centrality of music to TV aimed at somewhat older kids and the emphasis on pop music genres specifically. Pop music helped Disney attract older children with maturing tastes, but by incorporating pop music into its live-action shows Disney also contextualized these shows within a history of children's television.

It may be that Disney could also get away with even more of "an edge" in its pop products than mainstream teen pop could. All the extra-musical television and film narratives and visual depictions that emphasized childhood and family carved out some breathing room for the music to be more conventionally pop. The "school" of HSM did a lot of work contextualizing the musical performances within an already-safe and adult-monitored space of childhood. If Britney Spears's video for ". . . Baby One More Time" went out of its way to highlight the disjuncture between the pop song's sexual and romantic thrust and the school setting for racy effect, HSM worked to naturalize musical performance within the halls of school, literalizing it even in the plot's focus on an actual school musical. Similarly, the fact that the Jonas Brothers were real-life siblings still under the care of their parents positioned their pop songs in a family context. And the simple fact that the Cheetah Girls were associated with Disney positioned them as a kids-first act. Rather than a children's television island being intruded on by unaccountable Top 40 outsiders, homegrown acts, even if their content was not radically different, did not pose the same threat. By building alternative channels for circulating their music, Disney capitalized on its marginalization as a resource for mitigating moral panic.

Still Too Childish

Disney's tween music was clearly trying to straddle a difficult boundary between childhood and pop music. It largely did so by retaining as many features of conventional pop as possible, while scrubbing the most problematic elements—especially explicit sexuality—and integrating it into the narrative of live-action shows about children. In some cases it also added a small number of references to childhood and children's lives, like school and friendship, while avoiding overly childish topics. (Of course, it avoided young-child topics like trains, dinosaurs, and bedtimes, but it also largely avoided topics relevant to older children, like sleepovers or parents, that would position children in subordinate, familial roles.) While this mostly resolved (or at least forestalled) the problems created by airing Britney Spears's explicitly sexual MTV videos, it created another problem. By removing the explicit sexuality, including some mentions of childhood, and using younger performers, despite all its contrasts with traditional children's music, the music was quickly coded as being by and for children and was refused airplay on mainstream radio.

The conventional business model in the music industry was to promote album sales with radio airplay of hit singles. This approach changed substantially during the 2000s as record sales diminished (Knopper 2009), but it was never a viable model for children's music. Children's music had never had access to radio airplay, so it never had the ability to create massive hit songs. As A&M's director of children's marketing, Regina Kelland, said, "It's very difficult to achieve the normal gold and platinum levels since there's no radio airplay" (Zimmerman 1992). (Notably A&M represented Raffi, whose success made labels think maybe they could develop a hit-record model for children's music.)

But Disney was not only shooting for the "gold and platinum levels" of record sales with child audiences, but also aspiring to "launch some of its acts into the mainstream, adult audience and all" (Dodd 2007). Just as Torrie Dorrell described for MMC, however, traditional radio airplay was closed to these acts, because they were seen as "kids' music." Despite their extraordinary sales, Hilary Duff and Miley Cyrus struggled to get their music on the radio, as did Justin Bieber and Taylor Swift, all of whom spent years fighting radio programmers' perception that they were "too young" for Top 40 airplay (Price 2006; Stern 2013). But by 2006 Disney was uniquely situated to deal with this problem. Instead of mainstream radio or MTV, its singles and music videos were in heavy rotation on Radio Disney and the Disney Channel. And "with virtually no radio support" (Sisario 2006: E1), *High School Musical* was the top-selling album that year (Werde 2006).

In contrast to 1993, when MMC was unable to achieve breakout success, the Disney Channel, now much more widely available on basic cable, offered a range of popular original shows, and Radio Disney was widely available across the country. Furthermore, in the 1990s Disney's focus on animated films and its traditional products meant it was unwilling to commit to live music acts, but by 2006 the whole company threw its support behind these new products rather than leaving them to succeed or fail on their own. Breaking through to "a broader pop audience" was a secondary consideration—"the gravy," according to Bob Cavallo (Sisario 2006). The exclusion from Top 40 radio likely contributed to adult perceptions of the Disney acts as "safe." Despite their similarities to contemporary pop, they still circulated in a largely separate kids-only network, and so they sidestepped, for a while, concerns about children's participation in traditionally adult public spheres. In effect Disney built out an entire alternative media ecology that paralleled, but did not often interact with, mainstream music and media. Kids could participate in their own walled-garden version of popular culture and, through their marginalization, even claim a sort of subcultural capital and authenticity. In this sense, being too childish for mainstream media was a virtue.

These acts would eventually break into the mainstream. Radio executives eventually recognized not just their popularity, but the growing demographic importance of younger audiences and their strong connection to these artists (Stern 2013). To a surprising extent these artists achieved mainstream success without breaking ties with their children's media roots. *High School Musical* stars Zac Efron, Vanessa Hudgens, and Ashley Tisdale (among others) began to have independent careers subsequent to *HSM*, but for years they also continued to star in *HSM* sequels and routinely appeared on major awards shows in their capacity as *HSM* stars. They did not seem to feel a need to strongly split from Disney. The Jonas Brothers' early success depended on marketing through the Disney Channel, including guest appearances on *Hannah Montana* and starring in a Disney Channel original movie, *Camp Rock*. Unlike many of the other Disney personalities, they started as a music act, without the awkward baggage of a kiddie TV show to hold them back from mainstream popularity. Nonetheless, despite achieving widespread success and an apparently easy route to freedom from Disney, in May 2009 the Jonas Brothers returned to the Disney Channel with a silly, gag-filled half-hour sitcom of their own, *JONAS L.A.*—clearly treating the Disney connection as a resource rather than a burden. Miley Cyrus stopped recording as Hannah Montana in 2010, but the show continued to air new episodes through 2011, and Cyrus remained with Hollywood Records through 2013. Her 2009 single "Party in the USA" peaked at number 2 on the *Billboard* Hot 100 chart and played widely on Top 40 radio that summer, as the third season of *Hannah Montana* aired on the Disney Channel. Eventually Cyrus, Lovato, and others would publicly break with Disney. But their mainstream success was not foreclosed by their affiliation with Disney.

A Kids' Pop Format Meant a Girls' Pop Format

With its turn to pop music, Disney was chasing tweens, and they got girls. When the kids' TV networks were pursuing tween audiences through the 1990s, their campaigns were directed at "kids" with "sophisticated" tastes, and Nickelodeon was celebrated for addressing girls and boys together. On the other hand, by 2009 the Disney Channel's audience was so dominated by girls that Disney created a new channel, Disney XD, to try to win back boy viewers (Barnes 2009). Disney's turn to pop music was not intended to be a turn to girls. But Top 40 pop is defined in large part by female audiences (Weisbard 2014). By fully committing to pop music, while refusing the puerile humor or oppositional politics of Nickelodeon's approach, the Disney Channel's ultimate gendering was overdetermined. The contrast with the music artists who did appear on Nickelodeon in the mid-2000s is instructive. The Naked Brothers Band and especially Drake Bell made guitar-driven rock that sounded, if anything, conservative, dated, and male. The website *AllMusic* compared the Naked Brothers Band to Jimmy Buffett (Erlewine 2007) and Drake Bell to Paul McCartney (*AllMusic* 2005)

Eric Weisbard's account of radio formats—Top 40, adult contemporary, rhythm and blues, album-oriented rock, country—and the creation of "multiple mainstreams: distinct, if at times overlapping, cultural centers" offers a way of understanding Disney's cultivation of tween pop music. Weisbard writes that "the logic of formats celebrated the skillful matching of a set of songs with a set of people," while "the logic of genres ... celebrated the creative matching of a set of songs and a set of ideals" (2014: introduction). From this perspective, genres establish and enforce musical criteria for inclusion, prioritizing authenticity and fidelity. Formats, by contrast, emphasize people rather than music, crossing genre boundaries without reservation in pursuit of audiences. Generating new audiences—identifying existing groups but also working to create or shape coherent groups from messy sociology—is central to the logic of formats. Weisbard argues that radio program directors have "strong business reasons to experiment with untapped consumer segments, to accentuate the 'maturation' of a buying group with ... music to match" (2014: introduction). Furthermore, as Weisbard's history makes clear, age has always been as important to the commercial logic of formats as issues of race, class, and gender that more visibly structure the fault lines among rock, Top 40, and rhythm and blues, from the 1950s emergence of rock 'n' roll to the 2000s establishment of Latin radio in the United States (see also Keightley 2001).

Through the early 1990s US children's music was a genre, or a small handful of genres—folk revival, musical theater, perhaps bubblegum pop—which had little or no interaction. Radio Disney, by contrast, programmed oldies, novelty songs, and 1990s teen pop in the same playlists, investing much more in matching itself to a particular audience than considerations of musical style or genre. The work Disney did in the decade between the creation of Radio Disney in 1996 and the launch of *High School Musical* in 2006 was to build a kids' pop format. The logic of "crossing over" is a characteristic dynamic of formats' fluid boundaries, and Top 40, especially, capaciously includes hits from country, hip-hop, rock, and R&B that are not overly fixed to the authenticating criteria of their genres. The process by which Disney's tween pop acts were successful first within Disney's tween media enclosure and later crossed over to mainstream airplay is characteristic of emerging music formats. The logic of crossing over also helps make sense of why Disney's pop acts helped define the Disney Channel so strongly as a girls' channel. Developing music acts that might "launch . . . into the mainstream, adult audience and all," means, in effect, developing pop acts that can appeal to an already-gendered Top 40 format. Crossing over to mainstream pop is a pervasively gendered process. Weisbard describes numerous examples, from the pop-friendly rock/rap band Linkin Park refusing to do events at Top 40 radio stations to preserve their masculine rock credibility, to female country artists from Dolly Parton to Taylor Swift having to break with country's masculinist hard-core factions to pursue their pop careers. The development of tween pop, then, was the natural extension of a logic already built into commercial radio and music production, and the strong connection Disney articulated between tween audiences and pop music was itself a significant force in gendering tweens feminine. As Weisbard argues, "Formats did not just sell music—they normalized it. Formats did not just sell products—they touted categories of consumers" (2014: introduction). What Disney did was normalize pop music for kids, and, even more, articulate the category "tween" as culturally, not just commercially, meaningful.

The Disney Channel would ultimately become so thoroughly identified with girls that its parent company would decide to create an entirely new television channel to pursue boy audiences, having given up on the possibility that any changes to the Disney Channel itself might ever bring boys back. By tracing the commercial logic of Disney's simultaneous turn to tween audiences and pop music, I want to underscore the important ways by which the construction of tween audiences as girls—now fully accomplished, and simply an unmistakable fact of the matter—was specifically not the motivation for many of the key moves in this history, and can meaningfully be seen as unintentional. Disney, like all its competitors, was chasing older kids, and kids with more "sophisticated" preferences. In practice that ended up meaning "girls," and it is important to see that Disney's turn to pop music contributed to that outcome. That a corporate strategy oriented to finely calibrated age gradations would result in a commercial formation that was broadly inclusive across a range of ages but was strictly and definitively gendered tells us something interesting about age and gender both.

The tension between "mainstream" and children's music is, significantly, a tension about the relationship between children and the wider public sphere of consumer media. Thus Disney's ability to launder pop music and make it appear appropriate for children had a lot to do with containing its musical products within a bounded sphere of media distribution and consumption. By restructuring children's music as a commercial music format, Disney articulated the relationship between children and the mainstream as a conventional one, more like the (fraught but intelligible) tensions between rock, country, or hip-hop authenticity and mainstream Top 40. Top 40 music formats, especially, have always been ready to follow profits, which means inclusively welcoming—or appropriating—rock 'n' roll, R&B, hip-hop, country, and Latin music into the mainstream fold. If welcoming (or appropriating) tween artists reflected the same logic, that also meant that childhood, at least within a sphere of entertainment media and consumer culture, had been configured to fit within familiar models of cultural identity.

Pop music let the Disney Channel split the difference somewhat: while Nickelodeon's brand—and appeal to older children—was based on explicit opposition between kids and adults signified through acts like humiliating adults by covering them in green slime, Disney always avoided explicit anti-adult sentiment and therefore was unable to make that sort of appeal to older child audiences. Pop music is already built around a logic of youth culture and subcultural affiliation, and by providing musical products very clearly defined as "pop music for kids" the Disney Channel was able to appeal to tweens as an independent subcultural group distinguished specifically from adults without making explicitly anti-adult statements. Ironically, in doing so they launched children's music acts into the mainstream and demonstrated new (old) business models for an ailing music industry.

THREE "HAVING IT ALL"

The Disney Channel's turn toward pop music during the 2000s was a calculated strategy to attract older child audiences with "mainstream" appeal, without dismantling core children's media business models centered on cross-marketing and merchandising, and without undermining central cultural markers of childhood. That aspirational business plan mirrored the aspirations to maturity identified by Daniel Thomas Cook and Susan B. Kaiser (2004) as central to the rhetorics of "tween" marketing and consumer culture. In this way Disney's goal of mainstream appeal was not so much an attempt to escape the confines of children's media as it was an effort to cultivate a productive tension between the "mainstream" and childhood as central to its vision of tween media. That tension, which built on a deeper cultural opposition between the sheltered domesticity of childhood and the wider public sphere of consumer media, was at the center of Disney's most prominent effort to break into the popular musical mainstream: the Disney Channel sitcom *Hannah Montana*.

Despite Disney's best efforts at threading the needle between children and pop music, that tension would also become central in *Hannah Montana* star Miley Cyrus's own public persona. In the spring of 2008, near the peak of her popularity, Cyrus did a photo shoot with Annie Leibovitz for *Vanity Fair*, in which she appeared without a top (though covered with a blanket) at age fifteen. The next year, at sixteen, Cyrus performed at the Teen Choice Awards by dancing with a pole and wearing a revealing outfit—which uncomfortable viewers interpreted as suggestive of exotic dancing. She received a lot of criticism from adults and fans alike for apparently exceeding the limits of age-appropriate behavior. One eleven-year-old told the *New York Times* in 2010, "I feel like she acts 25. She looks so old. She is too old for herself" (Holson 2010: ST1). At the same time, Cyrus's single "Party in the USA" was a major radio hit in the summer of 2009, and she appeared to have broken through to mainstream celebrity. The impossible position in which Cyrus found herself trying to reconcile sexuality, child audiences, and public performance was apparent in two contradictory responses from industry insiders to her "scandals." After the seminude photo shoot, a Disney Channel Worldwide executive told *Condé Nast Portfolio*, "For Miley Cyrus to be a 'good girl' is now a business decision for her. Parents have invested in her godliness. If she violates that trust, she won't get it back" (Greenfeld 2008). Compare that "business decision" with a comment from an editor at *US Magazine* in response to the Teen Choice Awards performance: "She already has this risque image, so it really wasn't much of a stretch. That's how Britney [Spears] took off. She was the good girl gone bad, and it looks to be working for Miley as well" (Kahn 2009). Despite Cyrus's clear success at accomplishing the Disney Channel's goal of transcending the boundaries between niche children's media and mass appeal by bringing together young listeners and mainstream audiences, the tensions inherent in such an accomplishment were potentially explosive.

Years later Cyrus would go on to distance herself from the show and Disney in more spectacular and strategic ways. In fall 2013 she joked on *Saturday Night Live* that Hannah Montana had been murdered. Also in 2013, as I discuss in the next chapter, her performance at the MTV Video Music Awards dramatically broke with the tame domesticity of her Disney image, rejecting Hannah Montana's "innocence" not just in its overt performance of sexuality and ironic use of childish teddy bears as props, but also in its appropriation and objectification of Black musical sounds, dance styles, and performers (Cottom 2013; Eells 2013; Platon 2013), claiming Blackness as part of a very clear racial coding that rejected the whiteness of innocence (Bernstein 2011). Such controversy is common for child stars, because of their contradictory demands of their roles as children and public performers (O'Connor 2008), to the point that Cyrus's experience of difficult transition from child to adult star almost followed a formula (Gevinson 2014).

But perhaps we risk learning too much from public scandal, especially scandals that so clearly mark a break between past and future. The real-life Cyrus made a decisive individual choice to resolve the contradictions between public performance and childhood innocence by disavowing her own childhood. From 2006 to 2011 Cyrus starred in a half-hour sitcom on the Disney Channel in which her fictional avatar dramatized a fantasy version of those very same contradictions. But rather than driving toward a decisive resolution or break, the fictional show *Hannah Montana* wallowed in its contradictions, milking them for drama and sentiment and making no effort to conclusively resolve them. Instead *Hannah Montana* narrated that tension between public and intimate life as characteristic of childhood, as the marker of an authentic and essentialized identity—less a contradiction than a confirmation. That Miley Cyrus grew up and chose adulthood by rejecting childhood tells us little about how the tensions at the heart of *Hannah Montana* would have addressed the lives of the millions of children who watched her on TV, attended her concerts, and listened to her albums in the middle of the decade. Those audiences have also grown older, but in 2006 Disney addressed them *as children*, not just as future teenagers and young adults. We risk losing sight of that extraordinary moment when we assume that its meaning was superseded and made intelligible only by later events. More importantly we risk shifting attention from children and back, again, as always, to adults, when we follow child stars across the threshold of their adulthoods, and then retrospectively interpret their childhood stardom from this side of that horizon.

And in 2006 *Hannah Montana* was truly extraordinary. The show ushered in a new era of children's media. Along with the television movie *High School Musical* and the pop-rock act the Jonas Brothers, *Hannah Montana* returned Disney to a level of commercial and cultural dominance with young audiences that it had lost since its heyday of animated musical films in the 1990s. In 2007 the *Hannah Montana* soundtrack album debuted at number 1 and spent seventy-eight weeks on the *Billboard* 200 chart (*Billboard* 2019a). A national concert tour sold out in minutes (Kaufman 2007), and a concert film sold out theaters nationally (Bowles 2008). Between its theatrical and home-video releases, *Hannah Montana / Miley Cyrus: Best of Both Worlds Concert Tour* earned $65 million domestically and set box office records for normally slow midwinter releases (*Box Office Mojo* 2014). The show effectively transformed Disney's music business and rapidly accelerated a decade-long shift toward pop music genres and multimedia tie-ins across the children's music industry (Chmielewski 2007). Certainly *Hannah Montana* built on earlier Disney Channel successes like *That's So Raven* and *Lizzie McGuire* (Martin 2004), as well as teen pop heavily marketed to children in the 1990s such as Britney Spears and NSYNC (Knopper 2009). But it combined and transformed those predecessors, establishing a model of enormously successful multimedia celebrity acts, bridging film, television, and popular music, focused entirely on preadolescent audiences. When we talk about the changing fields of tween media and children's consumer culture, then, *Hannah Montana* is a pivotal text.

Not only was *Hannah Montana* a genre-defining tween media product, but its narrative revolved around the tension between childhood domesticity and public participation. The show's premise is that fourteen-year-old pop sensation Hannah Montana lives a normal life as middle-school girl Miley Stewart. The narrative conflict in the show builds around tensions between Miley's public and private lives, exploring in rich detail how having a public life disrupts Miley's "normal" childhood and is especially threatening to the intimacy of her friendships and peer relationships.[1] This seems broadly to allegorize children's changing relationship to media and public culture, but rather than reinventing the wheel in sorting through these questions as they applied to children, *Hannah Montana* borrowed and adapted its approach from another sphere with a long tradition of media dramatizing cultural anxiety around changing social boundaries: the post/feminist problem of "having it all," which addresses women's changing relationship to domestic and waged work. "Having it all" is a long-standing topic in debates about feminism and gender equality, as in a widely read essay in the *Atlantic Monthly* by US State Department official and Princeton University professor Anne-Marie Slaughter titled "Why Women Still Can't Have It All" (2012), about her struggles to reconcile the demands of professional success with her goals as a mother. Such "having it all" discourses often identify a conflict between "feminism" and "femininity" (Brunsdon 1991) that applies specifically to women in contemporary capitalism, in which an apparent incompatibility between public, professional roles as wage earners and heads of households ("feminism") and private, domestic roles as wife and mother ("femininity") places impossible, contradictory demands on women. In my analysis, *Hannah Montana* reworks "having it all" as a heuristic for thinking through problems of children's changing relationship to media and domesticity, drawing (sometimes forced) parallels between working women's struggles to reconcile work with family and tween girls' struggles to envision a place for themselves beyond the "separate spheres" of childhood domesticity and schooling, without giving up what is seen as valuable and desirable about childhood.[2]

While this chapter explores how problematics of gender can be adapted to the particularities of childhood, I do not propose that it is possible to fully tease age out from gender. The problem of tween consumption is already a problem of femininity, and tween femininity is also implicitly white, affluent, suburban, and consumerist, while childhood, too, is normatively constructed as feminine, white, affluent, suburban, and consumerist. My goal then is to locate childhood among the intersections of gender, race, and class in consumer media, and to point out how frameworks like postfeminism can travel, slip, shift, or adapt across intersecting categories of identity.

Media scholar Morgan Blue (2013) has convincingly analyzed *Hannah Montana*'s postfeminist vision of contemporary girlhood. In particular, Blue demonstrates that *Hannah Montana* uses conventional tropes of postfeminist media in ways that confine girls within their femininity and foreclose the possibility of girls' freedom and agency in areas other than consumption—just as postfeminism generally portrays feminism as "taken into account" by women who then set it aside to celebrate traditional femininity in a retrenchment of gender norms (McRobbie 2009: 12). Here I build on Blue's analysis to emphasize age as a key category of social identity and to see *Hannah Montana*'s adoption of postfeminist conventions not only as a straightforward application to girlhood, but also as an imperfect adaptation to childhood. "Having it all" discourses so specifically address the particularities of adult women's struggles around wage earning, child rearing, and marriage that they apply awkwardly, at best, to a childhood context defined as outside work, marriage, and reproduction. Nonetheless in its plot, characterization, and tone *Hannah Montana* was structured around a very familiar "having it all" formula, which suggests that something more complicated was at work. My argument is that the show used "having it all" as a heuristic for working through the relatively uncharted territory of children's changing relationship to media and public culture.

On the one hand, this approach implies that *Hannah Montana* is not original: it adopted conventional formulas from women's media to work through familiar problems of public/private tension. On the other hand, media that narrates and struggles with the problem of children's public lives might have very different implications than media that narrates this problem for women. Marshaling conventionally postfeminist "having it all" discourses to envision a public life for children requires a much more creative, open-ended, and future-oriented imagination of possibility for children in the world, in part because the idea of childhood in public is implicitly unrealistic, fantastical, or destabilizing. Dominant ideologies around family and work treat children as fully private and domestic. The historical project of children's withdrawal from wage earning and confinement within consumerist domesticity has been intensified and more fully realized in the last generation, with the sacralization of childhood playing a key role in the retrenchment of patriarchal family values and reaction against women's increasing role as wage earners (Pugh 2009: 20). Furthermore, childhood innocence is central to ideologies of racial and class superiority, especially as rhetorical appeals to childhood allow for the coded reinforcement of patriarchal, bourgeois, and white supremacist projects (Bernstein 2011; Zelizer 1985). Of course many actual children work and are economically productive both inside and outside the home, but ideologies of childhood innocence either ignore such activities or treat them as pathologies that further justify social stratification and hierarchy. Allowing for the possibility of public or professional intrusions on protected childhoods—of children "having it all"—potentially threatens a core justification for the patriarchal family and risks eliciting discourses of anxiety, moral panic, and even vicious reaction against perceived threats to social authority.

Disney has long been invested in "family values" that stabilize the patriarchal, white, middle-class family (Giroux 1999), and *Hannah Montana*, which narrated the experiences of an affluent, white patriarchal family to mostly affluent, white child audiences, was no exception. Why, then, did one of the most prominent examples of children's media in the last decade so visibly probe the contradictions of this ideology of (white, affluent, feminine) childhood domesticity as its structuring conflict? It may be that thematizing childhood as anxious and contradictory encouraged a retrenchment toward "authentic" (and thus domestic) childhood, rather than necessarily leading toward autonomy for children and destabilization of their status within the family. The experience and narration of the self as contradictory and problematic is an unexceptional, even conventional, characteristic of public claims of minority-group affiliation. Lauren Berlant (2008) points out, for example, that negative affects are central to the production of an intimate public femininity, which claims its publicness precisely through appeals to domestic authenticity. Similarly, Michael Warner argues that "self-alienation is common to all of the contexts of publicity," such that "at the very moment of recognizing ourselves as the mass subject . . . we also recognize ourselves as minority subjects. As participants in the mass subject, we are the 'we' that can describe our particular affiliations of class, gender, sexual orientation, race, or subculture only as 'they'" (2002: 171). That experience of self-alienation through the recognition of oneself as affiliated with a publicly mediated group is perhaps *necessary* to the establishment of a coherent and self-ordering market demographic.

The children's media market needed children to think of their childhoods as a source of authenticity (naturally based in the reproductive family and characterized by same-age friendships), but also as a problem (vulnerable and full of contradiction). This meant simultaneously doubling down on the nuclear family as the site of authentic childhood while in the same gesture envisioning forms of childhood subjectivity that directly undermined the family's necessity. But this is a trick that women's media had productively worked out for generations: simultaneously positioning the heterosexual family as the highest object of individual desire while narrating stories of work and friendship that would seem to expose the family as obsolete. If encouraging the growth of children's media meant encouraging children's identification as subjects whose public and private lives are in contradictory tension, postfeminist women's media provided proven scripts for that goal.

"HAVING IT ALL" IN WOMEN'S MEDIA

Hannah Montana adapted a framework that had been worked through in women's media over two decades, responding to the concern that women's participation in wage labor threatens intimate domestic relations. The classic examples in feminist media studies are the television shows *Ally McBeal* and *Sex and the City* and the book and film series *Bridget Jones's Diary* (see, e.g., Genz 2010; McRobbie 2009; Moseley and Read 2002). Moseley and Read (2002) contrast *Ally McBeal* with earlier shows like *Murphy Brown* and *L.A. Law*. Those shows had previously been identified by Dow (1996) as examples of prime-time television in which "the main conflict for female characters is between career and personal happiness . . . [which] are mutually exclusive, as are feminist and feminine identities" (Moseley and Read 2002: 231). *Ally McBeal*, by contrast, "does not centre on a conflict between career and personal life, but instead on the struggle to hold them together. . . . The distinction and conflict between public and private and feminist and feminine identities is irrevocably deconstructed and integrated. . . . Ally has a successful career, but her personal life, unlike Murphy Brown's, is filled with warmth and friendship as well as loneliness and struggle" (232). Genz generalizes from Ally McBeal, Carrie Bradshaw (*Sex and the City*), and Bridget Jones a theory of the "postfeminist singleton": "the young, unattached, and mostly city-dwelling woman who is caught between the enjoyment of her independent urban life and her desperate yearning to find 'Mr. Right' with whom to settle down. The singleton's predicament centers on her recognition that 'having it all' implies walking a tightrope between professional success and personal failure, between feminist and feminine empowerment" (2010: 99). Earlier characters like Murphy Brown or Angela Bower from *Who's the Boss?* either forego marriage and motherhood or delegate domestic work to a live-in employee, choosing professional success over conventionally feminine motherhood. By contrast, the protagonists in the more recent examples are determined "*not to choose* between feminism and femininity, job and relationship" (Genz 2010: 113-14, emphasis added). But since the underlying conflict is a structural one that has not been resolved historically, materially, or culturally, the idea that women can refuse to choose may simply be a pipe dream or fantasy. One reading is that these media simply assume away the conflict and instead portray "the effortless realization of a postfeminist nirvana where women can 'have it all'" (103-4). Genz argues instead for a more optimistic, or at least more nuanced, reading in which "the postfeminist singleton expresses the pains and pleasures of her problematical quest for balance in a world where personal and professional, feminist and feminine positions are mutually pervasive" (104).

Whether highlighting struggle or resolution, these shows share a narrative technique for exploring women's refusal to choose between feminism and femininity: they collapse their protagonists' public and private contexts, treating their characters' professional lives as sites of intimacy. For example, Carrie Bradshaw, whose job is to write newspaper columns about her sex life, makes her personal life the basis of her work, while Ally McBeal's workplace is the site of a caring and intimate group of friends. This move sidesteps the problem of the family to which "having it all" originally refers. Instead it displaces intimacy onto nonfamilial relationships. These shows seem to envision friendship as a relationship that can accommodate care, dependence, emotional and financial support, and stability outside of heterosexual marriage, such that Gerhard (2005) goes so far as to argue for a queer reading of *Sex and the City*'s emphasis on stable friendships as an alternative or addition to marriage.[3]

Still, despite their protagonists' rich personal and professional lives, the narratives of these media revolve around (or at least repeatedly return to) a deeply felt absence of and desire for children and husbands. The feminism that makes personal and professional success possible in the first place seems in the same stroke to foreclose the sort of "essential" or "authentic" femininity embodied in roles like mother or wife that are still profoundly desired. On the one hand, these postfeminist media present a superheroic (or superficial) reconciliation of public and private. On the other hand, they lament a field of naturalized gender identity that is left behind. While we might describe these as questions about individual gender identity, what is specifically implicated are types of relationships: relationships like wife and mother that are presumptively stable, given, and natural but also strangely unattainable, versus unstable, chosen, and intensely felt relationships that characters desire, but never quite succeed, to convert into given naturalness.

What is fascinating in *Hannah Montana* is that it is built around an almost identical problematic, except the desired but unattainable relationship is not marriage or motherhood, but friendship itself. Friendship in *Hannah Montana* is a site of both given, natural supportiveness *and* unstable and occasionally desperate desire. Friendship is not just the relationship that combines and thus reconciles public and private, as it is in classically postfeminist texts. Here friendship is also the mode of intimacy that is most threatened by publicness. Rather than marriage or motherhood, friendship is posed as the role most characteristic of "essential" or "authentic" childhood. In the project of envisioning a public life for children, in parallel to or by analogy with the gendered problem of "having it all," the role of precarious but profoundly desired intimacy is filled by friendship as the site of vulnerability, anxiety, and desire.

CAN TWEENS HAVE IT ALL?

If "having it all" is the shorthand for an ongoing cultural conversation about public/private conflict for women, "tween" might be seen as shorthand for a parallel discourse about children. The in-betweenness foregrounded by the tween concept points to an incompatibility between the presumptive domesticity, dependence, and innocence of childhood and the (relative) publicness, independence, and worldliness of adolescence and its associated mass-mediated public youth culture. The oppositional terms here, while not identical with the tension between motherhood and work to which "having it all" might simplistically reduce, highlight similar themes. The relative independence of adolescence from the family is substantially linked to economic freedoms of consumption (Chinn 2008), in parallel to the apparent problem that independent economic success is said to cause for women's family success. The terms that contrast with economic independence—childhood and motherhood—both emphasize embedded familial relations, intimacy, and dependence. Very schematically, then, the tension implicit in the term "tween" poses the familial domesticity of childhood against the economic independence of adolescence, exposing an ideological binary of "private" versus "public" that may operate in parallel ways for preadolescent children as for working adult women.

It is important to my argument that *Hannah Montana* is a narrative of childhood more than adolescence, despite its characters' chronological age. (Miley is fourteen years old at the start of the show, which ends with her graduation from high school.) Marah Gubar (2003) points to the family as a key diagnostic of cultural constructions of age in her argument that the mouse-child protagonist of E. B. White's *Stuart Little* stages a drama of adolescence rather than childhood. *Stuart Little* emphasizes the boundary-crossing abjections of adolescence, especially in the protagonist's relation to his family, as his parents' "anxiety and discomfort lead them to encourage their son to embark upon dirty and dangerous adventures that basically constitute attempts to expel this disturbingly animalistic presence out of the family body" (100). More prosaically, *Stuart Little* is full of "many classic and discomfiting adolescent moments: first love, first date, first car wreck, and first job" (100). By contrast *Hannah Montana* never treats the nuclear family as specifically threatened, anxious, or discomforted. While it does depict Miley experiencing "firsts" like dating, notably her job is not a "first" at all, but something that precedes the show's timeline, and like her family it is a given and unquestioned part of her life. Her celebrity is firmly part of her childhood, it does not threaten her family, and she "grows up" in ways other than getting a job and becoming economically independent, since she has already reached those milestones. Were the fourteen-year-old character's public life to inspire conflict with her father, the narrative might be more simply recognizable as a story of adolescent angst and rebellion. Instead, *Hannah Montana* portrays "having it all" as a problem for friendship, a traditional site of childhood intimacy and desire. There is thus an important distinction between tween and teenager: however aspirational it is, tween is not simply the extension of adolescence downward, and its alignment with familial domesticity in media products like *Hannah Montana* suggests an investment in preserving and reproducing key elements of childhood, rather than simply growing out of them more quickly.[4]

In part this is another example of Disney effectively sidestepping a potential conflict. The problem consumption poses to families is that children's desires are oriented outward from the family, toward both friends and consumer products (Pugh 2009). But Disney is interested in addressing its audience as both children and consumers, and thus it poses those two desires—friendship and consumption—in a narratively productive tension. At the same time, Disney is invested in legitimating its own industry and in convincing morally panicky adults that popular music and other consumer products are not directly threatening to families. With popular music Disney already runs the risk of simply reproducing adolescent youth culture. Instead, despite the potential slippage of "tween" into "teen"—and the ubiquitous fears around "age compression" that such slippage is already occurring—for the balancing act of tween media to work, it needs to be firmly grounded in childhood. By naturalizing her family and refusing to treat it as a source of narrative conflict, *Hannah Montana* avoids becoming a narrative of adolescence and instead maintains its focus on public/private conflict as a problem specific to childhood. Furthermore, "having it all" discourses themselves emphasize traditionally "feminine" values like childbearing and care and are therefore symptomatic of a postfeminist political conservatism, or even of a public women's culture whose master trope is "complaint" (Berlant 2008). In the same way *Hannah Montana*'s vision of public childhood is deeply conservative, portraying an innocent childhood sphere of friendship and domesticity uncorrupted by consumption and publicness as an essentialized feature of "authentic" childhood identities.

INTIMATE FRIENDSHIP IN *HANNAH MONTANA*

Hannah Montana supports two contrasting interpretations. In the first, deep contradictions between public and private are effortlessly reconciled by consumption and "love conquering all." In the second, problematics of postfeminism are repurposed as problematics of childhood. From the latter perspective *Hannah Montana* did not so much narrate a simplistic morality play of gender-identity retrenchment as it posed and struggled with a fantastical but also deeply interesting question about what it might mean for children to be professionals or even heads of households and to have meaningful public lives without sacrificing the things that define them as "authentically" children: their embeddedness in familial relationships, their same-age friendships, their school lives, their consumer culture. If postfeminism negotiates a conflict between feminist empowerment and feminine authenticity, we can see something similar in *Hannah Montana*, where professional, economic, and cultural (if not political) autonomy is posed against "authentic" childhood. Where postfeminism portrays feminism as having "robbed women of their most treasured pleasures, i.e. romance, gossip and obsessive concerns about how to catch a husband" (McRobbie 2009: 21), similarly in *Hannah Montana* the possibility of a public, professional, economically independent life threatens the "most treasured pleasures" of childhood.

The first reading is suggested by the show's country-pop theme song, performed by Cyrus in a title sequence depicting Hannah Montana onstage before a crowd of excited child fans. The song poses two worlds and asserts that you can have them both:

> You get the limo out front
> Hottest styles, every shoe, every color
> Yeah, when you're famous it can be kind of fun
> It's really you but no one ever discovers
> In some ways you're just like all your friends
> But on stage you're a star
> You get the best of both worlds
>
> [...]
>
> Living two lives is a little weird
> But school's cool 'cause nobody knows
> Yeah, you get to be a small-town girl
> But big-time when you play your guitar
>
> [...]
>
> Pictures and autographs
> You get your face in all the magazines
> The best part's that
> You get to be whoever you want to be
>
> [...]
>
> Who would have thought that a girl like me
> Would double as a superstar?[5]

Certain lyrics celebrate authenticity: "small-town girl," "girl like me," "like all your friends," "it's really you." Others highlight the joys of celebrity. There is a hint of tension in the statement "living two lives is a little weird." But maintaining the secret ("school's cool 'cause nobody knows") resolves that tension entirely. There is a more indirect tension in the idea of an authentic self: phrases like "it's really you" imply an authentic identity that reads against "you get to be whoever you want to be." Looking more closely, the earlier line is also "you *get to be* a small-town girl"—so that "authentic" identity might itself be a choice. Combined with "hottest styles, every shoe, every color," we can see the core postfeminist trope of choice and empowerment through consumption (Gill 2007): choosing among two contradictory identities is as simple as choosing a pair of shoes, and Miley is privileged here specifically because she has a bigger closet full of shoes and identities. Realistically, being a small-town girl like all your friends should be directly incompatible with being a celebrity pop star with your picture in all the magazines. But the song simply assumes the contradiction away (do both!) and establishes the "situation" of the show as a classically postfeminist superficial reconciliation of public and private worlds.

If "The Best of Both Worlds" appears to assert the ease of "having it all," the tension of "it all" is between celebrity and school/friends, not work and family. While celebrity is similar to, but also much more than, wage-earning employment, school and friendship are very different from family, which the song never mentions. In particular, school and friendship are not obviously "private" or domestic, but instead have important components of publicness (Eckert 1996). Still, school is like the family home in being a site of paternal care and childhood dependence, and friendship is itself a central site of intimacy that, like family, may highlight mutuality in contrast to instrumental neoliberal individualism. As Valerie Hey writes, "Friendship demands a 'self' and the 'other.' Subjects cannot simply evade the regulation that flows from interconnectedness, mutuality and interdependence.... Taken together, young people's investments in the practice of compulsory sociability is so strong that no amount of neoliberalism is ever likely to overwrite it" (2002: 239). Such intense investment in sociability heightens the narrative stakes of friendship and situates it as a key site of both desire and anxiety, very much like the role of heterosexual romance in postfeminist women's shows.

By contrast with the theme song, the narrative of the show itself tends to suggest the second reading, especially as it spends a lot more effort fretting about tensions rather than assuming them away. The plot of the first episode opens with Miley's best friend Lilly, who does not know Miley is the famous performer, announcing a pair of tickets to see Hannah Montana in concert. Miley refuses to attend the concert to avoid revealing her secret identity, and Lilly, reasonably, is upset that her best friend will not join her to see their favorite act. Miley worries to her dad that if others found out then "no one would treat me the same" and "I'd never be 'just Miley' again."[6] The rest of the episode plays out around Miley's increasingly dramatic and ultimately unsuccessful efforts to conceal her identity from Lilly. When Miley does reveal her secret, Lilly is upset that she was not trusted from the start. Miley explains that "I thought maybe once you knew you wouldn't want to be my friend anymore, and you'd like Hannah Montana more than you'd like me." Lilly is sympathetic but affirms "that could never happen, Miley, don't you know that?" Miley agrees, and the friendship seems secured. But when Miley later shows Lilly her closet full of expensive clothes, Lilly fantasizes about telling their school friends. They argue passionately until Lilly calls Miley "Hannah," confirming Miley's worst fear of no longer being "just Miley." Finally they reconcile, when Lilly, again, affirms that Miley is her best friend, so for that reason she will not act on her admitted desire to use Hannah's celebrity for her own benefits.

There is no consumer delight here in choosing among an abundance of available identities, only anxiety at the risk posed by that abundance. Unlike the theme song where it is a simple matter of "school's cool 'cause nobody knows," here the possibility of Miley's secret being discovered is not just "a little weird." Instead it threatens her intensely valued core identity as "just Miley," which is defined relationally, as her identity *for Lilly*: the full line is "if *she* knew the truth, I'd never be just Miley again." Miley's core identity, then, is tied up in her relationship with her best friend, and more generally in the types of relationships and social roles that are available in childhood settings like school and home.

Interestingly, her actual family is never an existential problem like this: perhaps more like Ally McBeal's or Carrie Bradshaw's friends, Miley's father and brother are a source of comic relief and sometimes frustration, but they are a stable and undramatic presence in her life. Conflict with her brother does not lead to anxiety about the loss of that relationship. If *Hannah Montana* sought to realistically depict the lived tensions of consumption for contemporary children, it would have treated the nuclear family as specifically threatened. Allison Pugh's (2009) research shows very clearly that many parents see children's consumption as a real problem for their families and that the values of consumption directly pit children's friendships and peer communities against their families. Instead *Hannah Montana* depicted the patriarchal nuclear family as a source of stability and security for children, while treating friendship—the conventional site of children's consumerist pleasure and interest—as the relationship that is threatened by consumerist desire. The show tried to have it both ways: to flirt with publicness as an existential problem for childhood, without problematizing the patriarchal family or giving up its implicit identification with childhood. Miley's best friendship looks more like the romances in those postfeminist dramas: it is a deeply felt, emotionally fraught, and intensely valued relationship whose stability and continuity is desired but, despite all Lilly's protests to the contrary, clearly *not* assured. Instead it is vulnerable and requires continual reaffirmation. Just as the precariousness of romance thematizes the difficulty of attaining a satisfying intimate life for the postfeminist singleton, here a parallel desire for a satisfying intimacy is staged in a childhood context through the precariousness of best friendship.

Rather than consumption being the magic tool to resolve all contradictions, Hannah's material excess elicits an overabundance of desire in Lilly that again threatens to destabilize the friendship. We might continue the comparison with heterosexual romance narratives: tween girls like Lilly are often culturally stereotyped as overwhelmed by consumer desire. To the extent that that desire is *for* celebrity bodies like Hannah's, we might liken the construction of tween consumer desire to constructions of masculine sexual desire (cf. McRobbie and Garber 1976). Rosalind Gill (2007) argues that postfeminism requires girls and women to internalize the male gaze and self-objectify, resolving the problem of objectification not critically but passively by accepting objectivity as an authentic form of subjectivity. This is done primarily through consumer practices of clothing and decorating the body. Lilly's desire for Hannah presents a strikingly similar situation, even with consumer apparel at its center. Were Miley to follow the scripts of Gill's postfeminist sensibility, she might internalize her objectification under Lilly's consumer gaze and treat Hannah as a full-time authentic self. Instead she strongly rejects that option. Whether that reflects a critical sensibility toward postfeminism is less interesting to me than the way that the friendship itself is charged here with these problematics of desire and objectification.

Morgan Blue notes that Lilly is a tomboy who never lives up to the standards of "feminine propriety" set by Hannah/Miley (2013: 71). Once privy to Miley's secret, Lilly takes on a secret identity as well, the camp/drag Lola. Lilly/Lola's femininity is awkward and visibly performative: "As Lilly attempts to comply with Miley's sense of feminine propriety, she performs an exaggeration of youthful femininity in a collection of wigs, but tends toward the boyish—tomboyish—in relation to Hannah's masquerade of girlishness. In this way, Lilly's Lola disguise can work as a foil to Miley's Hannah, never threatening to displace Hannah's idealized girlhood" (71). I want to consider Lilly's tomboyishness in light of *Hannah Montana*'s format as a classic network-era live-audience family sitcom (Newman 2009). With her boyish puerility, her awkward physicality and slapstick humor, her repeated threats to publicly embarrass Miley/Hannah, her inability to meet class-based standards of feminine propriety set by her partner, and her personal failure to control her impulses and desires, Lilly conforms to the classic *male* sitcom archetype of the "working-class buffoon" who always embarrasses and disappoints his more refined wife (Butsch 2011). The plot of this first episode, in which intimate trust is unintentionally and incompetently betrayed but ultimately reaffirmed (while reserving the possibility that future episodes will return to the buffoonish character's bumbling failures), rehearses a family sitcom cliché. By comparing Lilly to buffoonish husbands I do not wish to suggest that her gender performance is radically nonconforming. I agree with Blue that her tomboyishness ultimately supports rather than undermines the show's hegemonic femininity. Rather I want to highlight the adaptation of explicitly domestic televisual roles—buffoonish husband, properly feminine wife—into this very different context of childhood friendship.

Noting the homology between friendship and romance here, we can read the episode's resolution as a conventional statement of "true love conquering all": in the course of the episode, Lilly asserts once that she would never prefer Hannah to Miley. She then reveals through her actions that this is not actually true. But then, despite failing to act on her initial promise, she is able to permanently heal the relationship by simply restating her commitment to Miley: "you're my best friend." This is unsatisfying for a conclusion that attempts to secure Miley and Lilly's friendship as the basis for the ongoing show. But it is also a standard formula of romantic narratives in which love is valued as the pure expression of interior feeling and is therefore demonstrated by passionate affirmations rather than actions. In friendship or romance, love may be sentimentally valuable precisely because it is not pragmatically or instrumentally valuable.

That age and not just gender is at stake here is confirmed over the course of the series, in future seasons and episodes. While Miley repeatedly "comes out" to select friends, she continues to closely guard her secret, which is a source of conflict and threat for her "normal" childhood of school and friendship. Miley Stewart can never come out to the whole world, because if she did so *she would stop being a child*. Unlike adult celebrities who publicly reveal details about their intimate romances and private lives to build sympathetic identification with audiences, it is not possible to be both an international pop star *and* a small-town girl who is just like her friends with a normal school life. But the latter is what it means to fit the cultural construction of childhood, just like motherhood and marriage are constitutive of culturally constructed femininity. In the series' last season, Miley does finally reveal her secret to the world, but only at the point when she and her friends will leave for college, which is to say, when they officially terminate their status as children. She does this because her secret creates problems for her friends—delaying Lilly's entry into college and getting Miley/Hannah's boyfriend into trouble with fans when he is caught with Miley and accused of "cheating" on Hannah. But also because the cost no longer exceeds the benefit: there is no more "authentic" childhood to be threatened by publicness. Thus when Hannah reveals that she is actually Miley on the *Tonight Show with Jay Leno*, we might note a shift into a much more conventional postfeminism: the public Hannah is integrated with the private Miley in the classic postfeminist move of resolving public/private conflict by collapsing them onto one another. Miley incorporates her professional identity into her private life; Hannah publicly reveals her private identity in her professional life. Upon entering adulthood, Miley can now pursue the model of Carrie Bradshaw, as a woman whose private and public lives are fully integrated by wholly publicizing the private.

CONTRADICTION AND CONSUMER CHILDHOOD

To summarize, *Hannah Montana* poses an idea very similar to "having it all" in its theme song and motivating situation. It then focuses on the implications of that idea for the "best friend" relationship between Miley and Lilly, which is narrated through recognizable if out-of-context tropes of romance, desire, objectification, domesticity, love, and even marriage. Miley's anxiety is not around finding and keeping a romantic partner or whether her profession will allow her to bear children and be a good mother. Instead she is anxious that her public, professional life will create deep problems for the most strongly felt intimate relationship in her life, her best friendship with Lilly. This fear is shown to be essentially valid, overcome only by the superheroic intensity of the friends' feelings for each other. To be sure, romantic friendship between girls is not a new theme (Faderman 1981), and it may be commonplace for girls' peer culture to focus on the vulnerability of emotionally heightened friendships (Thorne and Luria 1986). Borrowing from adult women's genres has a long history in girls' television (Seiter 1993).[7] What I think *is* interestingly new is the focus on mass-mediated public life as the specific threat to the intimacy of Miley and Lilly's friendship.

In conventional postfeminist media, "having it all" discourses allow three possible responses: accepting the incompatibility of work and family and choosing just one of them, superheroically/superficially collapsing the two and refusing the choice altogether, or highlighting the struggle, contradiction, and anxiety that the pursuit of "it all" creates in individuals' lives. The latter two are most visibly on the table in *Hannah Montana*. Genz argues for understanding the postfeminist singleton as embodying the third, emphasizing the struggle rather than resolution of contradictions at the forefront of postfeminist narratives. I read Blue as emphasizing the second, when she writes that "tensions between normative girl identities and celebrity or star personae, and between authenticity and performativity, are repeatedly raised and then mitigated in the series' continued attempts to reproduce and normalize celebrity girlhood" (2017: 51). Blue continues: "Hannah may trouble an otherwise stereotypical character. But she can do so only as long as Miley Stewart professes her preference for the 'normal' life over the particularly feminine excesses of celebrity. . . . There is minimal disconnect, then, between Miley's 'two worlds'" (2017: 51). But Miley does not merely *prefer* a "normal" life, as Blue puts it. Instead the stakes of that desire for her are clearly profound and even existential, raising questions about the very conditions of possibility of her life, and while the show very clearly raises these tensions, they are not so easily mitigated.

It is true that the theme song simplistically asserts the ease of achieving the "best of both worlds," and the first episode superficially resolves the threat posed by Hannah's celebrity to Miley and Lilly's friendship. But simplistic "happy endings" that purport to resolve thorny narrative problems need not have the last interpretive word. For example, in a related context of girls' literature, feminist readings of the *Anne of Green Gables* series have long emphasized the ultimate assimilation of the independent and not-romantically inclined protagonist into a stifling conventional regime of heteronormative romance. But in a contrasting approach, which resonates with my reading of *Hannah Montana*, Gubar emphasizes the books' portrayal of conflicting desires and "the extraordinary extent to which the *Anne* series dramatizes the *effort* its female characters must make to conform their unruly desires to the dictates of heterosexual romance, to close the gap between what they want and what they are supposed to want" (2001: 47). The *Anne* books spend so many pages attending to the solidary, intimate, and pleasurable relationships among its women characters that it is fair to think that their bulk might balance the narrative weight of a romantic conclusion and that despite their "happy ending" the books strive to articulate the value of intimacies other than heterosexual monogamy.[8] Jack Halberstam writes, similarly, about the endings of contemporary animated films for children: "along the way to these 'happy' endings, bad things happen to good animals, monsters, and children, and failure nestles in every dusty corner, reminding the child viewer that this too is what it means to live in a world created by mean, petty, greedy, and violent adults" (2011: 186). In the same vein, despite *Hannah Montana*'s happy ending, the issues it grapples with at length, in rich, character-driven detail—"along the way" to its romantic resolutions—are the worry, tension, and contradiction that Miley's two lives pose for her intimate relationships. What is not simplistic or superficial in the show is the depth of feeling expressed by Miley and Lilly for one another, the intensity of Miley's anxiety and fear for her relationship, and the richly detailed imagination of everything that could go wrong by connecting Miley's two worlds. Carol Dole writes that "the tortuous, even tortured, endings of all these chick flicks make clear that we do not currently have complete cultural consensus on whether women can have it all" (2007: 75). In *Hannah Montana*'s tortuous vision of the impact of publicness on its protagonist's intimate childhood, it does not so much reveal the lack of cultural consensus on that question, but rather it struggles to give form and shape to the question itself.

FOUR   THE WHITENESS OF TWEEN INNOCENCE

The Disney Channel and other kids' television networks have long been affirmative about racially diverse casting. Most of the Disney Channel's shows and movies with ensemble casts, including *Hannah Montana*, had nonwhite secondary characters, and several prominent shows like *That's So Raven*, *Wizards of Waverly Place*, and *Sonny with a Chance* starred African-American and Latina actors. Sarah Banet-Weiser (2007) and Sarah Turner (2014) maintain that these efforts at multiculturalism by children's TV networks have the effect of flattening racial difference into an affluent suburban milieu. They argue that, by treating Black, Asian, and Latinx actors as all interchangeably affluent and suburban, the effect is to collapse racial and ethnic difference into middle-class whiteness. Nonetheless the Disney Channel demonstrated a greater commitment than broadcast networks did to representing "diversity" by regularly including actors of color in prominent positions onscreen (Valdivia 2008).[1]

If one important critique of tween media is that diverse casting is mostly a fig leaf, a superficial acknowledgment of racial difference that ultimately reaffirms existing social hierarchies and stratification, I want to go a step further, to argue that tween music was deeply invested in whiteness as a foundational value. Rather than comprehensively overview various representations of racial difference in the tween music industry, I focus here on a particular formation of whiteness—constituted primarily in opposition to Blackness—as an ideological foundation for the investments in feminine innocence that significantly undergirded the tween music industry in the 2000s. The construction of tweens as girls at a fraught moment of transition is authorized by a deep-seated racial logic of innocent and vulnerable white femininity. But these core racial values were actively obscured by superficial gestures like diverse casting. The construction of tweens as primarily an age category had the effect of obscuring the equal, or even greater, importance of consumerism, gender, and race to that construction. But among those traits there was an additional ordering, such that the gendered and consumerist construction of tweens was much more visible than the implicit racial logics. In this chapter, then, I seek to bring out the submerged racial logic by which tween innocence was visible as a distinct investment in whiteness, and to see how negotiations of whiteness provided significant material for tween celebrities to manage the development of their careers.

I pursue this goal by focusing on a comparison between Miley Cyrus and Taylor Swift as they both transitioned from tween star to successful mainstream adult artist. At transitional moments in their careers, race was made visible in ways that it had not been in their earlier careers. For Cyrus, the contradictions of Disney childhood and mainstream pop maturity forced a decisive rupture, in which she embraced, appropriated, and fetishized African American performance styles as a way to fully separate herself from her earlier image. By contrast, Swift's slow transition to an adult career went much more smoothly. Without the baggage of the Disney brand, Swift was conceivably in a different position than Cyrus and less constrained by the ideological investments of commercial children's media. But instead of embracing mainstream freedom, Swift continued to emphasize her age and to claim the innocence of childhood for herself, well into her adult career. The comparison with Cyrus helps highlight Swift's long-standing investment in a particular version of white femininity that foregrounds innocence, youth, and vulnerability. While Cyrus explosively broke with her child-aligned persona by dramatically claiming tropes of Black culture and performance, Swift retained her commitment to innocent white femininity as she grew older, smoothing her transition to adulthood by, in some ways, rejecting certain expectations of maturity and reinvesting in whiteness and youthfulness.

Methodologically, in this chapter I seek to read backward, looking at these artists' performances of adulthood to see in relief how important unmarked whiteness (Lipsitz 2006) had been to the media construction of tween innocence in these artists' younger personas. For many artists, especially women, the transition from child star to adult artist can be laden with scandal and moral panic around sexuality. The very public "breakdowns" of

Britney Spears and Lindsay Lohan in the tabloids in the 2000s established a formula into which other performers' experiences were commonly seen to fit. Observers were quick to identify a Spears- or Lohan-esque spectacle when Disney Channel star Demi Lovato struggled with mental health issues in 2010, when *High School Musical* star Vanessa Hudgens had revealing photos leaked online, or when Miley Cyrus performed what many saw as too sexualized a dance or posed for partially nude artistic photos for *Vogue* (Greenfeld 2008; Greenblatt 2010a; Holson 2010; Johnston 2011; Keating and Zeidler 2007). I normally resist focusing on later events in child artists' lives, because the excessive demands of tabloid scandal and media spectacle on our attention can prevent us from seeing clearly the experience of child stars and child audiences in the years prior. That a child or teen star later experiences scandal does not necessarily provide any retrospective insight into their or their audiences' experiences during the time they were child stars—except perhaps that the experiences of child performers and audiences are, by definition, finite. Presentist bias is especially hard to resist in the context of the individual life course of a celebrity, where the linearity of biography seems so clearly to sequence causes and effects, and when over a century of psychoanalytic thinking has ingrained habits of mind that see a child's experience as the efficient cause of adult behavior and inclination. But this way of thinking cannot help but to subordinate the experiences of children to their future adulthoods, treating them only ever as "becomings" who live for another, future self, rather than as self-invested "beings" (Qvortrup 1994). Miley Cyrus, Justin Bieber, Taylor Swift, and other 2000s-era tween artists continued to have public careers in the entertainment industry after the peak of their tween stardom. But Swift's overwhelming success, Cyrus's energetic provocations, and Bieber's relative ignominy need not reveal anything about these artists' contributions and reception in public culture in 2009, when they were major figures in the tween media industry. History and biography are full of as much contingency as causality. In this chapter I look to Cyrus's and Swift's later careers because they do expose at least one thing in their earlier careers that was, if not hidden, then at least largely unspoken: a racial logic that undergirded their tween celebrity with a core investment in whiteness. My goal here is to read backward, even to reverse the direction of causality or interpretation, to see adult experiences revealing something about childhood rather than to see in childhood an explanation or cause of the adult experience.

MILEY CYRUS: TWEEN INNOCENCE AGAINST MUSICAL BLACKNESS

In 2010 Miley Cyrus released *Can't Be Tamed*, her last album under contract with Disney's Hollywood Records. It was widely seen as an effort to break out of her Disney persona, to be more edgy, rebellious, and adult. The video for its lead single, "Can't Be Tamed," showed Cyrus as a dark bird-monster in a cage, and it was both more sexualized and angrier than her previous work. Media scholar Morgan Blue notes that one interpretation of the video is as a "cry for recognition as a serious artist, as an adult, rather than as 'just a girl'" (2017: 175). Critics highlighted her effort to break from Disney and especially her intensified adoption of sexual imagery, noting that she was "strenuously distancing herself from the days of 'Hannah'" (Donahue 2010), with a "new, raunchier image" (Petridis 2010); "sexier," "steamy," and "officially making the move from teen queen to rock star" (B. B. Smith 2010); and "yet another Radio Disney pop starlet shedding off her family-friendly image to become a sexually-charged pin-up that's ready to enter the fray against all of those mainstream pop divas that inspired her" (Sawdey 2010). But most critics also agreed that she was unsuccessful: "her first rebellion didn't work" (Unterberger 2013); "despite her best rebellious efforts, Miley's just not (yet) that thorny a girl" (Greenblatt 2010b); and "her much touted 'adult' musical direction might not be all that adult" (Petridis 2010). Her efforts to break from Disney were "growing pains," and her claim of an independent musical identity were a "'don't call me Hannah Montana!' cris de coeur" (Greenblatt 2010b). Blue points out that the dramatic costuming of the "Can't Be Tamed" video might just as easily be read to mean "that Cyrus might be an asexual or pre-sexual girl *masquerading* as a sexual woman" (2017: 176). Cyrus visibly tried to break with her childish image by emphasizing sexuality and aggression, but she failed.

Somehow the wholesome, family-friendly, and childish themes of Cyrus's Disney career were not seen as being in such strong conflict with the sexuality, aggression, and nightlife themes of *Can't Be Tamed* that they could not coexist. Her efforts to adopt rebellious sexuality could even be seen as charmingly immature playacting. While sexuality is often understood as incompatible with childhood innocence, the sexualization of girlhood and the eroticization of innocence are in fact commonplace features of US public culture (Cook and Kaiser 2004; Egan and Hawkes 2008; Kincaid 1998), and Cyrus's experience suggests that her increasingly sexualized performance did not ultimately threaten or contradict her established persona as a tween Disney star.

But eventually Cyrus *did* succeed at breaking fully from her Disney persona, three years later with the release of her 2013 album *Bangerz*. Like *Can't Be Tamed*, *Bangerz* was rebellious, sexual, aggressive, and dark. What made it stand out from *Can't Be Tamed*, and what allowed Cyrus to fully claim a provocative new standing in mainstream adult popular music, was not simply more of what she had already tried, but the foregrounding of a critical new element: race. *Bangerz* forcefully incorporated Black musical genres, performance styles, and performers as part of its intensified investment in rebelliousness, sexuality, and aggression. In a spectacle of racial appropriation and objectification, Cyrus staged an extreme break with her past by posing racial Blackness, especially Black female performance and sexuality, in direct opposition to childhood innocence. Many scholars and critics have commented on the symbolic violence of Cyrus's racial appropriations and the long history of white performers reinforcing racist conceptions of Black culture, especially Black sexuality, by mimicking Black performance styles. My contribution in what follows is to explore how, in Cyrus's version of this long-standing pattern in American culture, *childhood* specifically was represented as the term posed in opposition to the portrayals of Black female sexuality that were widely seen to be provocative, edgy, and abject. Noting this dynamic allows us to look back to Cyrus's earlier career as a Disney star to bring its implicit investments in racial whiteness into much clearer relief. And it provides some insight, I hope, into the ways that cultural constructions of childhood innocence are raced white—that is, a cultural bias that refuses to treat Black children as "innocent" and denies them access even to the paternalistic privileges of protection, aestheticization, and desire that accrue to childhood in American culture—and how such constructions also inform the racial logics of "adult" media and performances.

In August 2013, seven years after *Hannah Montana* first aired on the Disney Channel, Cyrus performed at the MTV Video Music Awards (VMAs) to promote *Bangerz*. Her performance that night was intentionally provocative, absurdist, and racially charged. She emerged from the belly of a giant robot teddy bear. Grimacing with her tongue out, she was costumed in furry teddy-bear lingerie and surrounded by dancers wearing full-body, cartoonish teddy-bear costumes—calling to mind and parodying juvenile imagery from the children's television that she was dramatically leaving behind. Behind her, a line of Black women dancers wore skintight leggings and enormous plush bears on their backs. When the dancers turned around, their bodies were obscured entirely by the bears on their backs so it appeared to the camera that the bears were dancing. These dancers

Figure 4.1 Still from telecast of the 2013 MTV Video Music Awards, performed at Barclays Center in New York City, aired August 25 (Viacom Media Networks, 2013).

joined Cyrus at the front of the stage as the music for her single "We Can't Stop" started (figure 4.1). In the center of a circle of Black women, Cyrus started "twerking"—adopting a dance style from Southern Black American dance culture (Gaunt 2015). The contrast between Cyrus's thin white body and the bodies of the full-figured Black dancers was brought to the forefront when she walked across the stage to where a much larger woman waited, also wearing skintight pants, with her back turned to the audience as Cyrus mockingly slapped her buttocks. The extreme exoticization of the Black women performers was dramatically juxtaposed onstage with the childish imagery of the plush bears and life-sized animal costumes. These tropes of childishness appeared out of place and inappropriate, adding to the performance's cultivation of over-the-top absurdity and provocation. No white performers besides Cyrus appeared onstage until the beginning of the next song, when Robin Thicke, a white R&B singer known for a performance style strongly influenced by Black singers, came out for a duet.

This performance inspired controversy. Many observers responded to Cyrus's sexually explicit performance with Thicke in the following number, a performance of Thicke's controversial anticonsent song "Blurred Lines," while others defended her choice to affirmatively display her own sexuality and rejected "slut-shaming" criticism (e.g., Dries 2013; Goldberg 2013). This debate traced a long history of discourses about the sexualization and objectification of white female performers, which dialectically explores the question of whether women's sexualized performances can ever be autonomous and empowering or if they are intrinsically alienating because they appeal to the objectifying male gaze (e.g., Dibben 1999).[2] Within the contours of that debate, Cyrus's provocative performance rejected the constraints of feminine sexual propriety that had been forced on her by the media's hypocritical virgin/whore obsessions and by the conservative disciplining of the Disney star machine. That rejection was a claim of autonomy and self-determination against patriarchal control and a celebration of female sexual desire and display.

But that discourse of female sexual empowerment versus objectification had, at best, severe blind spots to race, which other critics noted. *Bangerz* explicitly adopted Black musical styles. Cyrus's songwriting team reported that she had told them, "I want urban, I just want something that just feels Black" (Platon 2013). "We Can't Stop" was originally intended for the Black artist Rihanna (Vena 2013), whom Cyrus was seen to be consciously emulating. The video for "We Can't Stop," which was released months earlier, had already been criticized for its racial appropriations. After the VMA performance, the same line of criticism was broadened and intensified. In a widely cited online essay, sociologist Tressie McMillan Cottom noted that "Cyrus' performance was not just a clueless, culturally insensitive attempt to assert her sexuality or a simple act of cultural appropriation at the expense of black bodies.... She is playing a type of black female body as a joke to challenge her audience's perceptions of herself while leaving their perceptions of black women's bodies firmly intact. It's a dance between performing sexual freedom and maintaining a hierarchy of female bodies from which white women benefit materially" (2013). Kyra Gaunt (2015) argues that Cyrus's portrayal of twerking, like many other mass-mediated portrayals of African American dance forms, was directed primarily to non-Black audiences. Such portrayals flatten and obscure local meanings and motivations for dance or musical styles in the contexts where those styles originated and continue to be practiced. This collapses particular meanings into hegemonic "stigmatized and stereotypical views of musical blackness, childhood adolescence, and black girls' sexuality" (2015: 247).

These criticisms echo bell hooks's critique of a long history of "white European fascination with the bodies of black people, particularly black female bodies" (1992: 63). As hooks has argued, contemporary media portrayals of Black female sexuality build on a long history in which white racial identity has been reinforced by "projecting onto black bodies a narrative of sexualization disassociated from whiteness" (62), while Black women's bodies have been put "on display ... to entertain guests with the naked image of

Otherness. They are not to look at her as a whole human being. They are to notice only certain parts. . . . [T]he black women whose naked bodies were displayed for whites at social functions had no presence. They were reduced to mere spectacle" (62). Cyrus's embrace of twerking and focus on the bodies of her dancers was one more instance in a long history of portrayals that, as hooks puts it, call "attention to the body in a manner inviting the gaze to mutilate black female bodies yet again, to focus solely on the 'butt'" (64). Cyrus's performance played on prevalent prejudices of Black female sexuality and Black music as deviant, uncontrollable, and animalistic—when the performers carrying bears strapped to their backs turned around, they were literally objectified, replaced in the camera's view by giant plush toys.

With *Bangerz* Cyrus not only staged this very conventional spectacle of Black women's sexualized bodies, she also participated in another, parallel tradition of white artists who commodify and appropriate Black culture (Brooks 2010). Here hooks's critique of Madonna's "provocative" performances from the 1980s, which were intended to titillate and scandalize white audiences, is equally relevant to the spectacle of race and sexuality Cyrus played out in 2013 (1992: 157–64). Cyrus embraced postracial mixing and fluidity in interviews (Eells 2013; Gevinson 2014), and like Madonna, she seemed motivated to link her adoption of Black musical styles to her flexible sexuality, in a sort of generalized capaciousness encompassing gender, sexuality, and race (Petrusich 2015). When, for example, *Rolling Stone*'s Josh Eells challenged her on the politics of her racial portrayals, she specifically pivoted to sexual politics as evidence of her racial openness: "Meanwhile, she argues, the idea that she's somehow playing black is absurd. 'I'm from one of the wealthiest counties in America,' she says. 'I know what I am. But I also know what I like to listen to. Look at any 20-year-old white girl right now—that's what they're listening to at the club. It's 2013. The gays are getting married, we're all collaborating. I would never think about the color of my dancers, like, 'Ooh, that might be controversial'" (Eells 2013). Gaunt similarly notes Cyrus's place in a long history of white artists "trading up" in their careers by appropriating Black musical styles, particularly in their transitions from adolescent to young adult celebrity personas (2015: 258).

While many were critical of Cyrus for the racism of her performance, another set of responses circulated objecting not to her racism but to her embrace of Black music. The day after the VMA telecast, "memes" pointing out the contrast between Cyrus's performance to country music conventions and normative ideals of rural white femininity began to circulate on Facebook and other social networking sites. One image showed Cyrus

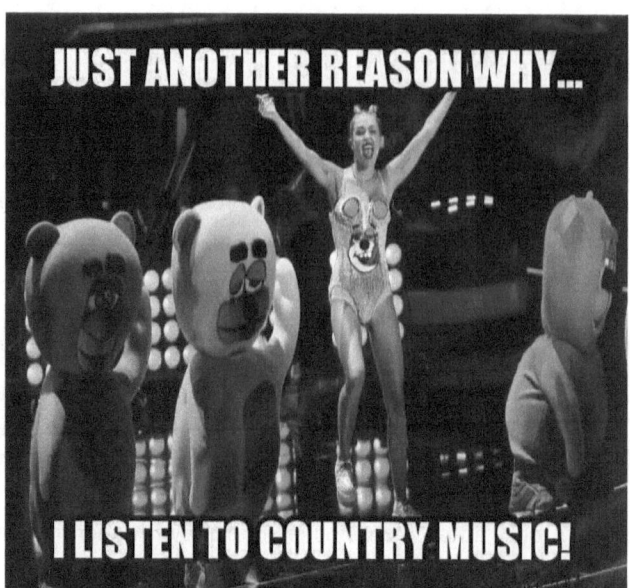

Figure 4.2 Image posted on August 26, 2013, to Facebook page for "Country Music Fan" (no longer accessible).

onstage surrounded by life-sized dancers in bear costumes, with the caption "JUST ANOTHER REASON WHY . . . I LISTEN TO COUNTRY MUSIC!" (figure 4.2). Another image showed Cyrus in front of a Black musician, with her eyes closed and mouth open, holding a foam finger between her legs. This still from the VMAs was cropped and placed next to a promotional photo of country singer Miranda Lambert, a leading figure in a traditionalist country music movement, standing outdoors and wearing jeans, boots, and a large belt buckle, while resting a rifle on her shoulder. The caption read "LESS MILEY MORE MIRANDA" (figure 4.3). These images posed an explicit contrast between Cyrus's 2013 performance and the figures of Lambert specifically and "country music" generally. Cyrus had been associated with country music herself—her father, Billy Ray Cyrus, was a popular country artist in the 1990s, and her first recordings were in a pop-country style. The image of Miranda Lambert participates in a common country music trope of the tough rural woman.[3] And despite historical connections and stylistic similarities between country and R&B (Pecknold 2013), country music is strongly associated with conservative, white, rural American culture and social groups (Fox 2004) and directly contrasted in the public imagination with African American genres of hip-hop and R&B. The image of Lambert in particular suggests an ideal of white femininity that is directly opposed to the version of femininity performed by Cyrus. Of course,

Figure 4.3 Image posted on August 26, 2013, to Facebook page for "Southern Charm Traditional Wear" (no longer accessible).

representations of female country performers wearing revealing clothes and performing in sexually suggestive ways are not at all uncommon in country music either, so it is notable that the creators of this image macro chose a photograph of Lambert that highlighted rustic toughness rather than glamorous femininity, to more strongly emphasize the contrast.

These internet memes are especially pointed in light of the racial portrayals of Cyrus's prior career as a Disney star. Her Disney Channel show, *Hannah Montana*, had focused on an affluent white family, and it explicitly foregrounded the sort of Southern white femininity that these internet responses posed in contrast to her VMA performances. Blue (2017) notes that the show explicitly thematized whiteness in its emphasis on the Stewart family's Southern roots, with accents, geographical references, country music artists as guest stars, and even "white trash" relatives. Blue also points to "the campy, excessive Southern White femininity that inspired Hannah Montana's blonde wig and feminine, often pink, always sparkling costumes" (2017: 75). These portrayals framed whiteness as one "ethnicity" among many, as guest stars like Dolly Parton as "Aunt Dolly" performed caricatures of Southern culture for laughs in much the same way that the character "Rico Suave," an academically advanced younger student from a rich Latinx family, performed an exaggerated Spanish accent. The show also placed country music front and center, which Aaron Fox has argued "is widely understood to signify an explicit claim to whiteness, not as an unmarked, neutral condition of lacking (or trying to shed) race, but as a marked, foregrounded claim of cultural identity" (2004: 44). In the tradition of classic Disney films, the primary nonwhite characters in *Hannah Montana* were villains or antagonists—Rico Suave is a constant adversary, as are Amber and Ashley, the overweening popular girls at school who bully Hannah and Lilly, and who were played by Black and Asian American actors. *Hannah Montana*, in fact, stood out among its generation of Disney Channel products for the strength of its investment in whiteness.

The extreme provocation of Cyrus's VMAs performance went well beyond the sincere interest in and appreciation for Black music and culture that she claimed for herself, and even beyond the normal demand for spectacle and controversy at televised awards shows. It is clear that one thing she was doing was breaking irrevocably with her past. That past was widely understood as an association with "Disney," which brings childhood and femininity to the fore. Disney goes to great lengths to sublimate race by including many performers of color in its products. But if Cyrus was motivated to break from Disney by claiming Black female sexuality, that opposition suggests that whiteness was more central to Disney's semiotics than it conventionally allowed. That is, on a map of cultural identities, Cyrus's performance locates Black female sexuality as fully opposite white feminine childhood. Since whiteness works to make itself invisible (Lipsitz 2006)—or, as in *Hannah Montana*'s portrayals of Southern culture, as just one ethnicity among many—the deep investment in whiteness of 2000s-era tween media may only be visible in the motivated rejection of it by an artist looking to fully transition to a new phase in her career. Cyrus made this explicit, when, asked about the criticisms of her racial portrayals with *Bangerz*, she replied with a rejection of Disney: "I don't give a shit. I'm not Disney, where they have, like, an Asian girl, a black girl, and a white girl, to be politically correct, and, like, everyone has bright-colored T-shirts" (Farrow 2014).

Cyrus's performance is *explicit*, not just in the sense that its content is vulgar or mature, but also its representations are unsubtle; much is directly stated, and little is implied. Gender and sexuality are explicitly thematized at the surface of the performance, which is unquestionably *about* the sexualized female body. Race is explicitly thematized at the surface of the performance, which is unquestionably *about* African American music and dance styles, the status of Black women's bodies as objects of sexual desire and abjection, and white artists' and media corporations' attempts to gain financially and culturally from Black people's labor and performances. In this mix of in-your-face signification, the performance is also unquestionably about age and childhood, which are also explicitly thematized along with race and sex. The VMAs performance is full of markers of childhood, especially the ironic teddy bears. Full-sized costume animals performing pop music—as in the Kidz Bop video for "Since U Been Gone"—are a long-standing convention of the iconography of children's media. The bears' outlandish appearances clearly stand in for the childishness of the prior career from which she was forcefully breaking away. Depicting those animals as drunk or high, licking their lips and participating in a spectacle of racial and sexual provocation is an explicit and forceful rejection of the "innocence" of children's media, and by extension of Cyrus's own prior persona.

Much incisive criticism has explored issues of race, gender, musical style, and performance in Cyrus's recent career. My contribution here is narrowly to foreground the function of age in the mix with race and gender in Cyrus's cultural production around the release of *Bangerz*. Many respondents noted that this performance was part of Cyrus's effort to "challenge her audience's perceptions of herself," as Cottom puts it. And age was often noted explicitly, especially in reference to her previous affiliation with Disney. Cyrus's turn to a team of hip-hop songwriters, for example, was seen as part of a project of "breaking actress/singer Miley Cyrus out of her bubblegum Disney shell and into the spunky young woman she has always been" (Platon 2013). And writing in *Vice* Wilbert Cooper described "Miley Cyrus 2.0, the former Disney *Hannah Montana* starlet who's transmogrified into a sexed-up, ganja-puffing, white-washed Rihanna. . . . another child star getting ready to rebel against [her] child-friendly image" (2013). But the relationship of age to race and gender is not incidental to the cultural logic of Cyrus's performance. Rather, it is central, and her appeal to or appropriation of Black musical and performance styles in 2013 tells us something important about that relationship.

Returning to her prior effort at "rebellion" with *Can't Be Tamed*, we can see how *Bangerz* dramatically escalated a rejection of Disney childishness that had begun three years earlier specifically by claiming Blackness as the opposite of childhood in the ways it did. Sexualization was not enough to reject childhood, but adding race to sex intensified that cultural logic. Critic Andrew Unterberger argues that the main contrast between *Can't Be Tamed* and *Bangerz* was Cyrus's increased "control": "she's being similarly rebellious, but now feels firmly in control of her music and her image, representing herself in a way that feels unique to her, and only vaguely related to any of her peers" (2013). Unterberger narrates Cyrus's development between the two albums as a path from aimless immaturity progressing to goal-oriented adulthood. But the individual adult "control" that Cyrus asserted in *Bangerz* was framed, decidedly, as control *over* Black musical styles and Black performers' bodies.

The negative space created by the figure she deployed onstage at the 2013 VMAs was precisely the 2007 figure of Miley Cyrus as innocent, white, feminine, and asexual. That is also a racialized image, but when it stands by itself on television and onstage in 2007, its whiteness is unmarked, even hidden. On the other hand in 2007 age and gender were marked and explicitly foregrounded. But whiteness is the condition of possibility for those dynamics of childhood and femininity to take place, for the question of public and private childhood to be staged. Partly because posing publicness as a problem confronting children depends on an understanding of childhood as innocent, private, and vulnerable, and that understanding of childhood, especially in the United States, has always been a privilege of whiteness (Bernstein 2011). Which is to say, innocence historically is not granted to Black children, girls or boys. Instead Black children have been treated as older than they are, as threatening and criminal rather than as threatened and vulnerable (Epstein, Blake, and González 2017; Goff et al. 2014; Morris 2016: 34), and certainly not the figures of futurity to which national ideologies cling (Edelman 2004; Muñoz 2009). The "having it all" discourses that *Hannah Montana* adapts to girlhood have always centered affluent white women. So in Cyrus's flailing efforts to claim Black bodies and Black cultural forms for her own purposes, we can see how important ideologies of whiteness were to her previous status as a tween celebrity.

TAYLOR SWIFT: TWEEN INNOCENCE AS WHITENESS

If Cyrus exposed the racialization of tween innocence by setting it against Black musical forms, Swift's career highlighted the affirmative investments in whiteness presupposed by tween innocence. In 2014, a year after Cyrus released *Bangerz*, Taylor Swift's video for "Shake It Off," the first single from her world-conquering fifth record *1989*, was criticized for its offensive depictions of Black women's bodies and African American music, dance, and fashion. In a scene widely read as a parody of Cyrus's appropriation of twerking, Swift, dressed in cut-off jean shorts, an animal-print jacket, and gaudy jewelry, tries to keep up with a group of Black women dancers, clearly

Figure 4.4 Still from video for "Shake It Off" (Big Machine Records, 2014, dir. Mark Romanek).

ridiculing their sexualized emphasis on butt shaking and highlighting her own distance from that sort of sexuality (figure 4.4). Critic Sady Doyle suggested in response that, while Swift had a long history of denigrating other women for being overly sexual, "Shake It Off" was notable for being "one of the few times Swift has ever acknowledged race in her work" (2014). But in fact, going back to some of the earliest moments in her career, it is almost impossible to disentangle Swift's investments in femininity and childhood innocence from parallel investments in racial whiteness. In this section, then, I try to narrate Swift's career as a series of returns to the core values of childhood and whiteness—or childhood *as* whiteness.

Swift's transition to an adult career was strikingly different than Cyrus's. If Cyrus broke from the figure of the sexually innocent (and sexually vulnerable) white girl through her appeal to the hypersexualization of Black bodies, Swift made use of the same logic to pursue the opposite goal. Rather than dramatically breaking with her tween-pop past, Swift claimed youthfulness and innocence for herself far into her period of remarkable mainstream success. She did not embrace Black musical culture like Cyrus, but instead actively and continually reinvested in racial whiteness as a legitimating and valorizing position. My argument here is that Swift's career shows how these two core commitments—to childhood innocence, on the one hand, and racial whiteness, on the other—are not just paired or complementary, but are instead deeply integrated and mutually constitutive.

Throughout her career Swift consistently presented herself within a narrow range of vulnerable, white, innocent femininity well into the period that she was one of the very most successful artists in the music industry. In a sense, Swift never did actively "transition" from tween star to adult artist. Instead she made strategic use of the intersections of vulnerable white femininity and childhood innocence to ease the transition to adult pop artist. Rather than making a clean break and forcing the issue as the contradictions became overwhelming, as Cyrus and earlier artists did, Swift massaged the contradictions by explicitly and implicitly claiming childishness and vulnerability well into her adult career. Her stylistic location in country music facilitated this by giving her access to a particular formation of white femininity constructed specifically in terms of grievance and vulnerability that would have allowed her to push against the sexualization and display that is expected of female pop artists. (And unlike Miranda Lambert and others, Swift never adopted the toughness or rusticity made available by country music for herself.) As Robin Bernstein notes regarding the nineteenth century that "innocence was raced white" (2011: 4), Swift's example shows clearly how twenty-first century constructions of feminine innocence have continued to be raced white.

Swift started performing at ten years old, had a songwriting contract at age thirteen, and signed with the small Nashville record label Big Machine Records at fifteen (McNamara 2007b). She released her debut album in 2006, when she was sixteen years old, and it reached the top of the country music charts the following year. Even though Swift achieved her earliest popularity at sixteen and seventeen, somewhat older than other young music performers at the time like Cyrus or Justin Bieber, her age was prominent in her celebrity persona, and she was variously called "precocious" (J. A. Baker 2008) and a "teen princess" (Rosen 2008: 89), and her music was "country as teenpop" (Baron 2008). Age was seen as a potential liability by Big Machine head Scott Borchetta, who told *Billboard* at the time that "he knew [promoting Swift] wouldn't be easy because country programmers are hesitant to play teenagers" (Price 2006). Her early success was commonly linked to a presumed youthful, tween audience, and she was described by handlers and journalists alike as having a connection to young audiences who were otherwise inscrutable to adult artists and industry professionals: "she has a preternatural gift for knowing exactly what her fanbase wants" (Keefe 2008); "teen fans are living life through her songs" (Williams 2009); "she very much lives in her demographic.... She's a great focus group in herself" (Tucker 2008a). Similarly, Swift's self-presentation in songs, videos, and interviews emphasized childhood and youth as key parts of her celebrity persona, even though she was less strongly associated with the tween music movement.

At the very beginning of her career, in the images associated with her first album, Swift was framed in a visual style recognizable as a mode of Nashville country music glamour—more polished and less campy than the elaborate Southern affectations of Hannah Montana's Dolly Parton cameos, and more refined and much more expensively dressed than the rural toughness of Miranda Lambert. In album art and music videos, she was styled in evening gowns or prom dresses, with heavy makeup and elaborately styled hair, as in the video for "Our Song," which depicted Swift putting on makeup and a prom dress in an expensively appointed bedroom, then lying in a bed of rose petals, and finally wearing an evening gown and long gloves onstage while performing the song. This presentation positioned her as a figure comparable to major established female country stars like Faith Hill, whose blond hair and glamorous feminine styling Swift echoed. Notably Swift quickly broke with that initial glamorous presentation and transitioned into the persona that would remain somewhat stable for years. This persona emphasized ordinariness, and even awkwardness, rather than glamorous femininity. As *Vanity Fair* described it, "Swift cultivates a gawky adorkability in her music videos, in which she often plays the unloved girl alone in her room pining over the cute guy" (Sales 2013). Ordinariness, even in combination with celebrity glamour, was an increasingly common frame for celebrity presentation (Gamson 2011). But Swift's emphasis on awkwardness, and her common narrative of subordination to more popular kids in school during her childhood, went beyond mere ordinariness (Comentale 2016). Instead Swift's self-presentation as less than fully in charge was closer to self-infantilization. The social difficulties of middle and high school were a central narrative trope of Swift's performance of "gawky adorkability." Even as her career progressed and she became an increasingly prominent celebrity, Swift continued to narrate her social difficulties in middle school in lyrics and interviews, and her songs continued to focus on school life, in songs and videos like "You Belong with Me," "Fifteen," and "Mean" (see Pollock 2014).

"Fifteen," for example, appeared in 2008 on *Fearless*, Swift's second album, just before she turned twenty. It is a song about the first day of high school, looking forward to romances and friendships that will occur over the next four years, but written from the perspective of someone who has just passed high school age and regrets incautious romantic or sexual experiences. "Fifteen" is simultaneously nostalgic and paternalistic, advising fifteen-year-olds against immodesty in the belief that "there's nothing to figure out," but at the same time wistful for the naive excitement and fantasy about a future that would ultimately be replaced by the world-weary retrospective viewpoint of a twenty-year-old.[4] Of course, the audience for "Fifteen" included very many fifteen-year-olds—not to mention much younger kids—for whom the account of high school would have been prospective rather than retrospective, and for that audience the wistful nostalgia would be projected forward rather than backward. In fact such anticipatory nostalgia may be characteristic of music targeted to tween or preadolescent audiences. Barbara Bradby identifies a very similar relationship of theme to audience in Britney Spears's early music, in which "very young girls were already rehearsing feelings of nostalgia for the loss of romance even as they explore what it will feel like to be an adolescent girl, herself rehearsing to be an adult woman" (2009: 185). Having high school as its explicit topic marked a song like "Fifteen" out as kids' fare as much as anything, and like Disney's *High School Musical* and *Hannah Montana* it was part of a tradition of media set in high school but aimed at middle-school or younger children. As "Fifteen" took the very moment of the beginning of high school as its subject, its attention lingered on the pivot between childhood and adolescence that was also the focus of tween discourse.

During the rollout of *Fearless*, Swift began to relate stories about being bullied and isolated in middle school. She told *Philadelphia Magazine*, "In middle school, my friends decided I was weird, and they didn't like my hair. They ditched me and talked behind my back" (Rys 2008). When the scale of Swift's celebrity began to attract mainstream attention, *Vanity Fair*'s Nancy Jo Sales noted that the tabloid criticism Swift began to receive ironically mirrored Swift's backward-looking school narratives, such that "the source of her appeal has always been her ability to dig deep into her youthful feelings and reveal them in all their painfulness" (2013). This connection between "appeal" (to a broad public) and "painfulness" (as a very interior and particular biographical experience) is the basis of public intimacy, in Berlant's sense: "intimate spheres feel like ethical places based on the sense of capacious emotional continuity they circulate, which seems to derive from an ongoing potential for relief from the hard, cold world. Indeed the offer of the simplicity of the feeling of rich continuity with a vaguely defined set of like others is often the central affective magnet of an intimate public" (2008: 6–7). In all the talk about Swift's easy connection to her youthful "demographic," we should recognize this as the core move: not just claiming shared youthfulness with her audience, but framing that youthfulness as a source of a very specific shared and difficult emotional experience of the world as a "hard, cold" place that produces biographies that are simultaneously collective and individual, a presentation of youthful suffering that clearly strives toward public intimacy. It is really not clear whether "Fifteen" sincerely advises younger girls to be cynical about boys to avoid early sex and heartbreak, or if it savors and celebrates the pleasure of crying together with a female friend over shared loss and regret, articulating a "normal" biographical trajectory to which girls should aspire in order to be able to participate in the intimate publicness of sentimental genres of complaint and regret.

Fearless was the top-selling album of 2009, driven by the popularity of its third single, "You Belong with Me." By the summer of 2009 the song had established itself as a crossover phenomenon, the first since Faith Hill's "Breathe" in 2000 to simultaneously hold a place in the top five of the *Billboard* Hot 100 and Hot Country charts—and prior to that since 1984, with Willie Nelson and Julio Iglesias's recording of "To All the Girls I've Loved Before" the nearest example (*Billboard* 2009). Only a third of the airplay for "You Belong with Me" was on country radio, with the majority on pop and adult formats (Pietroluongo 2009). Reviewers repeatedly pointed out Swift's increasing orientation toward pop music rather than country. National Public Radio (NPR) noted that the recording "features a little twang in the vocal and a little fiddle in the instrumental mix. But what it really is, is a driving pop song about being out of place" (Tucker 2008b). *Billboard* called it "a driving country rocker with enough of a pop sheen to continue Swift's crossover success" (Williams 2009). *Rolling Stone* described the album as "quirky teen pop" and only barely country: "The only overtly country-ish things about *Fearless* are Swift's light drawl, the occasional reference to a 'one-horse town' and a bit of fiddle and banjo tucked into the mix" (Rosen 2008). And Tom Breihan in *L Magazine* noted, "There might be someone out there making better pop music right now, but I sure haven't heard her" (quoted in Baron 2008).

Right at this moment when Swift was being recognized as transitioning into a new adult, mainstream phase of her career, her celebrity presentation began to double down on its commitment to youthful feminine vulnerability and, at the same time, to be more explicitly framed in terms of race. Specifically she began to appear in situations in which her youthful feminine whiteness was put in direct contrast with adult masculine Blackness. And as her career continued, the release of each new "crossover album" was packaged with clear markers of investment in cultural whiteness and strong contrasts with Blackness. In June 2009 Swift's appearance at the Country Music Television (CMT) Awards show made it very clear where her cultural affiliations lay. The telecast of that awards show opened

Figure 4.5 Still from telecast of the 2009 CMT Music Awards, performed at the Sommet Center in Nashville, aired June 16 on County Music Television (CMT Productions, 2009).

with a pretaped video of Swift in minstrel hip-hop costume as "T-Swizzle," alongside hip-hop artist T-Pain, rapping "Thug Story," a song parodying her own "Love Story" (figure 4.5). In the video, set in a parking garage, she raps, "I'm like eight foot four, blond hair to the floor, you shorties never thought I dreamed about rapping hard core / No I ain't got a car, no I never really been in a club, still live with my parents, but I'm still a thug." The joke, of course, was how far removed Swift's cultural background was from hip-hop, and the incompatibility of her use of terms like "shorties" and "thug" with her admission of youthful innocence, living with her parents, and having no experience of adult nightclubs. The T-Swizzle performance highlighted just how incongruous popular Black musical styles like rap were at a country music event—and, more to the point, how incongruous they were with her own youthful white femininity. Performing on live television side by side with a Black male artist, in a dark, empty parking garage, and using terms like "thug" and "hard core," she called attention to the contrast between the setting of the clip and her "normal" environment of a sheltered suburban home overseen by protective parents. This prerecorded segment carefully managed the racial tension at its core, domesticating it through humor and airing it in the context of the CMT Awards where Swift could position herself as comfortably at home, and it allowed Swift and the show's directors prior control over the prerecorded segment. By contrast, two months later Swift found herself staging a very similar encounter with Black masculinity at another televised awards show, this time not as an ironically awkward send-up of her own racial positioning but instead as a deadly serious performance of aggrieved white vulnerability.[5]

At the MTV VMAs in September 2009, Swift won the award for Best Female Video. The video for "You Belong with Me" was a conventional narrative about high school romance that won over visually and conceptually groundbreaking videos by Beyoncé and Lady Gaga. While *Fearless*, and especially "You Belong with Me," were almost universally acknowledged as pop-focused efforts to cross over from country to mainstream pop, as Swift mounted the stage to accept the award she showed no sign of sharing that view. Instead, visibly overcome by the recognition, she began her acceptance speech with self-effacement and extravagant modesty, saying, "I always dreamed about what it would be like to maybe win one of these one day, but I never actually thought that it would happen. I sing country music so thank you so much for giving me a chance to win a VMA award." Unlike the critics, audiences, and radio programmers who had spent the year treating *Fearless* as a pop album, Swift suggested that the country music she recorded was so far outside the mainstream represented by MTV's awards show that she could not imagine winning (effectively staging the same commitment to genre essentialism as in her T-Swizzle performance, which purported to highlight her awkward fit in genres beyond country). Interjecting "maybe" into her dream of winning a VMA suggested that even in her dreams she was cautiously pessimistic. In her bearing and speech on this stage in front of an audience of mostly grownup celebrities, Swift performed humility, reserve, and modesty, positioning herself as subordinate, even submissive.[6]

This performance of innocent vulnerability, humility, and marginality was sharpened when rapper Kanye West upset the carefully stage-managed live telecast by running onto the stage and taking the microphone from Swift. West said, "Yo, Taylor, I'm really happy for you, I'm gonna let you finish, but Beyoncé had one of the best videos of *all time*. One of the best videos of all time." He shrugged and handed the microphone back to Swift, who was speechless. The surprised audience slowly began to applaud and then gave Swift a supportive standing ovation, while booing West.

Beyoncé's video for "Single Ladies" had been widely hailed as a singular artistic achievement, and West's claim that it was "one of the best videos of all time" was not controversial. But for weeks afterward West was widely vilified in the press, by other celebrities, and on the internet as a jerk to the young and sensitive Swift (France 2009). The event provoked what *Billboard* called a "national uproar" (Moody 2009), and Choire Sicha noted that the "outrage was insane and immediate, both at the show, where the booing was a little frightening, and online, where everyone speed-Tweeted their horror and disapproval" (2009). Writer Harry Allen (2009) documents a large number of public comments on social media expressing explicitly racist and violent sentiments toward West. West was forced to apologize multiple times, on his website, on the *Jay Leno Show*, and directly to Swift (Martens and Villareal 2009), and he later canceled a tour and left public life for a few months.

Swift's acceptance speech positioned herself as an underdog whose victory was unlikely because she was a country music outsider, which in turn positioned the VMAs as graciously opening itself up to outsiders. But since Swift's status as a crossover pop success was already well established, the much more salient reason she would have been an underdog and unlikely victor was that Beyoncé's widely acclaimed "Single Ladies" was nominated alongside her. The only reason Swift offered in her acceptance speech for why she was unlikely to win a VMA was because she was a country singer. But the suggestion there was that the VMA voters were, in effect, biased and unwelcoming to country music. And that, in turn, implies that Swift's video really was deserving of the award, and only prejudice might exclude her from winning. In a meaningful sense this is not modesty, it is aggrieved entitlement. This grievance and entitlement are almost literally identical to that narrated in the winning video for "You Belong with Me" itself, in which the desired love interest is unavailable only because of unfair prejudice against an awkward T-shirt- and sneakers-wearing girl who cannot compete with the cheer captain.

In 2009 Swift was one of a small number of the most successful artists in popular music, but still she was not seen, nor did she present herself, as someone who could stand up for herself or hold her own against a public challenge by a fellow musician. West's interruption reinforced the vulnerable outsider persona that Swift was already presenting in her acceptance speech, and it played into the narratives of bullying, insecurity, and grievance that Swift had spent years cultivating. More to the point, it also exposed the racial logic embedded in those narratives, where vulnerability and grievance were most fully activated as powerful cultural symbols that mobilized widespread outrage and scandal in the context of an explicitly racialized encounter between a young white female country singer and an adult Black male rapper. That is, the image of a Black male threat to a vulnerable white girl is part of a long-standing narrative template in US politics and culture, which the VMA incident played thoroughly into. And while the VMA incident was apparently spontaneous, it certainly conformed perfectly—even generically—to Swift's established racial presentations. If anything it simply reenacted the racial scripts already narrated in the carefully managed T-Swizzle performance, which hinged on the perceived incompatibility of public Black masculinity with domestic white femininity.

Swift and West inhabited opposing positions in a range of binaries, so outrage at a confident/adult/Black/male/hip-hop superstar aggressively dominating a meek/young/white/woman/country singer-songwriter was overdetermined. And West interrupted the awards show in support of another Black artist, who could reasonably be seen as having been denied deserved recognition for a widely celebrated work, in favor of a relative newcomer benefiting unfairly from sympathy due to her race and age. (Swift's sense that as a country outsider she could not win a mainstream award was wrong; the bias in this case was clearly working against Black artists, not white ones.) But West's own grievance in solidarity with another Black artist was simply ignored and dismissed, while Swift's grievance as a vulnerable white girl being threatened by an aggressive Black man was repeated, amplified, and savored by a wide range of audiences, celebrities, and journalists. A few commentators at the time identified the important racial underpinnings of the episode and its aftermath (Allen 2009; Powers 2009; Vozick-Levinson 2009), and West himself noted on Twitter a year later that the "media have successfully painted the image of the ANGRY BLACK MAN" (Hill 2010). If Swift's narrative of aggrieved innocent vulnerability had been seen as a core part of her appeal to "her demographic" of young audiences, the addition of this racial logic—of Black threat to white innocence—provided an entry point for adults to participate, and revel in, that narrative of grievance and vulnerability.

A year later Swift had not forgotten the incident with Kanye West. Instead at the following VMAs she performed a song called "Innocent" from her 2010 album *Speak Now*, ironically (and patronizingly) accusing West of being "still an innocent" (Dinh 2010).[7] The album expanded on "Fifteen's" skepticism toward maturity with the song "Never Grow Up" (including a verse specifically addressed to fourteen-year-olds), which one reviewer described as "so patently anti-adult that Swift advises the baby she's tucking in for the night to stunt its own growth before the kid has to experience future rejections or desertions" (Willman 2010). *Speak Now* also included the song "Mean," which doubled down on the awkward high school theme, narrating a spat with a critical reviewer as a story about school bullying (Vena 2010d). "Mean" positioned Swift as a child being unfairly picked on and posited an adult future as the solution to present-day bullying, childishly anticipating that "someday I'll be big enough so you can't hit me."[8] Again, in commercial terms Swift was certainly "big enough" not to be threatened by criticism. Even when the content of her songs was more aggressive and self-assured, this only served to intensify and concentrate the frame of childhood innocence, grievance, and vulnerability, envisioning escape from that vulnerability only in the constantly receding future.

Along with this intensified investment in childhood grievance, "Mean" also doubled down on country music and on explicit markers of racial whiteness. Unlike the almost incidental country twang provided by the banjo on "You Belong with Me," "Mean"—which reviewers described as "rootsy" (Caramanica 2010)—was arranged for an old-time string band, with banjo, mandolin, fiddle, and double bass. Moreover, while the video for "You Belong with Me" presented Swift in a white suburban family and high school setting, the video for "Mean" took that logic several steps further. While it included scenes with white actors performing as school kids being bullied or excluded—similar to the roles Swift played in the "You Belong with Me" video—Swift and the musicians were shown as a rural string band, performing in the dirt yard in front of a run-down farmhouse with storm clouds in the background (figure 4.6). The Depression-era dustbowl Plains imagery recalled the opening scenes of the 1939 film *The Wizard of Oz*, a reference that was also visible in her performance of the song at the Grammy Awards in early 2011, in which Swift and her band stood in front of a set made to look like the piled debris of a home destroyed by a tornado, and in her VMA performance of "Innocent" the previous year, which was described by *Time* as "a stormy, dreary background straight out of the tornado scene in *The Wizard of Oz*" (Friedman 2010). Depression-era dustbowl Plains poverty and Appalachian string-band imagery directly appeal to a specifically white cultural mythology—old-time music and Great Plains homesteading are both explicit symbols of whiteness in US iconography—and their pairing with narratives of childhood bullying only reinforces grievance and resentment as the key sensibility of racial whiteness. The video for "Mean" moves through period portrayals, next positioning Swift in the silent-film trope of the distressed damsel tied to train tracks by a mustachioed villain, and finally showing her in a 1920s flapper dress on a stage brightly labeled "Broadway." Thus the song's story of growing up and escaping bullying is narrated in the video as a move from rural poverty to urban glamour—white poverty being overcome through celebrity recognition. While "You Belong with Me" expressed a sort of aggrieved entitlement to romantic love, in "Innocent" and "Mean" Swift now responded to

Figure 4.6 Still from music video for "Mean" (Big Machine Records, 2011, dir. Declan Whitebloom).

perceived aggression from outsiders by doubling down on explicit representations of whiteness, even more than romance.

If *Fearless* was seen as a breakout crossover album, *Speak Now*, despite wallowing in childhood grievance, was described as a maturation: "Swift takes a step into adulthood" (Sheffield 2010); "Swift seems comfortable with the whole growing-up thing" (Willman 2010). But, again, when given the chance, the now twenty-year-old Swift went out of her way to reject that interpretation. When she won Song of the Year for *Speak Now*'s "Love Story" at BMI's annual songwriters' awards event, she bragged about having written the song after an "epic teenage tantrum" with her parents (Pederson 2010), framing her success again through her central narrative of awkward and fitful youth.

In 2012 Swift released *Red*, an album that was again seen by critics as a breakout pop record that would finally cement her status as the leading star in pop music. *Vulture* called Swift the "Reigning Queen of Pop" (Rosen 2013). NPR celebrated the album's "musical and lyrical leaps into full adulthood" and Swift's "sure, confident move into a mainstream pop sound" (Tucker 2012). MTV News called *Red* Swift's "most mature and accomplished album" and argued that she was "no longer content to be shoehorned into country, [and] fully embraces her pop side" (J. Montgomery 2012)—echoing the same themes of long-anticipated maturity and breakout mainstream/pop success that reviewers had noted in response to Swift's two previous albums. In February 2013 Swift performed the album's lead single, "We Are Never Ever

Figure 4.7 Still from telecast of the 55th Annual Grammy Awards, performed at the Staples Center in Los Angeles, aired February 10, 2013, on CBS (National Academy of Recording Arts and Sciences, 2013).

Getting Back Together," at the Grammy Awards in an elaborate Alice in Wonderland–themed stage performance (figure 4.7). In a sense this 2013 performance was like Cyrus's performance later that year at the VMAs, in that both artists ironically included life-sized fantasy markers of children's culture onstage with them. Swift's performance might have been a similar sort of disavowal of her youthful roots, finally affirming the transition into mature pop stardom that her critics kept expecting of her. But unlike Cyrus's intoxicated teddy bears, Swift's Alice imagery operated more as a literal staging of her commitment to childhood fantasy, even in the context of an otherwise realistic breakup single whose lyrical emphasis was much more about bringing the romantic target down to size than about expanding the imaginative scope for fantasy. The *Alice* set design let Swift dress in a full-length pure white costume and be surrounded by clowns and queens and animals and circus tricks. *Alice's Adventures in Wonderland* is the book that initiated the "golden age of children's literature," inspiring generations of adults to link childhood with fantasy (Wullschläger 2001). If Cyrus's teddy bears sent up childhood as plush saccharine infantile comfort and dependence, Swift's *Alice*, by strong contrast, affirmed feminine white childhood as the cultural repository of adventure and imagination.

A single Alice reference on its own is suggestive, but especially notable during the rollout of *Red* was that Swift continued to narrate herself to the press explicitly in terms of childhood and fantasy. In 2010 journalists noted that she was not yet twenty-one and old enough to drink. But by the 2012 release of *Red* she was twenty-two years old, fully an adult for the purposes of pop music. But still journalists were pointing out her "insistence on her own immaturity" (Rosen 2013). Swift had established herself as a writer of intimate romantic songs, and in the tabloid press she was seen involved in a series of ill-fated monogamous relationships. But when she was pressed on the question of the fantasy of that romance, she returned to specifically childhood fantasy. In an interview with the *Guardian*, when challenged on the idea that she is "peddling false fairytales to young girls," Swift latched on to the term "fairytales" and immediately contextualized the idea of the romantic heterosexual "happily ever after" as a concept from children's stories and related it to her own childhood experiences and to the idea of imagination, rather than, say, to women's romance genres: "A fairytale is an interesting concept. There's 'happily ever after' at the end, but that's not a part of our world. Everything is an ongoing storyline and you're always battling the complexities of life. But what I got from fairytales, growing up, was a beautiful daydream. I'm glad I had the craziest imagination and believed in all sorts of things that don't exist" (MacPherson 2012). This explicitly framed the heterosexual romances in her songs in terms of childhood, foregrounding a very different interpretation of romantic fantasy than that of conventional women's romance genres like those described by Janice Radway (1984) or Lauren Berlant (2008)—though romance and childhood may share narrative and ideological investments in dependence and paternal authority, perhaps. Swift's *Guardian* interview continued, even more explicitly thematizing childhood and fantasy: "I think there's something we have as little kids that goes away sometimes. I don't care about looking youthful forever, but I care about seeming youthful.... I want to believe in pretty lies" (MacPherson 2012). In another interview during this period Swift described her "style" to *Vanity Fair* as "Tim Burton-Alice in Wonderland-pirate ship-Peter Pan" (Sales 2013).[9] Just as *Speak Now* wrapped itself in *The Wizard of Oz* and childhood grievance, *Red*—again, Swift's unquestioned breakout record that solidified her as the leading pop star in US popular music—clothed itself in Alice in Wonderland imagery and narrated its worldly romantic themes as childish fantasies.

After this string of (disavowed) breakout albums, in 2014, Swift herself announced *1989* as her "first documented, official pop album" (Ryan and Mansfield 2014), and journalists once again repeated the story of her transformation from country singer-songwriter to world-dominating pop star, with headlines like "A Farewell to Twang" (Caramanica 2014), "Taylor Swift Shakes Off Country with First Pop Album" (Ryan and Mansfield 2014), "Taylor Swift Leaves Country for Pop on '1989'" (Miers 2014), and "Taylor Swift

Aims for Pop's Throne" (Powers 2014). Reviewers now were more likely to note Swift's long history of movement toward pop, but still the headlines strongly supported the narrative of *1989* as a breakout mainstream record, and Swift herself may have had to put her thumb on the scale with her "documented, official" comment, given how many times she had already made this move and asked the public to accept it.

But while *1989* was framed as Swift's full, final, complete break with country and maturation into her grown-up, mainstream music industry–dominating role, the culmination of a long series of crossover records, upon its release she again disavowed the competence and authority that would come with such success, influence, and widespread acclimation and retreated, again, into the white, feminine, youthful vulnerability that had so long dominated her self-presentation. If anything, she doubled down on white vulnerability as anti-Blackness in the video for the lead single, "Shake It Off," in which a succession of scenarios show her awkwardly failing to competently achieve a series of cultural performances. In the most prominent scene, mentioned earlier in this chapter, she is embarrassed trying to keep up with Black women's purported sexuality in a parody of hip-hop videos that was widely read as a send-up of Miley Cyrus's appropriation of Black musical and dance styles (figure 4.4, above). The "Shake It Off" video also included a parody of the related masculine hip-hop stereotype, with Swift wearing a hoody and holding a boom box on her shoulder (figure 4.8). Swift's purported ordinariness, then, was explicitly opposed to Black cultural forms, which were shown to be stereotyped, unrestrained, and gaudy. As the *New York Times'* Jon Caramanica noted, "Modern pop stars—white pop stars, that is—mainly get there by emulating black music. . . . Ms. Swift, though, is having none of that; what she doesn't do on this album is as important as what she does." He continued, cynically, "The singer most likely to sell the most copies of any album this year has written herself a narrative in which she's still the outsider" (2014: AR22).

The video's boom-box scene recalled not Miley Cyrus's escapades or any of Swift's other contemporaries or rivals so much as her own video from 2009 as T-Swizzle, in which she performed precisely the same parody of Black popular culture, with precisely the same effect: to authenticate her ordinary, awkward whiteness through explicit contrast to contrived, performative Blackness. Rachel Dubrofsky (2016) argues that performances like Swift's in "Shake It Off" prioritize ironic self-reflexivity as an expression of racialized personal authenticity (that is, Swift reveals her true self in the video by depicting precisely what she is not), in which whiteness

Figure 4.8 Still from video for "Shake It Off" (Big Machine Records, 2014, dir. Mark Romanek).

is confirmed as a form of transparency—self-reflexive disclosure, "not hiding anything" (2016: 185)—through contrast with racialized bodies that do not reflexively disclose their ironic interiority. In a similar vein Robin James (2017) argues that in an era of stylistic fluidity, the celebratory marker "post-genre" is applied most readily to white artists like Swift who perform their genre transcendence by enumerating, as Swift does in "Shake It Off," the range of musical styles that influence but ultimately do not constrain them. Post-genre designations, James argues, participate in wider "post-race" discourses about US transcendence of racial divisions and history. As James puts it, "Claims to genre transcendence are credible when they are made by artists who, like Swift, appear free of any particular social identity. In order to sound post-genre, one has to seem post-identity" (2017: 27), but this is a status ultimately granted only to white artists. In 2009 Swift performed her minstrel T-Swizzle routine to confirm her bona fides as not Black and thereby secure her status within country music despite already slipping away from the genre. In 2014 she recycled that same minstrel shtick wholesale, this time not to cement herself within one genre but to establish her escape from genre and transcendence to pop eclecticism—even though all she did was perform one more iteration of the awkward vulnerable whiteness that she had been performing since she was sixteen.

If one thing did change from the long-standing formula, it is that Swift finally dropped the overt markers of childhood from her self-presentation.

She no longer rhapsodized about childhood fantasy or wrapped herself in imagery from children's stories and childhood experiences. But by retaining that investment in childhood innocence for so long and pairing it constantly with whiteness, she extended and smoothed the period of her transition from tween celebrity to adult superstar. Central elements of the particular formation of cultural whiteness that Swift claimed are vulnerability and grievance. Significantly this is where childhood and femininity take on critical roles in the construction of white identity, because traditional constructions of childhood and femininity share "innocence" as a core structuring value, and innocence itself is fundamentally defined in terms of vulnerability, loss, and grievance. White resentment, perhaps, provides a scaffold from "child" to "woman," since in their cultural constructions the three terms have critical intersections. Or, more precisely, Swift positioned herself from the start right at one critical point of intersection between childhood, whiteness, and femininity, and her core investment in the trope of vulnerable grievance allowed her to move fluidly between the three categories, and eventually to use whiteness to transition seamlessly from child to adult celebrity.

CONCLUSION

American racial discourses have long framed youthful, white feminine bodies as the site of white fantasies of vulnerability to violent threats from pathological Black aggressors—the position Kanye West was read as filling in his 2009 encounter with Swift—and these fantasies provide a basis for framing white supremacy as self-defense and ressentiment. When I teach about the Swift-West VMAs incident in childhood studies classes at the University of Pittsburgh, I pair it with the "Gus chase" sequence from the 1915 film *Birth of a Nation*, a canonical instance of the US mythology of Black sexual threats to (sexually and morally) innocent white women that dramatizes fantasies of racial threats to the nation as a whole (see, among others, Carby 1985; Diawara 1988; Dines 1998; Merritt 1990; Wiegman 1993). In that sequence, Gus, a Black captain in the Reconstruction army (who is played by a white actor in blackface), pursues Flora Cameron, the white "Little Sister" of the film's hero, Ben Cameron, through the woods. Flora throws herself from a cliff rather than accede to Gus's romantic/sexual advances, and her death motivates Ben to organize his recently founded Ku Klux Klan to lynch Gus and rise up to overthrow the Reconstruction regime. At the start of the scene, Flora is depicted as especially childish, leaving off her chore of collecting water from a spring to play with and be charmed by a squirrel in a tree, as the film pushes hard on the long-standing association of childhood innocence with nature (Hendrick 1997). Certainly the context and the stakes are very different in the 1915 and 2009 media spectacles, but the relevant correspondence between the Gus chase sequence and the Swift-West encounter at the VMAs is not just the staging of Black, masculine aggression against youthful, white, feminine vulnerability, but also the power that sequence has to mobilize broad outrage and action in response to perceived and trumped-up Black threats against white girls' innocence, as audiences are inspired to rise up in indignation to protect the white girl and, just as importantly, vilify the Black transgressor.

Whiteness, femininity, and childhood are mixed up together in this paradoxical but long-standing claim to cultural power as perpetual vulnerability, grievance, and resentment. But in *Birth of a Nation* the vulnerability of white, feminine childishness is put in service to Ben Cameron's masculine, white supremacist ends—Flora's pain, fear, and interiority are largely beside the point of the film—while in Taylor Swift's celebrity persona and musical output a parallel claim to cultural power is made from the position and on behalf of the vulnerable, young white girl. What are the subject positions offered to women and children by the intersections of race, gender, and age in this cultural mythology of white grievance? Lauren Berlant (2008) shows that the "female complaint"—Berlant's term for the master trope of feminine grievance in women's genres—is largely about race, explicitly and implicitly. Women's genres seek out and foreground images of Black suffering as the ultimate source of pain and vulnerability in support of a sentimentality based around narratives of grievance and complaint. In Berlant's telling, narrative identification with Black suffering serves to confirm bourgeois white women's own moral, political, and cultural centrality in American culture. Taylor Swift's work participates fully in the same genres of romance, melodrama, and the gothic that Berlant's analysis places at the center of US women's culture, and Swift continually voices something very similar to Berlant's gloss of the female complaint, that "women live for love, and love is the gift that keeps on taking" (2008: 1). (In Berlant's telling, it is to increase the stakes and intensity of this emotional "taking" from people who are only trying to give love that women's genres turn to images of Black suffering for heightened emotions.) Insofar as male romantic partners—for whom women's love and compassion elicits only rejection and abuse, at least until the final happy ending (Radway 1984)—are the conventional source of women's grievance in romance genres, Swift's narratives of failed heterosexual romance explicitly recapitulated this core trope of the genre. But if, as Berlant points out, motherhood, and a mother's love for her children, is the other core identification and source of suffering in women's genres, Swift adopted the other role in the mother-child dyad, positioning herself as the vulnerable, dependent, suffering child. Swift has taken the romance convention of grievance against male partners and paired it with complaints about middle-school bullies—for whom a child's desire for friendship elicits only rejection and abuse. She voices a feminine complaint from a specifically and enduringly youthful, even childish, standpoint.

What happens to women's genres when they are voiced as children's genres? One change is that the racial logic shifts—from appropriation to opposition. There is a link between Swift's expressions of grievance, her investment in fantasy and childhood, and her positioning of herself in vulnerable relation to Black culture. In Berlant's central text, *Uncle Tom's Cabin*, white women readers are encouraged to identify with the Black mother's fear of the loss of her child to slave traders—with the goal of validating white women's moral and political centrality in US culture by centering their emotional sensitivity and leadership. As Berlant puts it, "Embedded in the often sweetly motivated and solidaristic activity of the intimate public of femininity is a white universalist paternalism, sometimes dressed as maternalism. As long as they have had a public sphere, bourgeois white women writers have mobilized fantasies of what black and working-class interiority based on suffering must feel like in order to find a language for their own more privileged suffering at the hands of other women, men, and callous institutions" (2008: 6). While in most ways, especially for its constant foregrounding of suffering through selflessness, Swift's body of work across a decade is almost perfectly conventional of the genre of women's complaint, it notably does *not* have the identification with Black feminine suffering that Berlant shows is so important to much of the rest of that genre. Instead it claims a different figure of suffering, grievance, and vulnerability: the fantasy of the innocent white victim of masculine Black brutality. It calls into being not the enduring "woman's culture" of American history, but an adjacent tween culture, which shares US women's culture's investments in whiteness, femininity, and grievance, and even its investments in childhood, though it locates itself in the position of the dependent, vulnerable, innocent child, rather than that of the child's caregiver and protector. By voicing a childish complaint, Swift drops the sentimental identification with Black female suffering through shared motherhood and instead fully claims whiteness—not white universalist paternalism but whiteness as anti-Blackness—because ultimately that is the racial logic that the innocence of the figure of the suffering white child offers.

In the next chapter I work through Justin Bieber's "self-infantilization" as a strategy of celebrity presentation. For Bieber self-infantilization emphasized immaturity and irresponsibility. Here we can see Swift doing something similar, but she emphasized different elements of childishness, especially innocence and vulnerability. The "innocence" that is ascribed to children is almost entirely constructed in the negative: it is the absence of experience, sexual desire, sin, temptation, knowledge, reason, self-control, socialization, the ability to harm. As James Kincaid has argued, this empty innocence is the cultural value at the center of constructions of modern childhood: "this hollowing out of children by way of purifying them of any stains (or any substance) also makes them radically different, other. In this empty state, they present themselves as candidates for being filled with, among other things, desire" (1998: 175). Kincaid's argument is about the eroticization of innocence, which is certainly relevant to Swift and other young performers, but more to the point here, this construction of innocence as emptiness has an inexorable logic of vulnerability and grievance. Innocence itself is a pure distillation of vulnerability, in that it is existentially threatened by any encounter with the world or any passage of time: any experience had, any knowledge gained, any reasoning cultivated, any desire acknowledged, is in the very act an erosion of the innocence that exists only in the absence of those things. If innocence is that which is most prized about childhood by adults, and innocence is itself unstable, constantly vanishing, an absence rather than a presence, then what is being valued is also something already lost. The valorization of innocence is effectively a discourse of grievance, as in Wordsworth's classic lines, which are full of resentment at the loss of innocence's transcendence and at confinement in the adult "prison-house":

> trailing clouds of glory do we come
> From God, who is our home:
> Heaven lies about us in our infancy!
> Shades of the prison-house begin to close
> Upon the growing Boy,
>
> [. . .]
>
> At length the Man perceives it die away,
> And fade into the light of common day. ([1807] 1992: lines 64–76)

This is why so much of Swift's narrative of childhood grievance is stuck in the past, or not quite in the past but in the strangely twisted subjunctive temporality of anticipatory nostalgia for future lost innocence, as in "Fifteen."

This construction of innocence as emptiness also racializes it as unmarked whiteness. Kincaid writes that we formulate "the image of the alluring child as bleached, bourgeois, and androgynous" (1998: 20), or as Robin Bernstein puts it, in the nineteenth century "sentimental childlike innocence manifested through the performed transcendence of social categories of class, gender, and ... race.... Innocence was not a literal state of being unraced but was, rather, the performance of not-noticing, a performed claim of slipping beyond social categories" (2011: 6). Bernstein, Anna Mae Duane (2010), and others have pointed out that the figure of the suffering, innocent child is classically white, while Black children have been depicted as invulnerable to physical and emotional harm, a trait that is often deployed for comic effect. The sexualized innocence that Kincaid describes is the same cultural formation as the racialized innocence that Bernstein analyzes, because both are founded on the logic of absence, disavowal, and concomitant vulnerability.

The racialization of innocence deposits white supremacist logics within deeply held contemporary values around childhood. Bernstein argues persuasively that childhood works as a sort of cultural archive of practices and values that have been nominally forgotten or sublimated by a mainstream adult culture. The repertoires of nineteenth-century minstrelsy—Stephen Foster's compositions, for example—still flourish in children's music and cartoons (Sammond 2015; Smolko 2012). Depositing such cultural repositories with children launders them of their associations with racial tyranny and violence—the association with childhood makes such traditions "innocent." Bernstein writes: "Childhood innocence provided a perfect alibi: not only the ability to remember while appearing to forget, but even more powerfully, the production of racial memory through the performance of forgetting" (2011: 8). Something like this may explain, in part, the deep investment in whiteness demonstrated during the tween moment. By embedding deep-seated mythologies about white feminine vulnerability in opposition to the hypersexualization and objectification of Black women's bodies, on the one hand, and Black male aggression, on the other, in apparently frivolous, consumerist, and infantilized tween media in the twenty-first century, US public culture, like the audience for the 2009 VMAs, is free to enjoy these traditional narratives while disavowing any culpability for their racial implications.

To summarize: we do not see explicit representations of Blackness in Cyrus's work until a moment of extreme effort to break away from her child-star persona, at which point she placed musical, visual, and embodied representations of Blackness at the center of a constellation of imagery that also emphasized sex, drugs, rebellion, and opposition to childhood innocence. This centering of Blackness as the core signifier of anti-innocence was deeply problematic for its recapitulation of narratives of Blackness as antisocial and abject. It also directs our attention backward to see more clearly the earlier investments in whiteness of a show like *Hannah Montana*: in explicit representations of racial whiteness like the Southern "white trash" performances of Aunt Dolly and the antagonist roles filled by actors of color, and in implicit representations, such as the show's centering of the racially flattened figure of the consuming bourgeois girl, the playful innocence of its childish humor, and its characters' dependence on paternalist parents, as well as the grievance and complaint foregrounded in the problem of "having it all"—a contemporary discourse of bourgeois white femininity about the simultaneous demands of caregiving and breadwinning—that is the show's core narrative trope. Cyrus's *Bangerz* moment drew heavy-handedly on long-standing and deeply embedded cultural narratives around Black femininity, sexuality, and objectification in order to break fully from the childhood persona that appears in relief as more deeply and explicitly invested in whiteness than may have been initially visible.

In parallel, we do not see explicit representations of Blackness in Swift's work until she begins to be pulled into the mainstream, interpreted by critics and audiences as having begun to secure her position as a major adult artist. If the gravitational force of Disney kept pulling Cyrus back into childhood, by contrast Swift orbited the mainstream, and her Top 40 success kept threatening to pull her fully into adulthood. At each of these moments, starting with the 2009 release of *Fearless*, she reinvested in narratives of childhood grievance and dependence, such as bullying by popular schoolkids and fights with her parents, and also began to situate herself in opposition to adult male Blackness: not just the perhaps unanticipated encounter with Kanye West at the VMAs, but also, just two months earlier, as T-Swizzle rapping alongside T-Pain at the CMT Awards. In future years, in defensive response against criticism and against the pull of the mainstream, she continued to pair references to childhood innocence and fantasy with the white cultural imagery of *Oz* and *Alice*, and later the explicit anti-Blackness of "Shake It Off." If for Cyrus Blackness was the maximal symbol of anti-innocence, for Swift anti-Blackness provided the ultimate symbolic confirmation of that innocence.

FIVE THE TWEEN PRODIGY AT HOME AND ONLINE

In 2007, when Justin Bieber was thirteen years old, he started posting home videos of himself singing and playing music on the video-sharing website YouTube.[1] The videos show him singing in the bathroom and playing guitar on his living-room couch, as well as competing in a local talent show and busking on the steps in front of a local theater in his hometown of Stratford, Ontario. These videos were very popular online and ultimately led to Bieber's discovery by a talent agent, after which he moved to Atlanta, signed a record contract, and began working toward his breakout commercial success in 2009, at age fifteen.

Along with Miley Cyrus and Taylor Swift, Bieber was one of the most prominent representatives of the explosion of young artists during the tween moment. Like Cyrus and Swift, Bieber's early reception was dominated by emphasis on his age, and his own celebrity packaging encouraged this focus on his youthfulness. But in important ways Bieber's portrayal as a child celebrity was very different from Cyrus's and Swift's, with his gender a key element of contrast. As a boy star, Bieber was put forward to girl audiences as a figure not for identification or aspiration but for objectification and desire. Unlike Cyrus and Swift, Bieber was portrayed as an exceptionally precocious talented musician and performer, a "prodigy" whose instrumental and vocal abilities—more than emotional resonance or lyrical depth—justified his dramatic success. Unlike Cyrus and Swift, he embraced Black musical styles from the very beginning of his career, framing himself within the established role of the white male R&B singer and conspicuously adopting Black artists as mentors and collaborators. And if *Hannah Montana*, like other tween media products, highlighted its protagonist's ongoing struggle to reconcile childhood intimacy with public participation, Bieber, by contrast, was portrayed as heroically resolving any potential contradictions between childhood and celebrity through his extreme talent. Central to this portrayal were emerging social media products like Facebook, Twitter, and especially YouTube. The same tools were frequently described as important to the success of tween artists like Swift in connecting to their similarly young fans, but in Bieber's celebrity persona those new media offerings linked with the cultural figure of the boy musical prodigy to provide a rhetorical framing of intimate childhood and public celebrity as not just compatible, but, if anything, exemplary of triumphant new structures of public culture in the twenty-first century. In this chapter I am interested in new media less as a "real" mediating structure, and much more as a rhetorical figure that was deployed as a solution to representational problems. The biographical detail that Bieber was discovered on YouTube is less interesting to me than the way the figure of YouTube was deployed after the fact to frame Bieber's relationships with his fans.

This chapter's central example, the 2011 concert film *Never Say Never*, presents his commercial success as a story of prodigious talent that is allowed by new media to remain sheltered in domesticity. This film, which depicted Bieber's summer 2010 tour, is a rich document that productively connects several strands in Bieber's career: his family life, his status as a child, his early performance ability, his use of the internet, and his commercial success. If *Hannah Montana* posed the tension between childhood embedded in family domesticity and the dramatic publicness required by commercial musical success as the driving tension motivating the intimate publicness of tween identification, *Never Say Never* does, perhaps, the opposite. The film acknowledges the tension between childhood—and especially the negative traits of dependence, immaturity, and irrationality—and the public exposure and economic power of celebrity. But *Never Say Never* identifies these tensions not to struggle with them but instead simply to overcome them. It offers two tools for their resolution: first, "prodigy," an established discourse about the pairing of childhood and supposedly adult levels of ability, whose logic of individual talent *Never Say Never* adapts to a wildly different context of commercial media; and second, the internet, especially video-sharing tools like YouTube, which offers a vision of intimate one-to-many and many-to-many communication that seems to overcome barriers between public and private and allows Bieber's public success to be presented as though it is embedded within comfortable family domesticity. If *Hannah Montana* wallowed in childhood as a source of emotional intensity, and Taylor Swift carried childhood innocence with her into her adult career as a talisman of whiteness and femininity, *Never Say Never* treated childhood as the basis for a narrative of heroic achievement—*almost* a bildungsroman, but without the protagonist's progressive development toward adulthood or maturity.

At least in part this is possible because Bieber's gender gave him access to a subject position—the white male R&B singer—from which he could performatively transcend racial boundaries, rather than be threatened by them. And this brings up an important point about gender, race, and childhood: the "innocence" that so constrained Cyrus and Swift but also intensified their investments in racial whiteness is very different for girls than for boys. The sexual innocence imposed on girl celebrities ultimately, and ironically, demands a sort of maturity based in bodily self-discipline, propriety, and restraint. Bieber, on the other hand, is not innocent as much as "immature" or "puerile"—that canonical trope of undisciplined masculine childhood play and bodily freedom. Puerility revels in following unrestrained play well past the limits of social propriety. In Natalia Cecire's (2012a) telling, puerility may well be bound by the internal rules of a game but it is not, importantly, restrained by social norms like those of bodily propriety. In *Never Say Never*, Bieber's puerility is so excessive and unrestrained that it threatens to overtake itself and harm the source of his own prodigious talent, his singing voice, a situation that the film shows eventually requiring adult intervention. *Hannah Montana* treats Miley as the author and protagonist of her own development, guided but not directed by well-meaning adults. *Never Say Never*, by contrast, revels in the profound immaturity of Bieber's overflowing talent, and it focuses intently on paternalistic intervention and authority. If *Hannah Montana*'s Miley works hard on an unsolvable problem, Bieber does not work hard at all but nonetheless succeeds remarkably, and that confirms his tremendous talent.

Playful unrestrained puerility justifies Bieber's investment in Black musical styles and genres, as his embrace of R&B is seen as following logically from his pursuit of vocal mastery. If Cyrus's and Swift's presentations of innocent white youthful femininity were implicitly and explicitly contrasted with Black femininity and threatened by Black masculinity, Bieber's early career showed almost the opposite. In the YouTube home videos that got him discovered, he primarily performed songs by Black R&B artists including Chris Brown, Ne-Yo, Brian McKnight, and Alicia Keys, as well as white R&B artists like Justin Timberlake and Elliott Yamin. Those musically demanding songs were especially effective at highlighting his ability as a singer, which was responsible for much of the early attention his videos received on YouTube. After being discovered, Bieber was famously mentored by the Black R&B artist Usher, and the featured guest artists on Bieber's debut 2010 studio album *My World* 2.0 were all African American: rapper Ludacris, rapper and singer Sean Kingston, and singer Jessica Jarrell. This is all to say that from the earliest moments of his career, Bieber surrounded himself with Black performers and embraced Black musical genres, especially R&B.

Of course there is a tradition going back to nineteenth-century minstrelsy of white male performers appropriating Black performance styles (Lott 1993), and specifically a tradition of "blue-eyed soul" that was codified in the 1960s and by 2009 was undergoing a revival as artists like Justin Timberlake, Robin Thicke, Elliott Yamin, and others reestablished white male R&B as a recognizable segment of the pop music market.[2] Darron Smith argues that embracing tropes of Blackness gives young white male performers like Bieber access to "coolness" coded as strongly masculine: "when white males perform (musically and physically) black music [they] are regaled by their fans, earning a legion of global followers and the spoils of fame" (2014). And Stephen Graham (2015) argues that "immersion" in Black musical styles provided Justin Timberlake a marker of credibility and also *maturity*—of having grown up from his early teen-pop career. Importantly that seriousness is seen to reflect *musical* immersion and acquired competence, rather than necessarily social or cultural immersion and participation. Mark Anthony Neal suggests, similarly, that while white hip-hop performers often lean on comedy, playing racial appropriation for laughs, "white male R&B singers . . . take the genre of R&B seriously" (2005: 371). That Bieber was fully committed to R&B performance styles from the earliest moments in his career, and that he made a visible effort to embrace Black mentors like Usher, suggests that his adoption of Black musical style may have been playful but was also *serious* in the same sense—not parodic like Swift's "Thug Story" or provocative like Cyrus's "We Can't Stop." Performing challenging R&B repertoire was what allowed Bieber to develop and showcase his vocal ability. So while Cyrus sought to highlight a contradiction between Black performance and childhood innocence in her 2013 performances, in Bieber's early career there was no implication that Black musical styles or Black performers conflicted with his youthful status. Rather, Black music offered a field for him to develop and put forward his musical mastery, and that pursuit of mastery justified navigating racial boundaries and appropriating and digesting whatever material he encountered, in a way that would have been closed to young female performers like Swift and Cyrus for whom racial boundaries were much trickier. Furthermore, the girl performers are characterized by extreme self-consciousness, while Bieber is shown as distinctly unreflexive. His talent, then, is portrayed not as the product of struggle with his circumstances but rather as the natural and unmediated expression of his puerile childishness, which allows the logic of appropriation to trump the logic of vulnerability (at least until it turns back on itself and requires adult intervention). If innocent tween femininity represents a sort of static rather than playful immanence that distills and intensifies racial whiteness, Bieber's immature tween masculinity reflects a converse principle of transcendence that expresses whiteness as a playful, unrestrained, and acquisitive appetite for whatever satisfies its mission of puerile expansion.

PRODIGY AND INEQUALITY

Bieber's reception commonly emphasized his musical ability, and frequently described him as a "prodigy" (e.g., Rayner 2013; Vena 2010a; Widdicombe 2012). By contrast, when the *New Yorker*'s Sasha Frere-Jones (2008) described Taylor Swift's "precociousness" in an article headlined "Prodigy," his account focused on the maturity of her songwriting and her ability to transcend the constraints of genre, rather than her abilities as a singer or instrumentalist, while at the same time an established strain of criticism highlighted her supposed "pitch problems" as a singer (Stimeling 2016). Bieber, on the other hand, was not widely celebrated as a songwriter or for the emotional connection his songs made. Popular uses of the concept of prodigy link musical, commercial, cultural, and social forms of exceptionality to age. In *Never Say Never*, representations and discussions of Bieber's talent slipped easily back and forth from musical ability to commercial ability—which itself is about eliciting desire, and ultimately record and ticket sales, from a mass audience—and ultimately the latter was what the film put forward as the true measure of his talent.

Popular and scholarly prodigy discourses are based on ideas of exceptionality that are increasingly formalized and quantified by contemporary social scientists. A particularly influential and revealing perspective is formalized by educational psychologist Françoys Gagné (2009), whose Differentiated Model of Giftedness and Talent (DMGT) distinguishes "gifts," or individuals' given natural capacities, from "talents," the cultural, social, and environmental situations that allow such capacities to be realized and made meaningful. This distinction is effectively equivalent to binaries of "nature" and "culture" that have come in for sustained critique by theorists in the humanities and critical social sciences (Butler 1990; Ortner 1972). Distinguishing "gifts" from "talents" raises similar questions, but Gagné's model offers a helpful presentation of how ideologically loaded concepts like "prodigy" are constructed and maintained. Here I am interested in tracking how discourses explicitly about or adjacent to the concept of prodigy adhere to Bieber and reveal important underlying ideas about the social relations expressed by tween music. In fact it appears to me that prodigy discourses during the tween moment made more sense as an ideology of capitalism than of musical ability—or of the ways that musical and commercial efforts were not separable in the capitalist context of the tween music industry.

Gagné defines talent quantitatively, as a position in a normal (bell-curve) distribution, which highlights a very narrow range of possible musical values and assumes extreme differentiation within mass populations in a way that resonates with the cultural logics of celebrity surrounding Bieber. The DMGT model defines gifted and talented people as "the top 10% of age peers" (2009: 63), and makes even finer-grained distinctions of "exceptionally" (1:10,000) and "extremely" (1:100,000) gifted and talented individuals (2009: 71). If extreme talent is defined as being more capable than 100,000 other people, that definition both assumes a very narrow understanding of musicality and builds social inequality and hierarchy into that understanding.

Gagné's model can only account for precisely measurable abilities and requires a very large population. Especially from a cross-cultural perspective, applying such criteria to music does not make sense. For example, musically (and otherwise) egalitarian and small-scale societies like the Kaluli of Papua New Guinea, described by Feld (1984), do not have large enough populations to support evaluations of "extreme talent," and despite moderate variation in musical interest among individuals, they do not seem to exhibit the normal distributions of ability that Gagné's model assumes (with identifiable top and bottom deciles, etc.). With this definition of talent, such a model would imply that there are no "extremely"—or perhaps even "moderately" (top 1 percent)—talented Kaluli musicians. Following the DMGT model, we might even be forced to argue that the Kaluli "talent development process" (Gagné 2009: 67) is *holding back* the musical development of its most musically gifted individuals. But for a community that appears to provide its members with a much more intensive and universal musical socialization than the educational systems of the large-scale capitalist societies that Gagné researches, this would seem to be a perverse result. Or as John Blacking asks pointedly, "Must the majority be made 'unmusical' so that a few may become more 'musical'?" (1973: 4).

This point is relevant not just to very small-scale societies or examples of significant social and cultural distance. Rather, it applies equally well to the musical communities of children on school playgrounds around the world. As Kathryn Marsh (2008) has documented extensively, children display remarkable musical skills in handclapping games and songs that can stymie even musically trained adults. Like the Kaluli there may be children who show more interest or ability in musical games. But children's musical communities are small (despite their transnational reach, they do not have transnational audiences or performance circuits), and their musical games are participatory, including children with wide ranges of ability in relatively large groups. So there is no sense in which any one individual could be extremely talented. In fact the very definition of musical success in these games, in which a group must cooperate to produce a collective accomplishment, precludes individual talent. If talent is demonstrated mastery or achievement, in this case it is a trait of groups and not individuals. Therefore, even in highly stratified large-scale societies we can still find communities organized around skillful musical activity in such a way that normal bell-curved distributions of ability do not make sense.

Gary McPherson and Aaron Williamon (2016) argue for looking beyond individual performance to musical abilities like appraisal, improvisation, and teaching. Such a proposal might make room for valuing the skills demonstrated in children's playground music. But the problem is less with expanding the set of measured traits than the assumption that relevant traits will or should vary across populations in precisely measurable rankings. As critical education scholars Hervé Varenne and Ray McDermott (1998) argue in a parallel field, quantitative measurements that define educational "success" through comparative rankings in effect *produce* the "failure" of unsuccessful schools or students. In this way a descriptive model can easily become normative or prescriptive, such that the existence of failing or incompetent individuals is built into a definition of success that treats normal distributions as given, leaving no room to envision a world of shared competence and collective accomplishment. Linda Kreger Silverman and Nancy B. Miller (2009) have put forward a convincing feminist critique of the standard emphasis in giftedness studies on measuring comparative achievement that parallels many of my objections here. Unlike the Kaluli, whom Feld describes as having "no investment in rationalizing differences in competence" (1984: 391), twenty-first-century American society is deeply invested in rationalizing such differences.

My argument, then, is not to do away with concepts like talent or prodigy, but to encounter them critically, identify their implications, and observe their effects. Divisions between children and adults are culturally and socially contingent, and not fixed by biology or development (Prout and James 1997), so discourses about children, such as evaluations of children's musical abilities, play an important part in creating the social roles that children inhabit (Gubar 2013). This means that the concepts contained in the term "child musical prodigy" as they are applied to Justin Bieber are of central importance for understanding the cultural phenomenon of his dramatic commercial success, and for extracting useful lessons from it about the values and norms that structure children's participation in public media. Setting these social scientific approaches aside as models and instead treating them provisionally as discourses that participate in a wider sphere of culture, we can see how concepts like prodigy are built around assumptions of unequal, hierarchical, and large-scale social structures. That perspective, then, helps set in relief the contributions of an idea like prodigy to forms of popular cultural celebrity in large-scale capitalist societies like ours. In *Never Say Never*, importantly, it is precisely commercial success that ultimately fits the quantitative definition of prodigy, and it is Bieber's ability to sell concert tickets that is ultimately seen to set him apart as being extremely talented at a prodigiously young age.

THE TWEEN PRODIGY

Bieber's major success began at age fourteen, so he may not fit a standard definition of a prodigy as "a child younger than 10 years of age who performs at an adult professional level in a highly demanding field" (Feldman and Morelock 2011: 212). In the home videos that originally attracted attention—some showing him as young as two years old—Bieber demonstrated tremendous ability for his age in singing, playing guitar, and especially playing drums. Even so, in the context of popular music—the particular "highly demanding field" in which Bieber performs—what it means to achieve an adult level of talent might not be a straightforward question, in part because Bieber's age was always foregrounded in his performances. In the home videos as well as his later recordings, Bieber's singing voice is identifiably that of a young boy. And many of the videos are set in spaces like Bieber's family living room, bathroom, and kitchen, which mark his status as a child. Where the settings may be age-neutral, the simple visual fact of Bieber's young body performing is not.

Even if we desired an evaluation of performance ability separated from markers of age or other identity, it might not be possible. In classical music it may be common to treat musical sound as separable from visual or embodied information, as in cultures of closed-eye listening or auditioning from behind a curtain, and part of what makes the idea of child prodigies thinkable could be that field's expectation that music can or should transcend particular embodied experience (McClary 1991; McMullen 2006). But video and images of performers are central to popular music. This may be increasingly true, as by 2012 the most common form of music listening for young people was the video-sharing website YouTube, in which music is usually only accessible along with video or other images (Nielsen Holdings N.V. 2012). Even outside of visual representations, Simon Frith has argued persuasively that gesture and embodiment are central to popular musical performance (1998: 191–98), so competent performances of popular genres almost require performers to musically signify embodiment, which is to say, to perform markers of sociocultural identity. But if performing one's body, so to speak, is central to popular music competence, that means that we cannot assess a performer's ability without reference to their particular forms of embodiment (even if those references are ironic, layered, or appropriative). Conventionally such embodiment highlights gender, race, and sexuality, but age has also been a key identity performed by popular musicians (Whiteley 2005).

In genres that foreground performances of sociocultural identity in place of or in addition to technical musical skill, the question "does this child perform competently at an adult professional level?" is probably not answerable. As audiences we cannot help but see a child performer as a child, so evaluations are always appended by ". . . for a child" and it is very difficult to fairly separate out our expectations about age. Certainly a major part of the appeal and interest that Bieber's early videos garnered on YouTube was in recognizing the performer for the child that he was, while at the same time Bieber's recordings were judged too young for airplay on Top 40 radio. When standards of performance already include reference to embodied age identities, musical competence cannot be separated out from those sociocultural values. This means that there may be no simple definition in pop music of "performing at adult levels." Bieber was a remarkably successful child musician in part because of his embodied performance of his young voice—something no adult-bodied person could do. Bieber emerged as a public figure at the peak of the tween moment, after many other artists had established popular music for children as a major segment of the music industry and a significant music format in its own right. So while his age might once have been a barrier to Top 40 radio airplay, it quickly became an asset, as radio programmers saw Bieber and other young musicians as "stars of their generation" who "deliver audience" (Stern 2013).

Discourses about age compression, of "kids getting older younger," often anxiously highlight a mismatch between mature content and children's developmental limitations (assumed to be fixed and given). But we might also see in age compression a discourse of precocity. That is, "getting older younger" quite clearly means achieving developmental milestones at ever earlier ages—not far from widely held definitions of a prodigy. In the particular discourse of age compression, the precocious unit is not an individual child but rather children as a demographic group or sociocultural identity. Concepts of prodigy or precocity are built into the idea of children's participation in activities for which they are conventionally understood to be unsuited. But on the mass scale at which popular media takes place, those concepts attach to groups rather than individuals, and discourses of precocity end up referring as much to the cultural blurring of boundaries between social categories like child and adult in age-compression discourses as to specific, measurable individual abilities.

As the ascendance of the term "tween" implied, what counted as childhood in consumer culture was somewhat in flux by the end of the 2000s. Children's media was never more prominent or visible to adults, and the increasing visibility of children's participation in popular culture was already being articulated by marketers and cultural commentators as a phenomenon of widespread precocity. Therefore, Bieber entered a popular culture environment in which being a child was a clear source of value and interest: not only did his unusual talent draw attention from impressed observers, but he also entered the market at a moment when child audiences were increasingly articulated as an identity group, and they were primed to seek out and recognize their own. The film *Never Say Never* staged these relationships in precise detail onscreen.

NEVER SAY NEVER

Never Say Never is structured around two main narrative strands. First, it is a biopic about Justin Bieber's rise to fame, and it includes a large number of home videos, photographs, and interviews with family and friends. Second, it is a concert movie documenting his 2010 summer tour, focusing on the lead-up to his first concert at Madison Square Garden in New York. The film consistently collapses these two strands into one another, so that Bieber's childhood and home life is continually invoked in representations of his celebrity performance, and representations of YouTube are used to link the two separate strands. The juxtaposition of Bieber's professional success with his youthfulness and family life is not unique to *Never Say Never*. Among other examples, that pairing was the central focus of a major *New York Times* profile that is thematically very similar to the film (Hoffman 2010). In focusing my interpretation on the single film, my goal is to explore in detail how these disparate strands of Bieber's life and career were rhetorically linked and accounted for in his commercial portrayals. My analysis here argues for the rhetorical importance of new media imagery in bridging Bieber's domestic and professional strands, because the film is so concerned to resolve that tension. Therefore the film is interesting not so much as a historical document but as an ideological one, which deploys notions of child prodigy for its own commercial ends.

These themes are clearly established in the film's prologue, which opens on a computer screen and follows an internet user browsing viral videos of wedding disasters and cute animals. Finally an email message reading "No words. Just watch." leads to a YouTube page with a video of Bieber, sitting on a drab living-room couch with a Bart Simpson poster behind him, singing Chris Brown's "With You" (figure 5.1).[3] The shot zooms in until the web page disappears and the video takes up the whole frame, and then cuts abruptly to a slightly older Bieber in a white jacket and the shaggy haircut he became famous for, apparently backstage at a concert. Black intertitles cut in reading, "IN TEN DAYS / A KID FROM A SMALL TOWN IN CANADA / WILL PERFORM AT THE WORLD'S MOST FAMOUS ARENA / MADISON SQUARE GARDEN / THIS IS HIS STORY." The YouTube video is intercut with images of Bieber walking toward the stage, while the soundtrack cuts jarringly between "With You" and sounds of a loud preshow audience, until both scenes finally fade together and then to white, and to the title sequence. This brief sequence, which returns at the film's climax, encapsulates the overall story: the juxtaposition of Madison Square Garden and a home video of a child's living-room performance, of "a kid from a small town" and "the world's most famous arena," with YouTube positioned prominently between. From the beginning of the film, Bieber's success is presented as prodigious (that is, unexpected or in tension with his status as a child) through the constant pairing of images of domesticity with im-

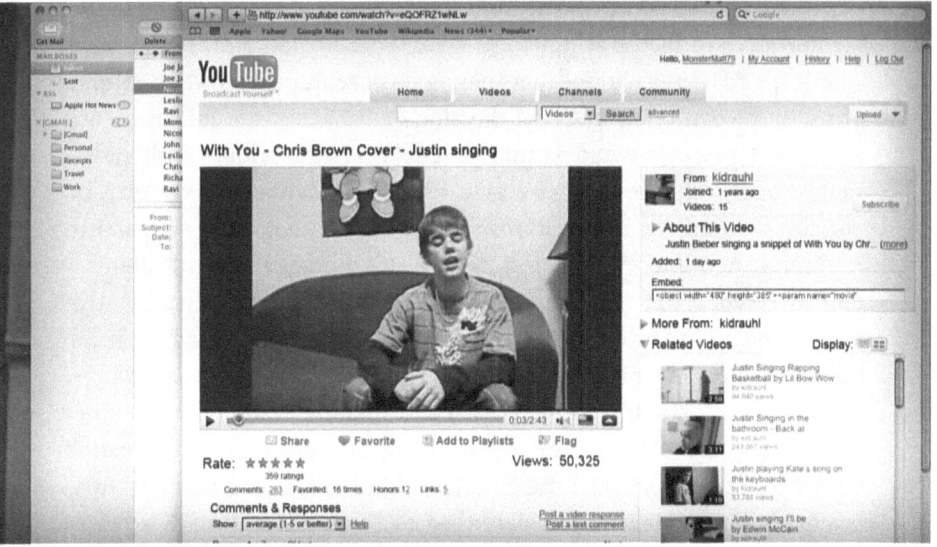

Figure 5.1 Bieber singing "With You," on YouTube, shown in web browser. Still from *Never Say Never* (Paramount Pictures, 2011, dir. Jon Chu).

ages of public performance, with YouTube as the medium that makes that exceptional or prodigious achievement possible and intelligible.

FAMILY

Following the title sequence, a brief scene of interviews with fans outside concert venues concludes with one fan saying, "He was just like a regular kid who had a dream and it just like came true." The film immediately cuts to a sequence of baby photos, home videos, shots of Bieber's hometown of Stratford, Ontario, and interviews with his mother, grandparents, coaches, and family friends, all of which emphasize the modesty of his upbringing, his strong bond with his grandparents, and his mother's commitment to his well-being despite the challenges of being a single mother. The film transitions to home videos of Bieber playing drums and interviews with his mother's musician friends. A neighbor describes his early interest: "Justin as a two-year-old would wander up to the stairs right in front of the drum kit, and just stare at Dan, the drummer in the band at the time. He would just be mesmerized. And he'd grab a pair of drumsticks and start hitting the stairs, and everybody noticed that his timing was amazing. Where does this talent come from?" He then describes Bieber at eight years old playing "jazz" at a church benefit, which was "quite difficult, but he was up for it." Home videos of Bieber at nine or ten years old soloing on the drums cut seamlessly to a brief shot of him soloing onstage during the concert tour. Thus, in the first few minutes of the film, Bieber's talent is quickly identified as both precocious and natural—a "gift" that he developed without lessons or many other resources—and it is situated in a domestic context, especially in strong familial relationships with his mother and grandparents.

Interestingly, Bieber's biological family—his mother and grandparents—quickly recedes from the film's focus. Instead the film immediately introduces Bieber's "road family," his professional tour staff, using both job titles and explicit kinship terms to identify their relationships to Bieber: Ryan Good is the road manager/stylist and "like the coolest older brother ever." Carin Morris "works wardrobe with Ryan, and she's just like Justin's big sister." Stage manager Scrappy says, "I kind of look at him like a little brother." Kenny Hamilton is described as "technically Justin's security guard, but Kenny is Justin's everything. . . . He lives on the bus with him." Hamilton himself tells the camera, "It's an uncle-nephew relationship. In my phone I have him programmed in as 'nephew.'" Bieber's manager, Scooter Braun (who, along with R&B star Usher, played the key role in discovering Bieber), is described as "in the road family definitely dad." He describes his job in parental terms: "ninety percent of my job is helping him become a good man. It's a family. So we're supporting each other, making sure the kid's okay." Finally voice coach Mama Jan (Smith) introduces herself: "I'm a fifty-four-year-old childless woman, and they call me 'Mama.'"[4]

While the tour staff are his employees, the film goes to great lengths to present them as caring authority figures and to present Bieber as very much a child. Throughout this sequence Bieber is portrayed not only as embedded in family relationships, but specifically as the child in a family, acting mischievously, joking, getting into trouble, and playfully wrestling with the "brother" and "uncle" figures, while the staff care for and discipline him. Even the one person not given an explicit kinship label, general manager Allison Kaye, is introduced as "the stern one" who intervenes when Bieber brandishes an electric clipper and jokingly threatens to shave his head, ordering him to "put that razor down right now!" Similarly Braun's introduction as "the dad" comes during a scene in which Bieber is shown sitting in the cab of a running forklift, apparently about to drive it, for which Braun then sternly rebukes him and physically carries him out of the vehicle (figure 5.2). This sequence concludes by returning briefly to

Figure 5.2 Scooter Braun lifting Bieber out of a forklift. Still from *Never Say Never* (Paramount Pictures, 2011, dir. Jon Chu).

Bieber's own family and home life when the tour arrives in Canada, mixing his real and professional "families." It shows Bieber's father (with whom Bieber did not live growing up) meeting the staff, a preshow prayer that includes his mother and father but in which only Mama Jan and other staff speak, and his father tearing up with pride during the performance. Mama Jan says in voiceover, "On the road with a group of people, it becomes a very functional dysfunctional family, all centered around one goal."

Conventional accounts of child stars commonly treat families as sites of social and developmental pathology, focusing on parental greed and exploitation (O'Connor 2008). But *Never Say Never* is keen to conflate Bieber's professional success and his status as a child in a family, so it may be that portraying his actual family at the center of that process would have raised concerns about exploitation and the commercialization of family intimacy (cf. Zelizer 1985). By treating Bieber's professional staff as family, the film strives to avoid commercializing the family, working instead to domesticate Bieber's commercial relationships.

IMMATURITY AND PATERNALISM

These representations of Bieber as a child in two families are part of a generally infantilizing portrayal of the star as distinctly immature—portrayed in ways that frame him more as a child than as the sixteen-year-old teenager that

Figure 5.3 "Mama" Jan, Allison Kaye, Scooter Braun, and Ryan Good tell Bieber they are canceling his scheduled performance. Still from *Never Say Never* (Paramount Pictures, 2011, dir. Jon Chu).

he was at the time. For example, after a concert, Bieber arrives at his grandparents' house and goes to bed in his childhood bedroom. He is shown playing and roughhousing with his childhood friends. His grandmother tells him he cannot go out until he cleans his room, and he and his friends relate a story about breaking a taxidermied fox with hockey sticks. At other times he is shown brushing his teeth or doing homework at night on the tour bus or being chided by a handler for eating doughnuts out of the garbage. Bieber's child fans also participate in his infantilization, describing him as "cute" and "adorable"—terms that refer simultaneously to objects of desire and childishness.

In fact, the plot of the film hinges on a moment in the lead-up to the concert at Madison Square Garden in which decisions about his own body and health are paternalistically made for him—despite his protests—which the film presents as wholly salutary. When Mama Jan asks Bieber if he has been taking care of his voice, which is showing signs of wear during the long tour, he responds seriously that on his trip home he talked more than usual, but he "wasn't screaming." The film then cuts to several shots of Bieber in fact screaming and yelling while playing with his friends—directly undercutting his claims and effectively calling him out for lying. This is surprising in a movie celebrating Bieber, but it fits the broader theme of immaturity. Not only is Bieber's puerile boyish exuberance an appealing

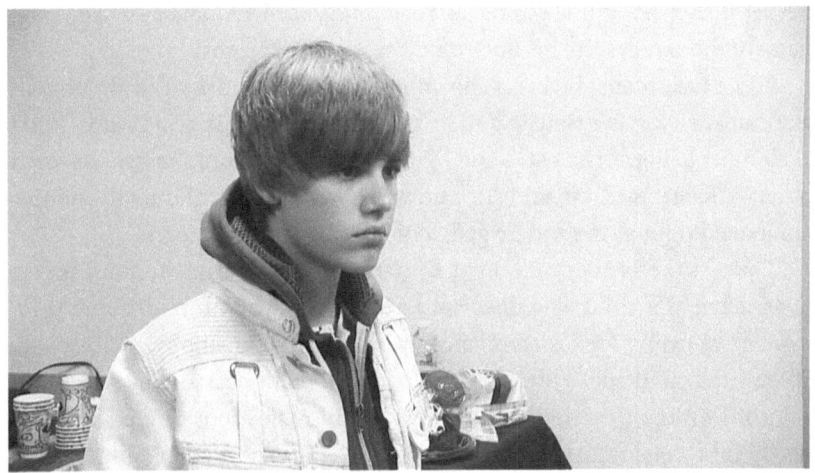

Figure 5.4 Bieber accepts their decision. Still from *Never Say Never* (Paramount Pictures, 2011, dir. Jon Chu).

part of his image, but his inability to responsibly care for his primary professional tool, even lying to avoid being caught, clearly positions his rebelliousness as childish and immature.

The tension between Bieber's repeatedly specified age and "professionalism" emerges here as a central theme. Earlier in the film Mama Jan noted that "one of the hardest things . . . for a kid on the road to understand is that he's a working man." A doctor called in to examine him tells Braun and Mama Jan, away from Bieber, that "we want him to be a healthy sixteen-year-old, but if he's taking on this career as a commitment it comes with obligations. There's a professionalism that comes along with it at any age where you have to make certain sacrifices, and that's why I think he has to cancel tomorrow's event." Another staff member is shown making a phone call to cancel the event, and then the decision to cancel a show is presented to Bieber as a fait accompli (figure 5.3).

He protests meekly: "There's gonna be a lot of kids that are gonna be let down." Braun says, "If I asked you [whether to keep to the tour schedule], you'll say yes, but then you'll destroy your vocal cords and we can't risk that."

And Mama Jan says, "I can't let you do that." She then asks, "Do you want to cancel seven shows, or move one now?" and Bieber meekly consents to "move one" (figure 5.4). Mama Jan continues aggressively to lecture Bieber about making "smart decisions." Then, moments later, a grinning

Bieber is shown begging Mama Jan to let him eat McDonald's chicken nuggets for dinner, despite his doctor's dietary proscriptions.

In the next scene, Bieber is shown playing video games while Braun tells the camera, "Justin's sixteen and he's just fighting to just be a normal kid. I remember being at the VMAs and Madonna came out and she gave a speech about Michael Jackson, and she said we took away his childhood, and Justin looked right at me and he goes 'don't let that happen to me.'"

Thus in the primary moment of narrative tension in the film, Bieber is depicted as a child who does not know his own best interests and is incapable of caring for his own voice. It is presented as wholly positive that these adults in Bieber's life—his employees, in many cases—make decisions for him, without his input and preempting his objections. It is an odd portrayal for a celebratory concert film. We might expect such a film to present its star as down-to-earth, ordinary, and accessible, and celebrities may be portrayed not just as ordinary or relatable but as distinctly flawed (as reality television portrays stars in fights, feuds, crises, etc.). *Never Say Never* does not simply show Bieber with charming foibles. It actively infantilizes him as not just fun-loving, playful, or innocent, but also as irresponsible, a liar, and incapable of making good decisions. These portrayals are put forward either with the assumption that they do not reflect badly on Bieber, or that their benefits exceed their costs. Their effect, which is to establish Bieber's celebrity persona as fully childish and puerile, must outweigh any negative implications.

COMMERCIAL SUCCESS AS PRODIGIOUS TALENT

Bieber's infantilization contributes to his portrayal as a prodigy by emphasizing the distance between his age and his accomplishments. His childish inability to care for his voice is the primary source of narrative conflict as the plot leads up to his performance at Madison Square Garden, which serves as the triumphal climax to the film. Selling out Madison Square Garden is presented as a measurable demonstration of Bieber's extreme talent, while Bieber's prodigy is presented now as a commercial, rather than strictly musical, accomplishment. In the lead-up to the Madison Square Garden concert, the film turns to interviews of established music industry executives who define selling out arenas as an extremely rare ability, even among already exceptional celebrities, and they further emphasize the uniqueness of Bieber's age. Tour promoter Randy Phillips says,

What happened with Justin Bieber has never happened before. Truly a phenomenon. Even groups like NSYNC and the Backstreet Boys took years. Justin is now in that rarified atmosphere: all these giant artists who sell out arenas every two or three years when they go on tour. Well, Justin is one of them now. He's become a member of that club. On his first record. In his first year and a half. I don't believe that's ever happened before.... The ultimate in our business is becoming an arena headliner: being able to sell out Madison Square Garden.

Producer and record executive LA Reid tells the camera, "Madison Square Garden represents the pinnacle of success for an artist. The Rolling Stones. U2. Michael Jackson. This is the big time. And for this *kid* to play Madison Square Garden, and he's the headliner? Give me a break, come on. This just doesn't happen."

Braun and Bieber then combine to narrate this particular accomplishment as entirely the product of Bieber's independent willpower and natural ability. Braun tells the camera, "A year and three days ago... we got invited to meet Taylor Swift at her sold-out show—first time she'd ever sold out the Garden.... Justin looked at me and said, 'I can do this.' And I said, 'Yeah, I believe you can do it.' And he says, 'No, I can do it in a year.'"

Bieber continues, "He kind of believed it but at the same time it was like... MSG is really hard to sell out. It's a really iconic venue."

Braun says, "He looked at me and he was like I can do this I don't care how hard I gotta work.... We wanted that Garden.... So we went on sale, and they called me and they're like, 'We're going to sell out this entire tour in two days.' I said, 'What about the Garden?' They said, 'The Garden? That sold out an hour ago.' And I said, 'What?' They said, 'Oh, yeah, we sold that out in twenty-two minutes.'"

To headline an arena—especially Madison Square Garden—is portrayed here as the highest measure of accomplishment in popular music. Phillips and Reid both emphasize the extreme rarity even of adults who succeed at this, and they marvel at Bieber's age and the speed of his accomplishment. And while interspersed comments from Bieber help establish the context, ultimately the climactic accomplishment is narrated by Braun, the adult, whose look of disbelief when he relates the "twenty-two minutes" figure expresses the sense of wonder that adults apply to child prodigies. The film pauses a moment after "twenty-two minutes" to let the enormity of Bieber's accomplishment sink in. Bieber himself is only allowed to ingenuously relate his guileless faith in his own abilities.

This is very clearly a prodigy discourse. It treats talent as measurable (through ticket sales) and defines categories of extreme talent in terms of statistical rarity. It also treats age as a normative precondition for ability, so the precocious achievement of extreme talent marks a child prodigy as the object of adult interest and even wonder. But at the same time, Bieber's *musical* abilities—established early in the film through home videos and testimonials—are no longer commented upon. Instead it is his commercial achievement that is so explicitly framed in terms of prodigy, even playing on a distinction between gifts and talents. Bieber highlights something like Gagné's "talent development" when he says he does not care how hard he will have to work. But ultimately the payoff is more than anyone thought to hope: not just selling out Madison Square Garden but selling it out in twenty-two minutes. Bieber's excess of gifts overflows any articulable goals of his "talent development" process. Thus, right before its climactic moment, the film provides a rubric for evaluating extreme talent (selling out Madison Square Garden) and then a precise quantitative measurement that locates Bieber within that rubric not just as a member of an elite group of performers, but remarkable even within that group.

The next minutes build to Bieber's entrance onstage at Madison Square Garden: backstage shots of celebrities; shots of crying fans; shots of the various "family members" backstage; and candid shots of Mama Jan giving advice. The film then pauses and cuts to a greenroom with Bieber, Usher, and Braun. Bieber holds his nose and drinks Usher's recommended energy drink, and calls it "dinosaur pee." He interrupts Usher's attempt at advice, reminding him (and us), "I'm sixteen, I always have energy." This moment of boyish play transitions to a sentimental preshow hug, in which Braun tells Bieber he is proud of him, "the little man in all of our lives."

And then the film returns to the shots from the prologue. Bieber puts on the white jacket he was wearing eighty minutes earlier in the film and says in voiceover: "I was once chilling in my room watching TV, just in a regular place. And now I'm in this big world living my dream, and you know doing what I love. And it's just crazy how it all came around." Off-camera fans begin to scream and chant his name. The film cuts quickly between tracking shots of Bieber walking toward the stage entrance, shots of the packed auditorium and the spectacle of lasers and smoke happening simultaneously onstage, and rapid-fire sequences of family photographs and stills from home videos. The film lingers on the wide-eyed faces of children in the audience and then pauses dramatically at the moment right before Bieber starts singing to linger on a few more of those photographs and home-video stills. And then finally it releases into the performance at Madison Square Garden.

YOUTUBE

There is a missing link here. The film's climactic scene returns to the opening: backstage at Madison Square Garden, the sound of fans cheering is heard over a montage of family photos. In the prologue, the juxtaposition of Madison Square Garden with childhood domesticity was presented as a problem: "A KID FROM A SMALL TOWN IN CANADA / WILL PERFORM AT THE WORLD'S MOST FAMOUS ARENA." But how do you get from the former to the latter? If anything, simply cutting back and forth between home and arena only highlights the contrast between the two spaces. But by the time the film finally returns to this scene, that tension seems to have been resolved. The key to that resolution, and the figure in the movie that ultimately mediates between public and private, family and commerce, childhood and celebrity, is the video-sharing website YouTube, and social media and the internet more generally.

The direct connections that the film continually makes between the disparate contexts of Bieber's public and private lives were explicitly modeled on the internet, in particular the "hyperlinks" among websites that connect bodies of information and spaces for participation. Director John Chu described how he incorporated these internet connections as a formal structure in the film: "If he's talking about his youth and talking about his magnetic smile, you start to hear 'U Smile' start to creep in the background and the underscore ... you see images from his life, and at the end of that song, the spotlight from the number connects with the spotlight of his tour bus and he goes back into his bed.... And there [are] hyperlinked ideas ... we're weaving in and out" (Vena 2010c). But more than just a formal device connecting various themes, the internet itself is a key figure onscreen. Besides titles identifying dates or individuals, the film only uses graphics and animation in reference to the internet. Certain shots overlay the YouTube logo and playback controls on the bottom, as though the video were being viewed through a web browser, with accelerating comments and views animated over all of that (figure 5.5). And Bieber's posts to Twitter pop up occasionally as bubbles onscreen.

Just before it arrives at the Madison Square Garden concert, the film relates Bieber's discovery by Braun, who explains how he stumbled across the online videos by accident and then convinced Bieber and his family to sign

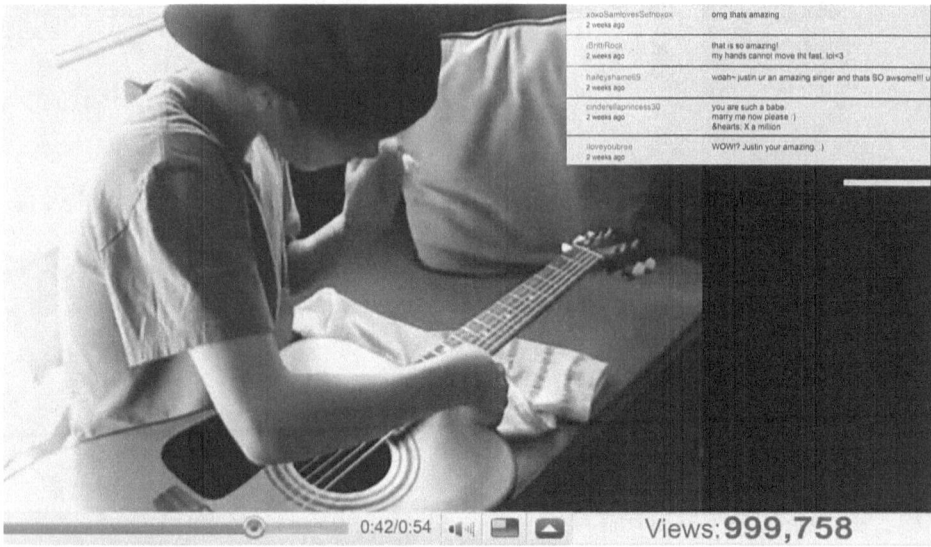

Figure 5.5 Representing YouTube on screen. Still from *Never Say Never* (Paramount Pictures, 2011, dir. Jon Chu).

with him and move to Atlanta. Cut among another home video of Bieber drumming on his guitar—with the YouTube logo and playback controls included at the bottom—Braun describes how he struggled to get Bieber a hearing from major labels. He presents YouTube as an explicit alternative to the child entertainment "machine" of Disney and Nickelodeon, specifically because young audiences were turning to the internet as a replacement for television: "Every label said, 'There's no platform for him. You need Nickelodeon or Disney, you need the machine.' Did you guys read the stats that kids are spending more time on the internet than they are watching TV? And the place where they're watching most of their videos is YouTube?" Earlier Braun told the *New York Times* that YouTube was central to connecting Bieber to his young fans: "I wanted to build him up more on YouTube first.... We supplied more content. I said: 'Justin, sing like there's no one in the room. But let's not use expensive cameras.' We'll give it to kids, let them do the work, so that they feel like it's theirs" (Hoffman 2010).

A relatively short segment built around the song "One Time" relates Bieber's rise to fame. Braun explains that radio stations would not play Bieber's young voice, so they toured constantly, and Bieber used the social media site Twitter to get his existing fans to show up for performances. Archival footage shows huge crowds filling malls and radio-station parking lots. Hamilton says, "At that point, no one really realized how powerful social networking was, or is." From images of malls and parking lots, the film moves to an establishing shot of an amphitheater packed full of thousands of screaming fans, while the soundtrack imperceptibly shifts from small local performances of this song to big public ones. At the same time graphics begin to pop up onscreen, portraying YouTube controls as though the shot is inside a web browser, and showing Bieber's Twitter conversations with fans nondiegetically with the filmed footage, in a graphic language that points away from the documentary realism of the rest of the film. The segment cuts to Kaye, the general manager, who argues that Bieber's fans feel a special ownership of him precisely because social media can let them bypass the normal mediations of the culture industries and consume his performance directly: "Justin's fans are the most loyal group of girls on the planet. They all feel a certain ownership of him, because they feel like they found him before Scooter found him, before the record labels found him. He belongs to *them*."

This is the key ideological moment in the film. While the prologue and climax juxtapose Bieber's home and professional life, this segment narrates a step-wise progression from his childhood living room to the in-person connections Bieber made with his fans at small regional shows to his mediated personal connections with fans through social media. And then, in an extraordinary and unique visual moment in the film, LA Reid says, "I've never seen fans like this," and the image swings away as if on a hinge to reveal a computer-generated mosaic of hundreds of YouTube videos of fans singing along with "One Time" in their own homes and backyards (figure 5.6). The images move and proliferate in a fantastic three-dimensional black space out of which a few stage lights shine in the distant background. As more and more YouTube videos fill the screen, individual frames grow smaller and smaller until they resolve into the individual pixels of a wide camera shot of Bieber's live performance of "One Time" onstage (figure 5.7). The fan videos appear again, now floating in Madison Square Garden's cavernous space above the live performance, singing *to* Bieber as Bieber sings to them (figure 1.5). The individual frames of fans' home videos move around each other like photographs hanging from a mobile, as though they share a real volume of space—a space that lays over the actual space of a large auditorium, whose stage lights intrude into the digital mosaic just as the home-video tiles float over the audience in the live performance.[5]

The home videos of fans singing along with Bieber clearly recall the home videos of Bieber himself singing along to other celebrities' songs. The mass audience is conceived as a collection of individuals, using digital

Figure 5.6 Montage of fan videos during "One Time" sequence. Still from *Never Say Never* (Paramount Pictures, 2011, dir. Jon Chu).

Figure 5.7 Montage of fan videos resolving into Bieber's onstage performance. Still from *Never Say Never* (Paramount Pictures, 2011, dir. Jon Chu).

animation techniques that allow the filmmakers to trace identifiable individuals as they join larger and larger groups. The mass audience in the auditorium is paired with the mass audience at home and online. Just as home videos trail Bieber's every footstep as he moves toward the public performance space, they follow the audience to that space as well. In this narration of Bieber's rise to fame, what makes his success possible is the steady agglomeration of intimate one-to-one relationships between performer and audience, all of whom are metaphorically located safely in their own family homes. Bieber sings from his childhood couch to fans who sing back to him from their own living rooms and backyards.

Jack Halberstam has suggested, in the adjacent context of animated films by studios like Pixar and DreamWorks, that digital animation offers unique tools for portraying mass social formations as "swarms" of collective action by bees, ants, fish, penguins, and farm animals: "CGI introduced numbers, groups, the multitude. Once you have an animation technique for the crowd, you need narratives about crowds, you need to animate the story line of the many and downplay the story line of the exception" (2011: 175). Of course, *Never Say Never* is offering precisely a story line of the exception. But when it finally needs to resolve the motivating contradiction that it sets up from the first moments, between Bieber as immature child in need of domestic confinement and Bieber as world-conquering pop star exploding beyond any conceivable limits, it turns to this digital animation of the online swarm of children singing along.

This digital mosaic scene puts forward a spatial metaphor of internet media and the relationship between performers and audiences. These online performances are presented as taking place in a three-dimensional, social, and participatory space, but one that is always linked to and enclosed in domestic safety. In the literal space of the auditorium, child audiences and a child performer gather outside their homes to participate in an activity that is, the film seems to want to say, effectively the same as that online space, which is itself comfortably embedded in individual family homes, as YouTube domesticates Madison Square Garden. Jon Chu described his interest in portraying a "digital lifestyle" (Vena 2010b). But there is nothing particularly "digital" about live concerts. Instead, this concert film proposes to narrate a "new" form of mass mediated relationality, with Bieber and his fans positioned at the forefront, in which the live concert is not conceived as the primary site of public performance and audition, the home is. The CGI "swarm" of YouTube videos floating together in the space of a concert venue offers a literal visual representation of the intimate public of a mass of individual children singing along together from the domestic shelter of their family bedrooms. If Kidz Bop's video for "Since U Been Gone" showed public musical performance as a childish fantasy, replete with stuffed animals come to life, *Never Say Never* took the intimacy and fantasy of that idea and literalized it through Bieber's own biography and representations of Bieber's fans.

PUBLIC AND PRIVATE IN CHILDREN'S NEW MEDIA

Bieber's portrayal as a prodigy works to infantilize and domesticate him, precisely because this is what makes his prodigy visible. Home videos, infantilizing portrayals, and constant contextualization within the "family" all provide the childish ground against which his prodigious commercial accomplishment is figured. But because his prodigious accomplishment depends on his cultivation of a large and engaged audience of children—it is effectively *defined* that way—the portrayal of Bieber as a prodigy entails representations of his relationship to his audience, and specifically a portrayal of his audience as a statistical/mass formation that reveals his prodigy by responding commercially to it. The home videos of fans appear inside the space of the auditorium, while there is no documentary footage of fans at home consuming Bieber's music or videos. Similarly Bieber's family is located mostly in the background of the film, while his professional staff are treated like family. Rather than simply conflating public and private, there is a directionality here. Tropes of family, domesticity, and childhood are projected onto public spaces, and very distinctly *not* the reverse. While moral panics about online media point to the risk of media commercializing or corrupting domestic values, here we have online videos being used to domesticate existing commercial and public spaces.

Popular music consumption often takes place comfortably within family homes and so may not immediately activate adult concerns. The tradition of "bedroom culture" has been identified as a historically important part especially of the social and cultural lives of girls, who are doubly subject to the surveillance and control entailed by ideologies of innocence and vulnerability (Baker 2004b; McRobbie and Garber 1976). Especially in its association with femininity and domesticity, such bedroom culture points to forms of public media consumption and participation that are already coded as potentially complementary to values of family and childhood. The portrayal of private bedroom performances fantastically overflowing into real public performances may now be a conventional, even genre-defining, visual rhetorical trope of tween media.

Like bedroom music listening, online media is also conceptually primed to do this work. Accounts of YouTube in particular emphasize its blurring of traditional boundaries: between public and private (Lange 2007), amateur and professional (Salvato 2009), "ordinary" and "extraordinary" (Strangelove 2011)—the latter two pairs in particular resonate with questions of prodigy. And scholars such as Henry Jenkins (1998) and danah boyd (2008) have argued that young people's enthusiasm for digital and online media in part responds to the closing off of public spaces like street corners and shopping malls to children's independent social activity and freedom of movement, and to increasing adult surveillance and control over children's activities. Young people's participation in the "networked publics" (Ito 2008a) of sites like Facebook and Twitter may accommodate the freedom of movement and independence of social activity that have been foreclosed elsewhere. In fact, Mary Celeste Kearney points to the complementarity between bedroom culture and new media technologies to argue that girls "are problematizing the conventional construction of the bedroom as private by using this space as not only a production studio, but also a distribution center" (2007: 137). The "One Time" montage of fans' YouTube videos plays on the conceptual bridge that domestic consumption and online media already provide to domesticate the public performance space of Madison Square Garden. The spatial metaphor of the montage, in which online videos interact in a three-dimensional social space, might be seen as an attempt to depict visually Kearney's argument that "contemporary female youth are not retreating to private spaces; they are reconfiguring such sites to create new publics that can better serve their needs, interests, and goals" (2007: 138). By contrast, Sarah Banet-Weiser argues that the same phenomenon—girls posting videos of themselves dancing and singing on YouTube—reflects the hegemony of corporate "brand" culture at all levels of personal life (2012: 51–89).

The clear parallel between home videos of Bieber and those of his fans links to a set of YouTube practices that emphasize "affinity" within social groups (Lange 2009). Online images of family domesticity, as much as they mark children as dependent, immature, and without agency, also mark children *as children*—that is, an authentic position that makes collective identification possible. While they are occupying adult spaces, Bieber and his fans are not simply becoming adults or trying to pass as adults. If anything the film presents them reveling in their childishness: not simply being absorbed into an existing adult public culture but building a particular form of publicness up around them, as children. The connections being made online are portrayed as entirely between children. Child audiences performing on and watching YouTube from their homes can directly connect to Bieber as a child himself performing on and watching YouTube from his home. YouTube literally mediates connections among children, but it also symbolically mediates the conceptual gulf between childhood and publicity by envisioning an intimate online public space grounded in domesticity.

What does "prodigy" do for Bieber? It highlights blurred boundaries between child and adult and between public and private. And it provides tools for making Bieber's particular configuration of childhood celebrity legible. "Prodigy" provides a conceptual scaffold connecting conventionally adult forms of success with childhood embodiment. Bieber's prodigy involves a complicated inversion of talent and childishness—or even talent *as* childishness. So rather than credentialing Bieber as fully adult, having surpassed certain developmental milestones and proven his exceptionality, here prodigy does the reverse. There is no aspiration to adulthood. Instead conventionally adult forms of popular cultural success are domesticated, or even infantilized—treated not as the hard-won endpoint of a developmental ladder, but as straightforward and unproblematically childish. Rather than discourses of prodigy providing rhetorical support for separating Bieber out from among his "peers," instead the very definition of his prodigy—headlining and selling out Madison Square Garden—requires his intense identification with other children. To be a prodigy in the terms set by commercial popular music is to cultivate such intense identification with a class of fans that they expend time and energy turning up to one's performances. That means that the rhetoric of prodigy that the film develops around Bieber hinges on a portrayal of his audience as the objects of his prodigious mastery, and YouTube is the rhetorical tool that enables that account.

AFTER THE TWEEN MOMENT

CONCLUSION

The tween music industry emerged slowly in the early years of the 2000s. It then exploded into public awareness in 2006 with *High School Musical*, and over the next few years tween artists would achieve extraordinary visibility and success. That expansive visibility presented conceptual and rhetorical challenges for representing children as celebrities and audiences, and the chapters of this book have explored the ways that tween media grappled with those challenges. By 2011, this explosive moment had started to calm. The most successful artists, like Miley Cyrus, Justin Bieber, and Taylor Swift, were now established and familiar acts—no longer an insurgency of kids breaking into mainstream awareness. Phenomena like HSM and the Jonas Brothers had faded back out of sight. Meanwhile, a second and third generation of young artists targeting young audiences were being put forward by television networks and record labels. This trajectory, from tentative early gestures to provocative mainstreaming to mature success, outlines what I have been calling the "tween moment": the decade from 2001 to 2011 that spans the cultural and commercial project of tween pop. The tween moment encompasses the early efforts to articulate tween pop as a music format made by Razor & Tie and Disney from 2001 to 2005, and the meteoric success of that format from 2006 to 2011. By 2011, in my reading, that project had been largely accomplished. Tween music was widely accepted as a legitimate music format within the music industry and by adult and child audiences. As the pressure to justify and even defend the tween project began to relent, new projects began to take shape.

In this conclusion I explore this periodization of the "tween moment" in two ways. First I return to the peak years of 2008 and 2009 to see more clearly how tween pop was staged as a social and political provocation within public culture. Second, I offer four examples in which the challenges that motivated tween pop's fraught representations during its peak years seemed to have begun to lessen around 2011, suggesting that we might reasonably see that year as the start of a new phase of tween pop. In my reading, during the tween moment the culture industries put forward a major social and historical claim, that children can and should participate in public culture. Building on a long cultural history posing childhood and publicness in opposition to one another, the project of the tween moment was to assert and perform their compatibility, and even complementarity. While that project seems to have significant historical and cultural stakes, its goal ultimately was much narrower: to carve out space for a commercial formation that sought to integrate earlier models of self-contained children's media within the broader structures of the rest of the music industry—in effect to articulate pop for kids as a music format like any other. The tween project achieved the latter goal; whether it changed long-standing US cultural norms about the public status of children remains to be seen.

TWEEN SOLIDARITY

At the MTV Video Music Awards in 2009, ten minutes after Kanye West took the microphone from Taylor Swift, two young people took the stage. Justin Bieber, at the time a fifteen-year-old singer who had only just broken out, and Miranda Cosgrove, the sixteen-year-old star of the popular Nickelodeon show *iCarly*, came out to introduce Swift's performance of "You Belong with Me"—the song whose video won the award for Best Female Video, precipitating the conflict with West moments earlier. But before launching into the scripted introduction, the very young-looking Bieber said, "First of all, I'd just like to say give it up for Taylor Swift. She deserved that award!" Cosgrove joined in enthusiastically: "Yeah! Whooo! Taylor Swift!" Cosgrove and Bieber went on to introduce Swift herself in a performance of the winning song. The first two people to publicly and individually stand up in defense of Swift after her run-in with West were children—younger than Swift herself. It seemed clear that Bieber and Cosgrove were claiming Swift as one of their own.

In public events in the late 2000s, there was a notable phenomenon of such expressions of solidarity among tween artists, who were beginning to appear in mainstream contexts like the VMAs. The Kanye/Swift encounter was highly racialized—posing adult Black masculinity against youthful white femininity in a long-standing binary opposition in American culture. Just as much as Bieber and Cosgrove interpellated Swift as one of them—highlighting her youth and participation in the tween culture industry that they unmistakably represented—in doing so they also interpellated themselves on the side of Swift's aggrieved whiteness. Expressions of solidarity among tween artists during these peak years of the tween moment would often revolve around a reactionary cultural political mix of whiteness, grievance, innocence, and childhood. These spectacles of confrontation with "mainstream" artists doubled down on youthful vulnerability and innocence as the definitive characteristic of public tween identity—ironically putting forward childishness itself as the basis for, in some cases, very aggressive sallies against putatively "adult" mainstream culture. These confrontations defined the peak years of the tween moment, and their disappearance after 2011 helps delineate the end of the tween moment.

A similar encounter the previous year, also at the VMAs, helps illustrate how these public expressions of solidarity among tween performers took shape during the tween moment. The 2008 VMAs were something of a coming-out party for tween celebrities and the emerging music format they represented. Miley Cyrus and Taylor Swift were both nominated for Best New Artist (which they lost to Tokyo Hotel), and the show included appearances by the cast of *HSM* and a performance by the Jonas Brothers. When the *HSM* actors Vanessa Hudgens, Zac Efron, Corbin Bleu, and Ashley Tisdale introduced a performance by Christina Aguilera, Efron commented, "The next artist hit the scene when she was just a kid," highlighting Aguilera's own start as a Disney Channel performer and implicitly linking the four contemporary Disney stars standing onstage to the established mainstream singer. Mentions of the tween acts consistently framed them as youthful subjects whose success remained displaced into the future. Announcing the Best New Artist Award, Chace Crawford noted, "Many of the past winners of this award went on to become icons like Nirvana, Alicia Keys, and 50 Cent," and when introducing the Jonas Brothers' performance, Taylor Swift asked the audience if they were "ready to make more entertainment history."[1]

The host, British comedian Russell Brand, continually noted the presence of these tween-oriented acts. In his opening monologue, he ridiculed the Jonas Brothers for wearing "promise rings," with which, along with several other contemporary Disney stars, they publicly expressed their commitment to abstain from sex until marriage.[2] Brand joked, "It is a little bit ungrateful, 'cause they could literally have sex with any woman that they want, they're just not gonna do it." These comments highlighted an underlying tension for many tween acts. On the one hand the Jonas Brothers' prominent association with the Disney Channel made it natural to locate them on the side of children, but at the time of the 2008 VMAs the three brothers were twenty, nineteen, and fifteen—the oldest, Kevin, was only two months from his twenty-first birthday. Gestures like purity rings clearly worked to reinforce the performers' status as members of a child-oriented cultural formation, despite their chronological age, by explicitly distancing themselves from sex. But they also raised sex as a topic, and Brand's joke targeted this underlying ambiguity directly by suggesting that the Jonas Brothers, rather than still "children," were individuals at an age when they "should" be having sex.[3] An important subtext of the joke was simply the awkwardness of tween acts appearing as full participants at a mainstream popular music awards show. Notably Brand's Jonas Brothers jokes were part of a monologue that was explicitly political and focused on the upcoming US presidential election. The discussion of the Jonas Brothers' promise rings segued directly out of a bit about the pregnancy of vice presidential candidate Sarah Palin's teenage daughter, clearly and explicitly positioning such Disney-based gestures toward sexual innocence in the context of a broader reactionary cultural politics associated with evangelical Christianity and the Republican Party.

Brand continued to riff on the Jonas Brothers' virginity throughout the show, until Jordin Sparks, who had won *American Idol* the year before at seventeen, came on to introduce an award. Sparks immediately moved to the microphone and said, to applause, "All right, I just have one thing to say about promise rings. It's not bad to wear a promise ring 'cause not everybody, guy or girl, wants to be a slut." Brand's joking criticism of the Jonas Brothers for being virgins was now being seriously thrown back at him in much stronger terms. Sparks stood up, publicly, in solidarity with other young artists, and suggested that their values might be significantly different, and preferable.

The next time Brand was onstage, he apologized: "I've got to say sorry, 'cause I said them things about promise rings. That were bad of me. I don't mean to take it lightly or whatever. I love the Jonas Brothers, think it's really good, and you know, look, let me be honest, I don't want to piss off teenage fans, all right? In fact, quite the opposite. So promise rings, I'm well up for it, well done, everyone. It's just, you know, a bit of sex occasionally never hurt anybody." In the days after the 2008 VMAs the Sparks/Brand dustup received a lot of media attention, and Sparks appeared on Fox News

Channel's *Hannity & Colmes* to be praised for her defense of reactionary sexual conservatism.

The run-in between Brand, the Jonases, and Sparks clearly sorted the participants into coherent, recognizable, and opposed groups, with the Disney Channel performers unproblematically slotted into an existing side in the culture wars. In my reading of the 2008 VMAs, age was clearly at play—the presence of several prominent tween performers seemed to require notice from Brand, and he framed their participation in terms of age and age-related topics like sexual innocence. Of course, the primary audience for provocative comedy like Brand's is youthful, and the audience for pop music generally and MTV in particular is also young, certainly overlapping in age significantly with the audience for acts like the Jonas Brothers (who were the Disney act that targeted the upper age range of the tween audience). And lest the culture war divisions obscure the age identification, Brand returned to the stage to emphasize that the powerful group for whom Sparks spoke was precisely an audience specified by age rather than political affiliation.

This incident prefigured the even more explosive West/Swift encounter at the VMAs the following year, and it seemed to establish a template for confrontation between tween and mainstream representatives in public forums. It did not produce quite the media spectacle as the West/Swift encounter would the following year, partly because it was establishing a template, and because Brand, Sparks, and the Jonas Brothers were not as famous or influential as West, Swift, and Beyoncé. In 2009 race was clearly a factor fueling the sense of scandal, but in this case Sparks is African American and Brand is white and English, so the racial markers did not reinforce or amplify the existing fault lines of cultural politics the way they would the following year. But even more than in 2009, this dustup explicitly tied the tween music industry's investments in sexual innocence and reactionary cultural constructions of childhood to contemporary US electoral politics.

It is worth noting how empowered these emerging young artists felt to break the script of the telecast and voice support for peers whom they perceived to be under attack. Swift was rendered speechless by West's interruption, and the Jonas Brothers' appearance in a carefully choreographed live performance prevented them from ad-libbing any comments had they wished to. But despite their own silence, which might have seemed meek or deferential, Sparks in 2008 and then again Bieber and Cosgrove in 2009 took the first available opportunity to speak out in response. In the core incidents (West's interruption, Brand's joke) age was all mixed up with race and sexuality and politics and genre, which themselves were mediated through the specificity of the individual actors involved. But these defensive responses on behalf of peers seemed much more clearly to express something like solidarity and shared group membership. If their ages and mainstream success made Swift and Sparks potentially more marginal figures in tween entertainment, the Jonas Brothers and Justin Bieber were full members, who were understood first and foremost as tween stars.

Tween acts' "power" derived substantially from the adults who mobilized on behalf of put-upon kids—very different from prior logics of youth-cultural defiance. The commercial interests invested in acts like the Jonas Brothers would have certainly felt along with Brand that the "teenage fans" were not an audience to be glibly dismissed, and Brand's apology after returning from backstage might well have been the result of direct or understood pressure from MTV and the other corporate backers of the VMAs. In addition to direct commercial interest, an unlikely resource in the emerging power of tweens was a widespread cultural logic that understood children as powerless, vulnerable, and even helpless. Sparks's "defensive" response—in my view, the most aggressive act described here—positioned Brand as the attacker, and an unprovoked attack on "children" by an adult (especially a rather disheveled, dangerous-looking adult) is, of course, unacceptable in polite society, because the power dynamics are asymmetrical: children are assumed to be unable to defend themselves against such attacks. The irony is that Sparks could and did defend herself and her peers.

The most visible spectacles of the tween moment expressed its core contradiction: childhood and publicness are in tension, and it took a certain rhetorical and conceptual alchemy to assert childhood *as* publicness, to claim power in public precisely through the characteristics of childhood that are seen to be the most at odds with publicness. At least for a few highly visible moments, the public intimacy that tween media cultivated, with its strong mandate to remain only "juxtapolitical," as Lauren Berlant (2008) puts it, stepped over the line into recognizable, explicit politics. But it did not stay there.

TWEEN POP AFTER THE TWEEN MOMENT

Moments of explicit confrontation and assertions of group identity were helpful for making visible cultural and conceptual investments that generally remain implicit. But these eruptions never defined the tween moment. They were not early expressions of a confrontational group identification that would continue to assert itself, nor did they signpost the future of children's participation in public culture. The tween moment was a cultural project, and it would eventually conclude. This book is about the coming-into-being of a particular cultural formation that built on long-standing cultural and commercial figurations of childhood, but, under the new label "tween," reworked and consolidated them into the logic of public identity. From this perspective the tween moment did not carve out new audience segments from a narrow age range; it rearticulated social and cultural categories like childhood and adolescence under new signs to shift the relative emphasis on characteristic traits (e.g., femininity over puerility) and foreground different projects (e.g., publicness over protection). Taking the raw cultural and commercial material of childhood, a category defined *against* publicness, and reworking it into a public identity that operates according to the logic of markets and media industries would naturally be fraught with difficulty. Thus the massive energy put into consolidating the tween as a commercial category defined primarily in relation to media, and especially popular music, found itself constantly grappling with contradiction and incompleteness in pursuit of some sort of synthesis—or at least getting people used enough to the contradictions that they stopped being bothered by them.

In my reading, the years 2001 to 2011 broadly frame the beginning and the end of that effort. My periodization starts with the release of the first *Kidz Bop* album, which can be understood as the first major gesture of the tween moment, when the Disney Channel was also just beginning to develop its in-house approach to pop. My periodization ends with Bieber's *Never Say Never*, which presented its star as triumphantly resolving the apparent contradictions of tween media. To the extent that I have engaged with texts that appeared after 2011, it has been to better understand retrospectively what happened *during* the tween moment, as with my discussions of Cyrus's and Swift's later careers, which serve as figures to expose the ground of the unmarked centrality of whiteness in the earlier construction of these artists' tween celebrity personas.

But while Cyrus and Swift were twerking, new artists continued to record and perform pop music for kids. So what happened after the tween moment ended? The tween music industry grew up. It stopped being an effort to produce something new and stabilized into the thing it had been working to become. Tween music became one more mature, accepted, and normal category of pop music. It no longer needed to foreground the challenges and contradictions of putting childhood forward as a public identity. It is beyond the scope of this book to comprehensively survey and characterize tween pop after 2011, but the four examples that follow help outline my sense that we entered a new period, and that the exigencies that motivated the forms that tween music took during the tween moment are no longer so urgent.

Kidz Bop Got Boring

Over the course of the tween moment, Kidz Bop's approach to representing children in relation to popular music shifted dramatically. Kidz Bop's innovation was to put children's anonymous collective voices at the center of pop music recordings. But later, Kidz Bop almost completely abandoned that model to focus on promoting specific identifiable children as singers and performers across a range of products, from recordings to videos to stage performances. If originally Kidz Bop put forward a quite literally "anti-celebrity" vision of kids' engagement with popular music, after 2011 it was fully invested in a celebrity model that no longer centered around musical representations of children's mass participation in public music culture. The history of this transition goes through a major effort starting in 2007 to invest in trendy video sharing and social media as a site for growth and audience engagement.

In early 2007, at the peak of the tween moment, Razor & Tie relaunched KidzBop.com as a video-sharing site for kids. The front page of the site showed row after row of videos uploaded by children who recorded themselves singing along to a favorite song, frequently to Kidz Bop recordings. Kidz Bop marketed this site as a "safe," kid-friendly alternative to video-sharing sites like YouTube that in the previous year had exploded in popularity and influence. KidzBop.com advertised to parents that "your child does not have the ability to enter or make public any text or video without it being reviewed and approved by our staff first" and that users could not post "personally identifiable information of any kind" on the site (Razor & Tie Media 2008). These policies, like those of many other child-focused websites, sought to conform with the requirements of Federal Trade Commission policies implementing the Children's Online Privacy Protection Act, which banned collection of "personally identifiable information" from children under thirteen (boyd et al. 2011; K. Montgomery 2007b).

With the site focused on anonymous kids sharing videos of themselves singing, Razor & Tie were tapping into the same cultural logic as the fantasy nightclub performance they articulated in the video for "Since U Been Gone" and the CGI masses of online video frames singing along with Justin

Bieber in *Never Say Never*: the idea that the anonymity and privacy of the internet offered a sort of reconciliation of children's public participation with the strong cultural norm that children remain sheltered in domestic anonymity. Press releases emphasized kids' active participation on the website, barely mentioning the core musical products: "The website allows kids to express themselves—as themselves—through unique online applications and proprietary functionality. Kids can star in video-based 'Web Shows,' challenge each other to 'Super Contests,' and build 'Fan Pages' as part of KidzBop.com's fun features. An introduction to social networking, the site also features a profile page for each member where they can chat with each other via a safe text messaging system" (Razor & Tie Media 2012). Despite clunky requirements that kids submit all their posts to moderators and choose text messages from lists of preapproved posts, the requirement that children not identify themselves resonated productively with the core conceit of Kidz Bop records, anonymous amateur children's voices filling in as the mass audience singing along to Top 40 pop songs.

In February 2014 Razor & Tie eliminated the video- and photo-sharing and social functions of their website. Shutting down the website only ratified a shift that had been almost fully achieved by 2011, when *Kidz Bop 20* was fully organized around an identifiable group of named and persistent child stars who served as lead and backup singers and performers on recordings and in advertisements, videos, live shows, and online. The transition had begun years earlier, and KidzBop.com could be seen as the central agent. The launch of the video-sharing site coincided with Kidz Bop's first live tour, which occurred in the summer of 2008 and followed the remarkably successful national tour the previous summer by Miley Cyrus / Hannah Montana, which had demonstrated the strong demand for live pop shows for kids. While Razor & Tie's business model had always been based on television advertising and direct marketing, during this period live concert tours were increasingly important to the business of pop music. Unlike recordings, which could be produced entirely with uncredited studio musicians, live shows required live performers. In 2009 Kidz Bop introduced the Kidz Bop Kids, a named group of child performers who appeared in advertisements and went on tours. (Kidz Bop records had always been said to feature the Kidz Bop Kids, but only now did that refer to a group of named, identifiable children. It wasn't until June 2009 that a separate web page dedicated to the Kidz Bop Kids appeared on KidzBop.com.) In 2010 Kidz Bop used the video-sharing platform to host a national singing contest to find the next iteration of the Kidz Bop Kids. While the earliest Kidz

Bop recordings featured anonymous professionals singing the lead vocals, confining the child singers to the group vocals in the choruses, during this period the lead vocals of Kidz Bop records increasingly featured individual child voices.

Journalist Jia Tolentino, in a sympathetic and insightful story in *Jezebel*, describes Kidz Bop's trajectory from its early focus on portraying children's voices as unmediated and amateur to its eventual adoption of a much more professionalized approach: "Their early albums used explicitly childish backing tracks, plus adults on lead vocals, plus kid voices occasionally chiming in. Then, they hit a brief period where they upgraded the instrumentation to a truer facsimile but let kid vocalists that truly sounded like kid vocalists—artless, gawky—take the lead. The effect was very dumb, and very wonderful. . . . Now, though, they are using kid vocalists like Matt and Bredia and Ashlynn and Grant, who know how to manipulate their voices like adults do" (2015). Similarly Josh Dean in *Bloomberg News* notes an "evolutionary shift from 'a generic CD box of cover songs,' as [Razor & Tie co-founder] Chenfeld refers to the original concept, to a carefully selected ensemble who represent the brand for three years." Razor & Tie's executives, Dean writes, "realized that the product would be even more attractive to its audience if those cheerful voices were attached to identifiable personalities. And so they shifted to a star-centric concept" (2015).

As Kidz Bop's model shifted increasingly toward this quasi-celebrity format of identifiable named performers, at least one element of the brand's underlying musical and cultural logic shifted. If the early Kidz Bop records highlighted the mass voices of anonymous child audiences as central to a particular experience of popular music, after 2011 this gradual shift toward identifiable celebrity singers had been completed and no longer seemed motivated around that particular intervention. Shutting down the video-sharing site simply confirmed that the vision of masses of children participating in pop music from their homes was no longer necessary to the legitimation and development of Kidz Bop as a brand. If early Kidz Bop put forward a provocative interpretation of pop music as public media, late-period Kidz Bop felt much more, in a word, generic: "What consumers see now is much closer to, say, the manufactured child prodigies turned out by the Disney and Nickelodeon assembly lines, which have produced Spears, Cyrus, and Ariana Grande, among others" (Dean 2015). Tolentino puts a finer point on it: "Kidz Bop's sound has started asymptotically approaching what the franchise by definition must differentiate themselves against, which is actual pop music" (2015). Other tween music acts that I discuss in this book did center on recognizable celebrity performers, and as Dean points out, Kidz Bop's transition is in part just a shift closer to the dominant business model in tween media. But texts like *Hannah Montana* and *Never Say Never* were also deeply invested in making sense of public child performance as a problem that required resolution. The more conventional, celebrity-focused acts addressed those issues narratively, while musically they pursued more conventional pop sounds. But Kidz Bop had always engaged with the same problem musically, through the relation and arrangement of child and adult voices in their recordings.[4]

In the early part of the decade the portrayal of child audiences as full participants in popular music was a pressing concern, to which Kidz Bop responded by representing children's anonymous, amateur, and collective voices as central to pop music recordings. By the end of the decade this issue had, apparently, stopped being so pressing, or had been overtaken by other pressures. Kidz Bop was able to organize itself around a much more conventional pop music configuration, and that allowed Kidz Bop to move away from technically complex, labor-intensive, and unique pop music business models, like direct marketing and online video sharing, and into a much more conventional model of releasing records anchored by recognizable celebrity performers and promoting them through videos and concert tours. Things seem to have gotten simpler, less fraught, and less interesting.

Disney Reconciled TV and Movie Musicals

In 2013 Disney released the animated musical feature *Frozen*. After years of weakness in its animated film business, in 2006 Disney had closed its traditional animation studios and purchased the computer animation studio Pixar, in an apparent effort to learn from that company's successes in making popular, sophisticated, and nonmusical children's feature films like *Toy Story* (1995) and *Finding Nemo* (2003). After a decade in which its animated musical feature films took backstage to its television products, *Frozen* represented a return to Disney's 1990s model of blockbuster animated musical features. By the end of 2014 *Frozen* had grossed $1.2 billion worldwide, making it the highest-grossing film released in 2013 (*Box Office Mojo* 2015), the highest-grossing animated film ever (Stedman 2014), and the fifth highest-grossing film of any category (Stewart 2014). The soundtrack had the second highest sales of any album in 2014 (Caulfield 2014)—it was barely knocked out of the top spot by Taylor Swift's *1989*—and was the top album on the 2014 *Billboard* Top 200 Albums list (*Billboard* 2014).

Despite its apparent resuscitation of the classic musical-theater model of Disney features, *Frozen* clearly learned from Disney's decade of pop music television. Most importantly, the songwriters of the movie's iconic song, "Let It Go," explicitly located the song within a lineage of female pop singer-songwriters, including Aimee Mann, Tori Amos, Adele, Avril Lavigne, Lady Gaga, and Katy Perry—and specifically as a break from Disney film traditions and the operatic and Broadway styles of previous Disney musicals (Zuckerman 2013). Every account of the film's development emphasized that the composition of "Let It Go" was pivotal to the development of the script and the overall conception of the film's narrative and themes (e.g., Ryzik 2014). Ryan Bunch notes that "Let It Go" appears in *Frozen* "more like a music video than a musical number" (2018: 96), and Jennifer Fleeger (2014) points out that the soundtrack recording of "Let It Go" departed from the Disney Princess musical formula by not resolving to the tonic harmony. Fleeger's interpretation emphasizes the psychological implications for the film's characterization of the protagonist Elsa, but it is worth noting also that pop songs, which prioritize repetition and recognition, have no strict conventions enforcing harmonic resolution. "Let It Go" was performed in the film by Idina Menzel, a Tony-winning Broadway performer. Disney also produced a music video and radio version of the song recorded by Demi Lovato, a prior Disney Channel star who had transitioned to a successful career recording Top 40 hits (Knopper 2014). Menzel herself was already something of a crossover success, with film and television appearances and a successful recording career outside Broadway. Disney had had record sales success with previous soundtracks, especially for *The Lion King*, for which pop star Elton John wrote and recorded songs. But Lovato, or even Menzel, singing "Let It Go" was stylistically, formally, and institutionally much different than Elton John singing "Can You Feel the Love Tonight" from *The Lion King*. For that matter, it was *much* different than career voice actress Jodi Benson singing "Part of Your World" on *The Little Mermaid*. Lovato, Menzel, and "Let It Go" all participated in a form of celebrity spectacle that was recognizably pop much more than Broadway. In 1994 the inclusion of Elton John was clearly meant to appeal to adults, as Disney still struggled with using "human beings" in its appeal to kids and did not make an effort to match female pop stars to aspirational girl audiences. If the 2000s were a period of decline for Disney films and ascension for Disney television and pop music, *Frozen* suggested a new model that combined hard-won lessons about narrative filmmaking learned from Pixar with hard-won lessons about kids and pop music learned from the

Disney Channel. While the tween moment was dominated by TV-based pop music celebrities, the dramatic success of *Frozen* pushed TV again to the backstage, recentered younger children as Disney's most profitable audience, and suggested that the pursuit of older child audiences was no longer the top priority of the children's media industries.

Black Performers Reclaimed the Spotlight

If Kidz Bop was no longer motivated by the musical challenge of representing kids' participation as mass audiences, a parallel dynamic was playing out in relation to the industry's investments in whiteness. During the peak of the tween moment, the most prominent artists, including Cyrus, Swift, Bieber, and the Jonas Brothers, were not just white but their celebrity personas were constructed around their whiteness in motivated ways. These artists deployed whiteness to reinforce their claims to innocence, domesticity, vulnerability, and prodigy. In effect whiteness provided a rhetorical bludgeon that deflected or mediated concerns about the assertion of children's public status. Notably, starting in 2010 and 2011, the Disney Channel began to invest in African American artists as lead performers in the pop-music-television model they had developed in the mid-2000s, and independent young Black artists emerged as well, building in part on the model established in previous years by tween artists. During those peak years that investment in whiteness was almost urgent, as the potential for reactionary moral panic constantly hovered around these child stars and whiteness provided a package of cultural tools that foregrounded and affirmed an ideology of childhood innocence. The emergence of Black artists as major figures in tween music in the early years of the next decade suggests that the urgency of whiteness may have calmed somewhat. Here I focus on the Disney Channel's shifting models of casting over the course of the tween moment, starting with "color-blind" multiculturalism that built out of the dominant approach from the 1990s, cresting into an intense whitewashing after the success of *High School Musical*, and finally transitioning into a new period of affirmative investment in Black stars.

Performers in kids' media in the 1990s and early 2000s were much more racially and ethnically diverse than mainstream adult media, especially on television, where tween media was centered. Many scholars have argued that "multiculturalism" in children's television from this period ultimately reinforced established racial hierarchies by reworking them through ideologies of "color-blindness" (see, for example, Banet-Weiser 2007; Turner

2014). One of the first artists to develop the tween music model on the Disney Channel was Raven-Symoné, the star of *That's So Raven*. Raven-Symoné, who is African American, led a racially diverse ensemble cast on television and was involved early on with the diverse ensemble girl group, the Cheetah Girls, the act that immediately preceded HSM and developed much of the model that would go on to be so explosively successful. The Cheetah Girls neatly fit the turn-of-the-century model of multicultural color-blindness, in which performers were clearly cast with a range of racial and ethnic identities.[5]

Then in 2006 HSM emerged as an unexpectedly enormous success, whose soundtrack was the top-selling album that year. HSM was developed along the earlier model, with an ensemble that included Vanessa Hudgens, of Filipino background, as the romantic lead, along with the African American actors Corbin Bleu and Monique Coleman among the six core cast members. HSM portrayed an affluent suburban high school, and musically it did not even make the gentle gestures toward ethnically marked genres that the Cheetah Girls did. Bleu and Coleman are not listed as the leads on any songs, and the one vaguely hip-hop song is sung by Efron.[6] The immediate follow-up to HSM was *Hannah Montana*, which was invested in very explicitly marked forms of whiteness, and, at the same time, Taylor Swift was releasing her debut album and topping the country music charts. During this peak period Disney continued to build around the Jonas Brothers, and then around Demi Lovato and Selena Gomez, who are Latina. Lovato was cast as Sonny Munroe, a white character from Wisconsin, in *Sonny with a Chance*, and Gomez was cast as Alex Russo, the daughter of an Italian American father and Mexican American mother, in *Wizards of Waverly Place*. Lovato also starred opposite the Jonas Brothers in the Disney Channel original movie *Camp Rock*.

In the larger trajectory of the tween moment, we can recognize again how tween innocence was constructed significantly in terms of whiteness as anti-Blackness. In the early part of the decade artists of color like Raven-Symoné and the members of the Cheetah Girls were important to Disney's initial exploratory investments in tween pop. But once HSM exploded in 2006 and tween pop fully took over the Disney Channel's business model, we see a retreat from foregrounding African American artists, and follow-up efforts that were much more anxious about casting actors of color, to the point of casting Latina artists as white characters in lead roles. Not only did African American stars largely disappear from the Disney Channel following HSM, but acts like *Hannah Montana* and the Jonas Brothers were much more explicitly committed to cultural formations strongly associated with whiteness. If Gomez and Lovato represented a sort of return to a semblance of the diverse casting that had defined kids' television previously, it was a tentative effort at best.

But starting around 2010 the Disney Channel began to put artists of color at the foreground again, investing heavily in African American performers in lead roles. In 2010 Zendaya was cast as one of two lead roles in the dance-based Disney Channel show *Shake It Up!* In 2013 she released a self-titled album on Hollywood Records and headlined a national tour. Then in 2014 she starred in the Disney Channel original movie *Zapped*, and in 2015 she starred again in another Disney Channel show, *K.C. Undercover*. In 2011 China McClain led the ensemble cast of the performance show *A.N.T. Farm* and in 2014 played the lead role in the Disney Channel original movie *How to Build a Better Boy*. Coco Jones was a featured contestant on Radio Disney's "Next Big Thing" competition in 2010, and she starred in the 2012 Disney Channel movie *Let It Shine*. She also released an album, *Made Of*, with Hollywood Records in 2013. Outside the Disney Channel, Cymphonique Miller (the daughter of rapper Master P) was cast as the lead in the music-focused Nickelodeon show *How to Rock* in 2012. The young teen R&B boy group Mindless Behavior released their first album in 2011 on Interscope Records, and that album and their 2013 follow-up both debuted in the top ten on *Billboard*'s Top 200 album sales chart. Also in 2010 Willow Smith, daughter of American actor and musician Will Smith, released her single "Whip My Hair" on Roc Nation (Jay-Z's label) in October 2010, shortly before her tenth birthday. The single was quickly certified platinum.

In all this we can see a shift in the presence and visibility of young African American performers in or around the tween music industry. But even more than just casting, the content of many of these artists' contributions engaged frankly and directly with race, which contrasted notably with some of the prominent tween acts that had immediately preceded them. Willow Smith's "Whip My Hair," for example, centers natural hairstyles in its empowerment message, and it was widely seen as a celebration of Black girlhood (Miller 2010). And the Disney Channel movie *Let It Shine* focuses on the status of hip-hop in an African American church.

Mindless Behavior offers a compelling contrast to Justin Bieber. By the time Mindless Behavior released their first album, *#1 Girl*, in 2011, Bieber had been putting forward his "blue-eyed soul" version of tween R&B for two years. Bieber's approach to R&B, however, was to carefully launder it through childish whiteness, foregrounding immaturity, dependence, and adorability. Mindless Behavior, on the other hand, did not claim any of those traits in their performance. The lyrics to their 2011 single "Mrs. Right," which described flying around the world seeking a girlfriend, were frankly sexual:

> Sassy little thing, like the way you talk,
> Heard you got the goods go ahead show them off,
> Take a picture quick, send it to my phone,
>
> [...]
>
> All my German chicks, let me kiss ya back,
> Open up your MacBook, put me on your lap,
>
> [...]
>
> Wipe me down wipe me down, if I like you, you wifey now[7]

The video for "Mrs. Right" featured the members of Mindless Behavior daydreaming in geography class about the girls they would meet around the world, opening with a series of girls in national costumes dancing to hip-hop at the front of the classroom, and concluding with a hip-hop pep rally in a darkened gymnasium. This video, by strong contrast to the approach of artists like Bieber at the time, did not dilute racialized presentations into generic "cuteness." Despite being visibly very young, the members of Mindless Behavior foregrounded a swaggering toughness and confidence much more than accessibility or cuteness. If Black sexuality, as we have seen in examples from Swift and Cyrus, was so easily posed against white innocence at the peak of the tween moment, then young Black artists frankly foregrounding an explicitly racialized sexuality in their work was a notable intervention, and one that, in my reading, would have been much more challenging to put forward just a few years earlier.

These were not attempts at color-blindness or multiculturalism, and unlike Swift's 2009 performance as T-Swizzle they were not parodies of Black music. While they may have adopted exaggerated or commodified markers of Black musicality, these performances were nonetheless earnestly and explicitly invested in Black music and performance styles. In addition to the tween music industry that had recently established itself, there is another context for acts like Mindless Behavior and Willow Smith: the long history of Black child performers in mainstream R&B and hip-hop, from R&B groups like the Jackson 5, New Edition, and B5, to hip-hop acts like Another Bad Creation, Kriss Kross, and Lil' Bow Wow. For that reason it may not be appropriate to label these acts as "tween"—especially as the tween music industry had spent the preceding five years defining itself in particularly racialized and gendered terms. But like the tween music industry at its peak, some of the Black artists who emerged in this later period were affiliated with kids' television networks, and others were not, and certainly the tween music industry was part of the broader context for these acts. It is notable, then, that not only the race of the artists being promoted, but also the salience of explicit markers of race in their musical and narrative contributions, shifted dramatically in the years immediately following the peak of tween music. If the early 2000s were characterized by multicultural color-blindness, and the late 2000s by white innocence and anti-Blackness, this later period seems to suggest a new engagement with race that did not just seek out flattened "diversity" but presented clear racial markers in prominent and even celebratory ways.

Childishness Went Mainstream

Finally, maybe kids really did get mainstream? Kids have long been important audiences for pop music. In the 1990s attempts to capitalize on that fact led teen pop acts like Britney Spears and NSYNC to cultivate relationships with television networks like Nickelodeon and Disney, but ultimately those efforts ended because these acts were seen as inappropriate for young audiences. One example from 2011 suggests to me that over the decade of the tween moment something may have shifted in broader public considerations of children's relationship to pop music. In 2011 eight-year-old Sophia Grace Brownlee and her five-year-old cousin Rosie McClelland became internet-famous when they posted a video to YouTube of themselves singing Nicki Minaj's hit single "Super Bass." This led to an appearance on Ellen DeGeneres's daytime talk show, where Minaj herself surprised the girls and sang "Super Bass" with them. Sophia Grace and Rosie went on to host a recurring segment on *The Ellen DeGeneres Show*, "Tea Time with Sophia Grace and Rosie," on which they spoke with other actors and musicians.

I'm interested in Sophia Grace and Rosie because their presentation as young girls highlighted many of the same elements of innocence and vulnerability that I discussed in relation to tween acts. The duo wore pink ballet outfits, with tutus and tiaras, for their first appearance on *Ellen*, and in their original YouTube video they used a jeweled pink toy princess scepter and a pink plastic recorder as their pretend microphones. Sophia Grace gamely plowed through lines like "he might sell coke" and "he a motherfucking trip" and "then the panties comin' off" with nonsense syllables, but she clearly articulated lines like "excuse me you're a hell of a guy" and "somebody please tell 'em who the eff I is."[8] A big part of the viral appeal of the video was the contrast between the girls' extreme presentation of white feminine innocence combined with a performance of a song that is very frank about sex and female desire. If anything Minaj's unapologetic expression of heterosexual desire as a Black woman presented the sort of cultural material that Miley Cyrus would later appropriate and caricature in her 2013 performance of "We Can't Stop" in her effort to finally decouple herself from Disney and white childhood innocence.

But by 2011 there were already some cracks in the wall separating white feminine innocence from Black musical sexuality. For example, Sophia Grace and Rosie's style of dress—their over-the-top pink princess dresses and tiaras and shiny accessories—fit right in to mainstream pop culture at the time. When Minaj joined Sophia Grace and Rosie on the set of *Ellen*, she was wearing a blue and blonde wig and a puffy pink flowered skirt with several gauzy layers. Ellen had the girls pick out their own over-the-top dress-up wigs, clearly modeled after Minaj's—pink for Rosie, and curly blonde with a giant lavender bow for Sophia Grace. Artists like Minaj and Katy Perry at that moment were bringing to the forefront a visual style that emphasized gaudy colorful childishness. Celebrities wore colorful wigs and princess-style dresses, in a trend that refracted its gendered visual style through Japanese and Korean popular culture. One of the "alter ego" characters Minaj used was known as "Harajuku Barbie," explicitly linking Japanese youth culture with US girls' toys.[9] Minaj's video for "Super Bass" had a pink toy-doll theme, and similarly that year the video and stage performances for Perry's "California Gurls" had a *Candyland* theme featuring cotton candy, gingerbread men, gum drops, and other colorfully childish trappings. Both artists explicitly played on the ironic juxtaposition of childish tropes with explicit sexuality. But in this context Sophia Grace and Rosie's YouTube video, and its perhaps unintentionally ironic juxtapositions, actually reproduced rather neatly the original aesthetic of Minaj's video: visuals of over-the-top pink girlishness paired with an audio track of assertive and explicit hip-hop. With bright neon and fluorescent colors, toys, candy, sparkles, and fantastically impossible dresses at the foreground of mainstream visual style in 2011, there was an explicit bridge to kids.

But look again at Taylor Swift in the summer of 2009, when the topic of her white vulnerability to Blackness was so foregrounded in her hip-hop performance as T-Swizzle and her perfectly generic run-in with Kanye West. Swift's girly innocence was framed specifically as anti-Blackness. That in 2011 the encounter between Black hip-hop and white girl princess culture was not only possible but also celebrated suggests again that something had shifted in children's relation to public culture.

✱ ✱ ✱

These examples—Kidz Bop becoming more generic; *Frozen* reshuffling the relationship of music, movies, and television at Disney; the (re)emergence of Black tween stars; and the mainstreaming of childishness—suggest that by 2011 the tween music industry confronted a new context. The concerns that motivated the specific representations of children in public that I have traced in this book seemed to have become less urgent. Launching a "new" music format organized around an audience demographic with a fraught relationship to mass media was a risky undertaking, and throughout the 2000s tween music represented itself in a way that both acknowledged and sought to transcend the implicit contradictions in its project. In part the changed situation of the next decade suggests that the project was largely successful: at least, the hint of moral panic no longer hovered quite so threateningly around pop music offerings for kids. Whether the tween music industry caused these changes or simply responded to them is unclear. Popular culture can be cyclical, and perhaps NSYNC's performance as toy action figures in 2000 (or even Britney Spears's sexy schoolgirl costume in 1998's ". . . Baby One More Time") reflected similar impulses. The 2000s were a reactionary cultural period overall, and popular music since 2010 has been dominated by women and artists of color. Perhaps all of the tween music industry's performative handwringing about the contradictions of domesticity and publicness did not affect anything beyond itself. The world changed around the tween music industry, and it followed.

My interests in all of this are less about whether the tween music industry effected a broader shift in the cultural construction of childhood, and much more about how they were motivated to work within that terrain in the first place. This short period of widespread cultural attention to children as mass media participants helps reveal the underlying contours of and relationships among categories like childhood, femininity, whiteness, and, not least, popular music. I have argued that the tween music industry was engaged in a historically significant project of reconceptualizing children's relationship to public culture, and to reshape childhood in the form of identity. It presented itself as transformative, but it likely did not achieve any real transformation in public culture or in children's lives. Instead this period of sustained grappling with the representational possibilities of childhood as an intimate public, which probed and tested weak spots in the construction of these cultural categories, had a much narrower goal, which it did accomplish: to establish one more music format in an already crowded popular music industry.

NOTES

Introduction: The Tween Moment

1 "What Time Is It," lyrics by Matthew R. T. Gerrard and Robert S. Nevil, © 2006 Walt Disney Music Company.
2 More details and findings from this study can be found in *Schooling New Media* (Bickford 2017).
3 Weikle-Mills identifies a similar tension between children's formal disempowerment and celebrations of their imaginative freedom in the eighteenth and nineteenth centuries: at the same time that dominant legal discourses fixed children's status as "irrational and incapable of action," artistic and cultural responses to influential liberal-democratic theories increasingly depicted "children's political actions, capacities, and responsibilities in an imaginary, literary realm" (Weikle-Mills 2013: 14). The dialectical history I am outlining here also has significant parallels to the argument made by scholars of seventeenth- and eighteenth-century literature that the modern public sphere and its associated subjectivities emerged in part as a result of the domestic confinement of women. This is a complicated and controversial account that I do not have the tools to treat fully here, but see Thompson (2009), N. Armstrong (1987), and McKeon (2005) for various perspectives that may offer useful lenses on twenty-first-century childhoods.
4 Friedan explicitly associates the confinement of women to domestic work with "immaturity" (1963: 79).
5 Weikle-Mills argues that infantilization is a particular practice that emerged as part of modern liberal-democratic political cultures: "Infantilization as a form of domination affecting specific groups rather than all political subjects [as under patriarchal regimes] was tied to the emergence of childhood as a special category for persons who were unable to participate in their own governance" (2013: 96).

6   Postman's book borrows heavily from an argument made by his PhD student, Joshua Meyrowitz, in a chapter of his dissertation, which would later become *No Sense of Place* (1985), an influential work of media theory.
7   Weikle-Mills argues what Berlant calls "infantile citizenship" is not new to the Reagan era but is rather "an integral and longstanding part of America's political history" (2008: 37) going back at least to the Revolution and founding. It is important to note the long histories of both infantilization panics and the real cultural phenomenon in which citizenship and social membership are envisioned as modes of childishness or dependence, what Weikle-Mills calls "affectionate citizenship" (2013). My goal here is to outline the eruption of a particular instance of this panic at the turn of the millennium, which coincided with other notable changes in cultural understandings of age and childhood, especially the development of discourses about tweens, and the contradictory phenomenon of children's domestic confinement and mediated freedom.
8   Psychologist Dan Kiley's *The Peter Pan Syndrome: Men Who Have Never Grown Up* (1983) had similarly linked supposed failures to achieve adult maturity with incomplete masculinity (see Kidd 2011: 86–88).
9   In 2008 reactionary *Washington Times* columnist Diana West published *The Death of the Grown-Up: How America's Arrested Development Is Bringing Down Western Civilization* (2008), a right-wing jeremiad about baby boomer immaturity somehow exposing the United States to the threat of global terrorism. Childhood scholar Gary Cross's version of this argument emphasized gender, identifying a widespread lack of maturity in men, which like Barber he blames substantially on "our embrace of a commercial culture that feeds on stunted human growth" (2008: 2). In 2009 the State University of New York Press published the academic collection *Perpetual Adolescence: Jungian Analyses of American Media, Literature, and Pop Culture* (Porterfield, Polette, and Baumlin 2009), and its contributions explored how the "myth of puer" (a Jungian archetype) defines contemporary American culture. In 2014 Stanford literature professor Robert Pogue Harrison published the more ponderous but ultimately similar *Juvenescence: A Cultural History of Our Age*.
10 By contrast Natalia Cecire (2012b) has argued persuasively that a significant strand of contemporary political discourse might reflect childish investments, but through the culturally *masculine* logic of "puerility"—an obsessive commitment to playful stakes-free rule following that characterizes journalism about statistical forecasting, for example—and not the infantilized femininity that Barber and the rest worry about.
11 In 2006 Walt Disney Records marketing executive Damon Whiteside described the *High School Musical* audience this way: "Our really core demographic . . . would be 8 to 14, though it can go younger, and there are probably some older kids buying it that wouldn't admit it. . . . And with the *Kidz Bop* albums, we have a little bit of the same audience, but we definitely skew older. I think *Kidz Bop* is an under-10 thing, and I think our majority is gonna be over 10, reaching into the 14s and 15s" (Willman 2006).

12 After Brown and Washton published reports on the tween market in 2001 and 2002 that uncritically passed along the age-compression narrative, their follow-up reports in 2003 and 2004 reversed course, noting that "tweens remain firmly anchored in childhood" (2003: 19). In fact they argued that due to undesired social changes—they cite divorce, bullying, and terrorism—"kids are getting older younger not because they want to but because they have to," and that kids turn to childhood, especially "the security and comfort provided by their parents and their home," as shelter against those challenges (209). Brown and Washton argued that tweens had effectively adopted for themselves adult anxieties about a threatening external world. Rather than clamoring for increased independence, they consented to their extended confinement in childhood and the home: "the desire of middle-schoolers to remain firmly entrenched in childhood has become even more apparent in recent years because tweens have come to perceive the world as a more dangerous place than before" (209).
13 In a cover story for *Newsweek*, journalist Abigail Jones (2014) suggests that the experience of being a tween girl is definitively about sexuality.
14 See Dueck (2013) for helpful theorization of the differences between face-to-face and stranger sociality.

Chapter One: Singing Along

1 *Kidz Bop* volume 1 was released in 2001. Another CD, *More Kidz Bop*, was released with a copyright date of 2000. That album is not included in the discographies I have consulted, and Razor and Tie's own self-description as well as contemporaneous reporting identify 2001 as the inauguration of the series. Very little information is available about *More Kidz Bop*, which appears to be a secondary release that may have gone to press too early. In any event, *More Kidz Bop* was not a significant release, and I stick with the standard dating of Kidz Bop to 2001.
2 See McNutt (2015) for a comprehensive analysis of Kidz Bop lyrics, which suggests that the recordings' lyrics have become more sanitized and conservative since 2009. I discuss Kidz Bop's changing approach since 2009 from a different perspective in the conclusion.
3 "1, 2 Step," lyrics by Alexander Phalon, Melissa Elliot, and Ciara Harris. © 2004 EMI April Music Inc.
4 Kidz Bop no longer hosts the video on its own website, but as of August 2019, the video can be viewed at https://www.youtube.com/watch?v=x5MC8u27prw. The DVD credits the video's production and direction to Wormseye Films, with no other information.
5 This idea of the interior of the home as the location for a portal to a fantasy space in which children have heightened value and agency is itself familiar from classic children's fantasy. In novels like George MacDonald's *The Princess and the Goblin* (1872) and C. S. Lewis's *The Lion, the Witch, and the*

Wardrobe (1950), the interior of the home is the site of access for a child—conventionally, a girl—to be transported to the magical world.

6   If media was fantasizing about children as pop music audiences, life would imitate art, and real-life opportunities for young children to attend live pop-oriented shows expanded dramatically during this period. Major media corporations put on national tours of acts like the Fresh Beat Band and Imagination Movers, and the "kindie" movement of independent children's musicians performing in pop genres also dramatically expanded the visibility of children's music and attracted large numbers of musicians to the field, including many, like Dan Zanes and Elizabeth Mitchell, who had prior careers as adult artists. The history of independent and commercial music for younger children is the subject of ongoing research.

7   Jia Tolentino, writing in *Jezebel*, agrees with me: "there are plenty of hits so saccharine that they almost sound better when sung by children—the Kidz Bop versions of 'Thrift Shop,' 'All About That Bass' and 'Happy' sound like final edits on the original tracks—and . . . most big-budget pop tracks are too hooky and also too generic to truly, even with kiddie alteration, sound bad" (2015).

8   Kidz Bop's portrayal of child and adult voices changed significantly starting around 2009, when the label reoriented the brand toward identifiable child singers and largely dropped the emphasis on mass amateur child voices. I discuss this development in more detail in the conclusion.

9   In *Never Say Never* Justin Bieber's manager related that radio stations refused to play Bieber's music, telling him "we don't play a young kid. Fifteen years old, he's got a young voice, that's not our thing." Taylor Swift struggled similarly, telling *Billboard* in 2006, "I've been trying to do this since I was 10. . . . So many people tell me that [country] radio won't play me because I'm too young" (Price 2006), and *Billboard* affirmed the "frequent difficulties for young, new female artists to break into country radio" (Hasty 2007). Eric Weisbard (2014) links Swift's difficulty getting radio airplay to Dolly Parton's struggles a generation earlier to be accepted by mainstream country radio because her femininity was linked to her mainstream crossover success as a concerning stretching or dilution of the genre's boundaries. And *Billboard*'s chart manager explained Demi Lovato's struggles to the *New York Times*: "Top 40 programmers are a little hesitant to play some of the younger Disney acts. . . . They may not appeal to older teens and people in their 20s" (Caramanica 2009).

Chapter Two: Music Television

1   In 1997 the television channel rebranded, dropping "the" from its name. I refer to it throughout as "the Disney Channel" rather than "Disney Channel" in deference to everyday language but without capitalizing the article, since it may or may not be part of the channel's official name.

2 Information for this section comes from interviews with a number of musicians and media professionals active in children's music during the 1990s, as well as a review of children's music articles in music industry publications like *Billboard* and *Variety*. Torrie Dorrell, who was a senior manager at Walt Disney Records from 1990 to 1994, was an especially important source of information about Disney's music business during this period, as was Moira McCormick, whose "Child's Play" column ran weekly in *Billboard* from 1992 to 2001 and chronicled the children's music and video business in great detail.
3 David Pierce, executive vice president of Sony Music Distribution in the 1990s, who later headed Sony Wonder, helped me understand the importance of retail home video in changing the children's music market in an interview conducted by phone on May 13, 2014.
4 In an interview twenty years later, Dorrell misspoke and called the series the "Live Artists Series." It was the Music Box Artists Series, and I have corrected that throughout.
5 The division of labor between Hollywood Records and Walt Disney Records was primarily that Walt Disney Records would release the soundtracks that came directly from the show and movie—*Hannah Montana*, *High School Musical*, *Camp Rock*—while Hollywood Records released the standalone music by Disney Channel artists.
6 Ironically, if Disney was seen as too immature in the 1990s while Nickelodeon had figured out how to connect with older kids, with musical programming, that relationship was inverted. While Disney focused on pop music for tweens, Nickelodeon led the way in developing pop musical programming for younger children. Not only was its preschool channel (Noggin, which became Nick Jr.) a primary outlet for independent children's music artists in the mid-2000s, in the late 2000s it also developed highly visible pop music–based television shows for younger children, in particular *Yo Gabba Gabba* and the *Fresh Beat Band* (which also emphasized outside sales opportunities, using the TV shows to heavily promote summer tours in 2011 and 2012, for instance). The toy-based fantasy cartoon shows were heavily criticized for their commercialization and violent content, and children's programmers had clearly backed off from that model somewhat (Mitroff and Herr Stephenson 2007). Shows like *Barney*, *Blues Clues*, and *Dora the Explorer* were also heavily merchandised, but their emphasis on learning curricula and prosocial messages helped counteract any concerns. If deemphasizing toy-based cartoons was partly a response to a relatively widespread critique of those shows as "thirty-minute advertisements," incorporating pop music created opportunities for integrating cross-marketing opportunities in less controversial areas.
7 This point was made emphatically in my interviews with Sony Wonder executives Ted Green (May 16, 2014) and David Pierce (May 13, 2014).

Chapter Three: "Having It All"

1. In general I refer to the character Miley Stewart as Miley, as she is mostly identified in the show, and the performer Miley Cyrus by her surname, Cyrus.
2. Melanie Kennedy makes a parallel but slightly different argument, that in *Hannah Montana* celebrity is offered as an "allegory for growing up female" (2014: 226).
3. If friendship is a deeply intimate site of desire in a long tradition of girls' narratives, it may be that the emphasis on friendship in shows like *Sex and the City* reflects not only a queer diminishment of patriarchal marriage and the family, but also a destabilization of ideologies of maturity or adulthood that align closely with patriarchal social structures, as *New York Times* film critic A. O. Scott has suggested (2014). If an emphasis on friendship reflects a broader process of "infantilization" of public life, it makes sense that resources developed in "adult" media should be ripe for reuse in children's media.
4. This is why I focus on the comparison to shows like *Ally McBeal* and *Sex and the City* rather than more contemporary examples of girls' media like HBO's *Girls* or the WB's *Gossip Girl*. Those newer shows are about mostly independent teenagers and young women who are rarely depicted in harmonious, dependent, and subordinate relationships to their parents, and instead represent what Rosenfeld (2007) has characterized as an "age of independence" in which grown children are independent from parents and extended families but do not have (and do not desire) dependents of their own. Shows like *Girls* do address maternity, reproduction, and fertility through frank depictions of birth control or abortion (Rossie 2014), but for the most part they depict young women for whom "having it all" is not a salient desire or a foundational problem. In fact, Projansky argues that postfeminist media has turned to girls and younger women precisely in reaction against media portrayals of women's work-life conflict, instead valuing girls who "are too young to have discovered that they 'can't have it all' and therefore are much more fun" (2007: 45). *Hannah Montana*, by contrast, addresses these problems head-on. Furthermore, the newer shows do not establish a binary division between separate contexts or competing values whose contrast structures their plots and characterization, while we see such a framework clearly in both *Hannah Montana* and many of the earlier women's shows.
5. "The Best of Both Worlds," performed by Miley Cyrus, lyrics by Matthew R. T. Gerrard and Robert S. Nevil, © 2006 Walt Disney Music Company.
6. "Lilly, Do You Want to Know a Secret?" *Hannah Montana*, season 1 DVD, directed by Lee Shallat-Chemel, teleplay by Michael Poryes, Gary Dontzig, and Steven Peterman (Walt Disney Studios Home Entertainment, 2008). Originally aired March 24, 2006, on the Disney Channel.

7   Seiter notes that 1980s girls' animated series like *My Little Pony* borrowed heavily from the television soap opera and the paperback romance (1993: 169).
8   In fact research with girl readers suggests that the romantic resolutions of the *Anne* series in particular may not have as much staying power or interest for audiences as the characters' preceding struggles (Hubler 1998).

Chapter Four: The Whiteness of Tween Innocence

1   On race and tween children's television, see also Blue (2017) and Griffin (2011).
2   The debate about objectification versus agency has taken on somewhat different contours around Black women performers, for whom the objectifying white gaze has a long and violent history, especially in the United States, but also for whom public performance has been an important site for asserting feminist claims (see, e.g., Davis 1998; hooks 1992).
3   On the figure of the "redneck woman" in country music, see Hubbs (2014: 107–30).
4   "Fifteen," lyrics by Taylor Swift, © 2008 Sony/ATV Tree Publishing.
5   In live performances Swift sometimes rapped, to similar effect. At a concert in 2007 a fan video records her performing Eminem's "Lose Yourself" at the start of the show, ending with the clear disavowal and transition, "Y'all ready to hear some country music?" (https://www.youtube.com/watch?v=v4WQPfMzK10, accessed August 7, 2019). And at a radio station interview in 2011 she was cajoled by the hosts into reciting Nicki Minaj's "Super Bass," which she concluded with a self-consciously embarrassed "uh oh" (https://www.youtube.com/watch?v=TSSwUzdk8rU, accessed August 7, 2019). These covers, like "Thug Story," performed whiteness, specifically by contrasting it with Black musical styles, as awkward, nerdy, and uncool, but also, for all that, authentic and open—a form of personal disclosure and vulnerability to embarrassment. "Thug Story" in particular is very similar to "Weird Al" Yankovic's 2006 song "White and Nerdy," which parodied rapper Chamillionaire's 2005 "Ridin (Dirty)" and linked whiteness and nerdiness together in opposition to cool, masculine Blackness (Kendall 2011). Yankovic, like Swift, used this parodic distance from Black culture to authenticate his personal whiteness, telling *Billboard*, "This is a song I was born to write. I've been doing research my entire life" (quoted in Kendall 2011: 511).
6   The 2009 Video Music Awards were held at Radio City Music Hall in New York on September 13, 2009, and were broadcast live on MTV. The telecasts are copyrighted by MTV Networks.
7   "Innocent," lyrics by Taylor Swift, © 2010 Sony/ATV Tree Publishing.
8   "Mean," lyrics by Taylor Swift, © 2010 Sony/ATV Tree Publishing.
9   Compare Swift's idealization of childhood fantasy to Cyrus's cynicism, as when Cyrus explained to Ronan Farrow, "I don't love kids. . . . I don't love them because, I mean, I think I was around too many kids at one point—

because I was around a lot of kids.... They're so fucking mean.... Sometimes I hear kids with their parents, and I want to go over and, like, smack them myself" (Farrow 2014).

Chapter Five: The Tween Prodigy at Home and Online

1. That original YouTube account, under the username "kidrauhl," remains active as Bieber's official YouTube site. Because YouTube lists videos chronologically, the earliest videos on the page are these home performances. As of November 2019 they can still be viewed at http://www.youtube.com/user/kidrauhl/videos.
2. A parallel trend of white women soul singers was also developing at this moment, with artists like Amy Winehouse, Joss Stone, Lily Allen, Adele, and others (see Brooks 2010).
3. The original video can be viewed on YouTube here: http://www.youtube.com/watch?v=eQOFRZ1wNLw (accessed November 13, 2019).
4. Jan Smith is only identified in the film as "Mama Jan."
5. There was apparently a contest encouraging fans to submit videos of themselves singing along to a different song, "That Should Be Me" (K. Warner 2010). That is a later recording that would not allow this connection to be made between Bieber's very early performances and his contemporary success. I have not found reports explaining how the filmmakers collected the videos that actually do appear in the film.

Conclusion: After the Tween Moment

1. The 2008 MTV Video Music Awards were held at Paramount Pictures Studios in Los Angeles on September 7, 2008, and were broadcast live on MTV. The telecasts are copyrighted by MTV Networks.
2. Hazel Cills (2018) provides a useful history and discussion of mid-2000s celebrity promise-ring culture.
3. Around the same time Swift herself explicitly said that promise rings posed a sort of trap, telling an interviewer, "I don't ever talk about how I feel about that sort of thing because it makes people look at me sexually, which has never been a goal of mine" (Rys 2008).
4. Interestingly, media scholar Myles McNutt's (2015) analysis of Kidz Bop lyrics suggests that song lyrics have also been increasingly sanitized since 2009, when Kidz Bop started to fully invest in identifiable child performers, suggesting that they really did become more musically conservative in this period, as the musical innovations and experimentation of their early period dropped off.
5. *That's So Raven* could be seen to continue a prominent trend of kid-oriented television shows starring Black actors in the 1990s, including Nickelodeon's *Kenan & Kel* (1996–2000), the Disney Channel's *The Famous Jett Jackson*

(1998–2001), and ABC/The WB's *Sister, Sister* (1994–99). From 2001 to 2005 the Disney Channel also aired *The Proud Family*, an animated sitcom about an African American family, and in 2007 the Disney Channel produced *Cory in the House*, a spinoff of *That's So Raven* starring Cory Baxter, which ran for two seasons. In Disney's pop music contributions specifically, however, Raven-Symoné was the only African American artist cast in a leading role until Zendaya in 2010.

6 Interestingly, and again suggesting HSM as a pivot between earlier and later models, the HSM soundtrack did include a version of "Get'cha Head in the Game," performed by B5, an R&B group with a young African American membership who had released an album in 2005. To my knowledge B5 were not promoted as part of Disney's marketing of HSM.

7 "Mrs. Right," performed by Mindless Behavior, featuring Diggy Simmons; lyrics by James Amankwa, Lakeisha Gamble, Goldie Hampton, John Maultsby, John Milsap, Walter Milsap, Candice Nelson, Daniel Simmons, Gregory Watts Jr., and Nathaniel Williams; © 2011 by Conjunction Entertainment, Diggy Music Publishing, EMI Blackwood Music, Warner-Tamerlane Publishing, Bootleggers Stop, Jerry Lee, and Universal Music Corp.

8 "Super Bass," performed by Nicki Minaj; lyrics by Esther Dean, Jeremy Coleman, Roahn Hylton, Daniel Johnson, and Onika Maraj; © 2010 by Artist 101 Publishing Group, Dat Damn Dean Music, Harajuku Barbie Music, Money Mack Music, Peermusic III, Songs of Universal, EMI April Music, FB Da Mastermind Music Publishing, and JMike Music.

9 The relationship of Japanese and Korean popular culture to US media, and especially children's consumer culture, is a long and important one, and the particular intersections with mediated femininity in the United States around 2011 merit analysis, but these topics are beyond the scope of this book. (For some useful approaches to these questions, see Allison 2006, 2008; Buckingham and Sefton-Green 2003; Ito 2008b; Ngai 2005; Plourde 2018; Tobin 2004; and Yano 2013.)

REFERENCES

Adorno, Theodor W. [1938] 1991. "On the Fetish Character of Music and the Regression of Listening." In *The Culture Industry: Selected Essays on Mass Culture*, edited by J. M. Bernstein, pp. 29–60. New York: Routledge Classics.
Allen, Harry. 2009. "'Is Kanye the New O.J.?': The *Real* Haters Appear, in Order to Protect Taylor Swift's White Womanhood from the Rape . . . Uh, the Rapper." *Media Assassin* (September 14). http://harryallen.info/?p=5154.
Allison, Anne. 2006. *Millennial Monsters: Japanese Toys and the Global Imagination*. Berkeley: University of California Press.
Allison, Anne. 2008. "The Attractions of the J-Wave for American Youth." In *Soft Power Superpowers: Cultural and National Assets of Japan and the United States*, edited by Watanabe Yasushi and David L. McConnell, pp. 99–110. Armonk, NY: M. E. Sharpe.
AllMusic. 2005. Review of *Telegraph* by Drake Bell. Accessed August 7, 2019. http://www.allmusic.com/album/telegraph-mw0000215559.
Anderman, Joan. 2007. "I Heard It on TV: CBS Heads into New Territory with Record Contracts Linked to Television, Itunes Downloads." *Boston Globe* (March 23). http://www.boston.com/ae/music/articles/2007/03/23/i_heard_it_on_tv/.
Anderson, Benedict. 1983. *Imagined Communities: Reflections on the Origin and Spread of Nationalism*. London: Verso.
Anderson, Kurt. 1997. "Kids Are Us: These Days, Behaving Like a Grownup Is Child's Play." *New Yorker* 73 (December 15), p. 70.
Armstrong, Nancy. 1987. *Desire and Domestic Fiction: A Political History of the Novel*. New York: Oxford University Press.
Armstrong, Stephen. 2009. "Scary Stuff: Disney Created Hannah Montana and This Britney-lite Has Made Billions." *Sunday Times* (May 3), pp. 4–5.
Baker, Joseph Anthony. 2008. Review of *Fearless* by Taylor Swift. *Entertainment Weekly* (November 5). http://www.ew.com/article/2008/11/05/fearless.

Baker, Sarah. 2001. "'Rock on, Baby': Pre-Teen Girls and Popular Music." *Continuum: Journal of Media and Cultural Studies* 15 (3): 359–71.

Baker, Sarah. 2003. "Research Report: Auto-Audio Ethnography; or, Pre-teen Girls' Capturing Their Popular Musical Practices on Tape." *Context* 26: 57–65.

Baker, Sarah. 2004a. "'It's not about Candy': Music, Sexiness, and Girls' Serious Play in After School Care." *International Journal of Cultural Studies* 7 (2): 197–212.

Baker, Sarah. 2004b. "Pop in(to) the Bedroom: Popular Music in Pre-Teen Girls' Bedroom Culture." *European Journal of Cultural Studies* 7 (1): 75–93.

Baker, Sarah. 2008. "From Snuggling and Snogging to Sampling and Scratching: Girls' Nonparticipation in Community-Based Music Activities." *Youth and Society* 39 (3): 316–39.

Baker, Sarah. 2013. "Teenybop and the Extraordinary Particularities of Mainstream Practice." In *Redefining Mainstream Popular Music*, edited by Sarah Baker, Andy Bennet, and Jodie Taylor, pp. 14–25. New York: Routledge.

Banet-Weiser, Sarah. 2007. *Kids Rule! Nickelodeon and Consumer Citizenship.* Durham, NC: Duke University Press.

Banet-Weiser, Sarah. 2012. *Authentic TM: The Politics of Ambivalence in a Brand Culture.* New York: New York University Press.

Barber, Benjamin R. 2007. *Con$umed: How Markets Corrupt Children, Infantilize Adults, and Swallow Citizens Whole.* New York: Norton.

Barnes, Brooks. 2009. "Disney Expert Uses Science to Draw Boy Viewers." *New York Times* (April 14), p. A1.

Baron, Zach. 2008. "Adventures in Taylor Swift Reviewing." *Village Voice* (November 19). http://www.villagevoice.com/music/adventures-in-taylor-swift-reviewing-6638518.

Barthes, Roland. [1972] 1990. "The Grain of the Voice." In *On Record: Rock, Pop, and the Written Word*, edited by Simon Frith and Andrew Goodwin, pp. 293–300. New York: Pantheon.

Beck, Richard. 2015. *We Believe the Children: A Moral Panic in the 1980s.* New York: Public Affairs.

Berlant, Lauren. 1997. *The Queen of America Goes to Washington City: Essays on Sex and Citizenship.* Durham, NC: Duke University Press.

Berlant, Lauren. 2008. *The Female Complaint: The Unfinished Business of Sentimentality in American Culture.* Durham, NC: Duke University Press.

Bernstein, Robin. 2011. *Racial Innocence: Performing American Childhood from Slavery to Civil Rights.* New York: New York University Press.

Bickford, Tyler. 2017. *Schooling New Media: Music, Language, and Technology in Children's Culture.* New York: Oxford University Press.

Billboard. 1995. "'The Lion King' Roars as '94's 4.9M Top-Seller." *Billboard* 107 (January 21), p. 57.

Billboard. 2007. "Year-End Charts." *Billboard* 119 (December 22), pp. 82–132.

Billboard. 2009. "Chart Beat." *Billboard* 121 (August 8), p. 33.

Billboard. 2014. "Top Billboard 200 Albums." *Billboard* 126 (December 20), pp. 106–7.

Billboard. 2019a. "Hannah Montana—Chart History." *Billboard*. Accessed August 7, 2019. https://www.billboard.com/music/hannah-montana/chart-history/billboard-200/song/514220.

Billboard. 2019b. "Kidz Bop Kids—Chart History." *Billboard*. Accessed August 7, 2019. https://www.billboard.com/music/kidz-bop-kids/chart-history/kids-albums.

Blacking, John. 1973. *How Musical Is Man?* Seattle: University of Washington Press.

Blassingille, Brandi Naomi. 2014. "Changing Faces on Children's Cable Programming: The Emergence of Racial and Ethnic Minorities as Lead Characters on Nickelodeon and Disney Channel 1996–2005." MA thesis, University of Texas at Austin.

Blue, Morgan Genevieve. 2013. "The Best of Both Worlds? Youth, Gender, and the Postfeminist Sensibility in Disney's *Hannah Montana*." *Feminist Media Studies* 13 (4): 660–75.

Blue, Morgan Genevieve. 2017. *Girlhood on Disney Channel: Branding, Celebrity, and Femininity*. New York: Routledge.

Bly, Robert. 1990. *Iron John: A Book about Men*. Reading, MA: Addison-Wesley.

Bly, Robert. 1997. *The Sibling Society*. New York: Vintage.

Bonilla-Silva, Eduardo. 2013. *Racism without Racists: Color-Blind Racism and the Persistence of Racial Inequality in America*, 4th ed. Lanham, MD: Rowman and Littlefield.

Boone, Pat. 1958. *'Twixt Twelve and Twenty*. Englewood Cliffs, NJ: Prentice Hall.

Bowles, Scott. 2008. "'Hannah Montana' Concert Film Earns Extended Theater Stay." *USA Today* (February 3). http://usatoday30.usatoday.com/life/movies/news/2008-02-03-boxoffice_N.htm.

Box Office Mojo. 2014. "Hannah Montana/Miley Cyrus: Best of Both Worlds Concert Tour (2008)." *Box Office Mojo*. Accessed August 7, 2014. http://boxofficemojo.com/movies/?id=hannahmontanaconcert.htm.

Box Office Mojo. 2015. "2013 Worldwide Grosses." *Box Office Mojo*. Accessed February 16, 2015. http://boxofficemojo.com/yearly/chart/?view2=worldwide&yr=2013&p=.htm.

Box Office Mojo. 2018. "Music Concert Movies at the Box Office." *Box Office Mojo*. Accessed January 17, 2018. https://www.boxofficemojo.com/genres/chart/?id=musicconcert.htm.

boyd, danah. 2008. "Why Youth (Heart) Social Network Sites: The Role of Networked Publics in Teenage Social Life." In *Youth, Identity, and Digital Media*, edited by David Buckingham, pp. 119–42. Cambridge, MA: MIT Press.

boyd, danah, Eszter Hargittai, Jason Schultz, and John Palfrey. 2011. "Why Parents Help Their Children Lie to Facebook about Age: Unintended Consequences of the 'Children's Online Privacy Protection Act.'" *First Monday* 16 (11). https://doi.org/10.5210/fm.v16i11.3850.

Bradby, Barbara. 2009. "Sexy (No No No): The Cool and the Hot in Female Popular Song." In *Dichotonies: Gender and Music*, edited by Beate Neumeier, pp. 175–95. Heidelberg: Universitätsverlag Winter.

Brennan, Patricia. 1988. "The Kids' Channel That 'Double Dares' to Be Different." *Washington Post* (September 25), p. Y8.

Brooks, Daphne. 2010. "'This Voice Which Is Not One': Amy Winehouse Sings the Ballad of Sonic Blue(s)face Culture." *Women and Performance: A Journal of Feminist Theory* 20 (1): 37–60.

Brown, Robert, and Ruth Washton. 2001. "The U.S. Tweens Market." Proprietary report. MarketResearch.com (February). http://www.marketresearch.com.

Brown, Robert, and Ruth Washton. 2002. "Special Youth Demographic Series: The U.S. Kids, Tweens, and Teens Market." Proprietary report. MarketResearch.com (November). http://www.marketresearch.com.

Brown, Robert, and Ruth Washton. 2003. "The U.S. Tweens Market." 2nd ed. Proprietary report. MarketResearch.com (April). http://www.marketresearch.com.

Brown, Robert, and Ruth Washton. 2004. "The U.S. Kids Market: Understanding the Trends and Lifestyles Affecting 3- to 12-Year-Olds." Proprietary report. MarketResearch.com (April). http://www.marketresearch.com.

Brown, Ruth Nicole. 2009. *Black Girlhood Celebration: Toward a Hip-Hop Feminist Pedagogy*. New York: Peter Lang.

Brunsdon, Charlotte. 1991. "Pedagogies of the Feminine: Feminist Teaching and Women's Genres." *Screen* 32 (4): 364–81.

Buckingham, David, and Julian Sefton-Green. 2003. "Gotta Catch 'em All: Structure, Agency, and Pedagogy in Children's Media Culture." *Media, Culture & Society* 25 (3): 379–99.

Bunch, Ryan. 2018 "'Love Is an Open Door': Revising and Repeating Disney's Musical Tropes in *Frozen*." In *Contemporary Musical Film*, edited by Kevin J. Donnelly and Beth Carroll, pp. 89–103. Edinburgh: Edinburgh University Press.

Butler, Judith. 1990. *Gender Trouble: Feminism and the Subversion of Identity*. New York: Routledge.

Butler, Judith. 1997. "Merely Cultural." *Social Text* 52/53: 265–77.

Butsch, Richard. 2011. "Ralph, Fred, Archie, Homer, and the King of Queens: Why Television Keeps Re-creating the Male Working-Class Buffoon." In *Gender, Race, and Class in Media*, 3rd ed., edited by Gail Dines and Jean M. Humez, pp. 101–9. Thousand Oaks, CA: Sage.

Cafarelli, Carl. 2001. "Overview: An Informal History of Bubblegum Music." In *Bubblegum Music Is the Naked Truth*, edited by Kim Cooper and David Smay, pp. 13–22. Los Angeles: Feral House.

Caramanica, Jon. 2009. "Tween Princess, Tweaked." *New York Times* (July 19), p. AR1.

Caramanica, Jon. 2010. "Taylor Swift Is Angry, Darn It." *New York Times* (October 24), p. AR1.

Caramanica, Jon. 2014. "A Farewell to Twang." *New York Times* (October 26), pp. AR1, AR22.

Carby, Hazel V. 1985. "'On the Threshold of Woman's Era': Lynching, Empire, and Sexuality in Black Feminist Theory." *Critical Inquiry* 12 (1): 262–77.

Caulfield, Keith. 2014. "Taylor Swift's '1989' Beats 'Frozen' as Top Selling Album of 2014." *Billboard* (December 31). http://www.billboard.com/articles/columns/chart-beat/6422411/taylor-swift-1989-beats-frozen-top-selling-album-2014.

Caulfield, Keith. 2015. "Most *Billboard* 200 Top 10 Albums by Artist." *Billboard* (November 12). https://www.billboard.com/articles/events/greatest-of-all-time/6760781/rolling-stones-most-billboard-200-top-10-albums-artists.

Cecire, Natalia. 2012a. "An A B C of Puerility: Anderson, Britten, Crane." *New Inquiry* (June 26). http://thenewinquiry.com/blogs/zunguzungu/an-a-b-c-of-puerility-anderson-britten-crane/.

Cecire, Natalia. 2012b. "The Passion of Nate Silver (Sort Of)." *Works Cited* (November 2). http://nataliacecire.blogspot.com/2012/11/the-passion-of-nate-silver-sort-of.html.

Chinn, Sarah. 2008. *Inventing Modern Adolescence: The Children of Immigrants in Turn-of-the-Century America*. New Brunswick, NJ: Rutgers University Press.

Chmielewski, Dawn C. 2007. "A Cinderella Story for Disney Music Group." *Los Angeles Times* (July 9). http://articles.latimes.com/print/2007/jul/09/business/fi-hollywood9.

Cills, Hazel. 2018. "The Rise and Fall of the Pop Star Purity Ring." *Jezebel* (January 18). https://themuse.jezebel.com/the-rise-and-fall-of-the-pop-star-purity-ring-1822170318.

Coates, Norma. 2003. "Teenyboppers, Groupies, and Other Grotesques: Girls and Women and Rock Culture in the 1960s and Early 1970s." *Journal of Popular Music Studies* 15 (1): 65–94.

Comentale, Edward P. 2016. "Dorking Out with Taylor and Kanye: Nerd Pop via Goffman and the Performance of Stigma." *Journal of Popular Music Studies* 28 (1): 7–32.

Cook, Daniel Thomas. 2004. *The Commodification of Childhood: The Children's Clothing Industry and the Rise of the Child Consumer*. Durham, NC: Duke University Press.

Cook, Daniel Thomas. 2007. "The Disempowering Empowerment of Children's Consumer 'Choice': Cultural Discourses of the Child Consumer in North America." *Society and Business Review* 2 (1): 37–52.

Cook, Daniel Thomas, and Susan B. Kaiser. 2004. "Betwixt and Be Tween: Age Ambiguity and the Sexualization of the Female Consuming Subject." *Journal of Consumer Culture* 4 (2): 203–27.

Cooper, Wilbert L. 2013. "Miley Cyrus Needs to Take an African American Studies Class." *Vice* (June 27). http://www.vice.com/read/miley-cyrus-needs-to-take-an-african-american-studies-class.

Cottom, Tressie McMillan. 2013. "When Your (Brown) Body Is a (White) Wonderland." *tressiemc* (August 27). http://tressiemc.com/2013/08/27/when-your-brown-body-is-a-white-wonderland/.

Coulter, Natalie. 2014. *Tweening the Girl: The Crystallization of the Tween Market*. New York: Peter Lang.

Cross, Gary. 2008. *Men to Boys: The Making of Modern Immaturity*. New York: Columbia University Press.

Danesi, Marcel. 2003. *Forever Young: The Teen-aging of Modern Culture*. Toronto: University of Toronto Press.

Davis, Angela Yvonne. 1998. *Blues Legacies and Black Feminism: Gertrude Ma Rainey, Bessie Smith, and Billie Holiday*. New York: Vintage.

Dean, Josh. 2015. "The New Kings of Pop: How Kidz Bop Took over the Music Industry." *Bloomberg Business* (April 17). http://www.bloomberg.com/graphics/2015-kidz-bop/.

Diawara, Manthia. 1988. "Black Spectatorship: Problems of Identification and Resistance." *Screen* 29 (4): 66–79.

Dibben, Nicola. 1999. "Representations of Femininity in Popular Music." *Popular Music* 18 (3): 331–55.

Dillon, Elizabeth Maddock. 2004. *The Gender of Freedom: Fictions of Liberalism and the Literary Public Sphere*. Stanford, CA: Stanford University Press.

Dines, Gail. 1998. "King Kong and the White Woman: *Hustler* Magazine and the Demonization of Black Masculinity." *Violence against Women* 4 (3): 291–307.

Dinh, James. 2010. "Taylor Swift Sings to Kanye West, Maybe, at VMAs." *MTV News* (September 12). http://www.mtv.com/news/1647666/taylor-swift-sings-to-kanye-west-maybe-at-vmas/.

Dodd, Claire. 2007. "Disney Eyes Lucrative Youth Niche." *Music Week* (May 12), p. 9.

Dole, Carol M. 2007. "The Return of Pink: *Legally Blonde*, Third-Wave Feminism, and Having It All." In *Chick Flicks: Contemporary Women at the Movies*, edited by Suzanne Ferriss and Mallory Young, pp. 58–78. New York: Routledge.

Donahue, Ann. 2010. "Girl, You'll Be a Woman Soon: With 'Can't Be Tamed,' Miley Cyrus Transitions from Tween Idol to Pop Star." *Billboard* 122 (June 5), pp. 17–19.

Dougher, Sarah. 2016. "When Loud Really Means Real: Tween Girls and the Voices of Rock Authenticity." In *Voicing Girlhood in Popular Music: Performance, Authority, Authenticity*, edited by Jacqueline Warwick and Allison Adrian, pp. 191–207. New York: Routledge.

Dougher, Sarah, and Diane Pecknold. 2018. "Not a Girl Band: Identity, Cultural Authority, and Musicianship among Tween Girls." In *Mediated Girlhoods: New Explorations of Girls Media Culture*, vol. 2, edited by Morgan Genevieve Blue and Mary Celeste Kearney, pp. 177–92. New York: Peter Lang.

Douglas, Ann. 1977. *The Feminization of American Culture*. New York: Knopf.

Dow, Bonnie J. 1996. *Prime-Time Feminism: Television, Media Culture, and the Women's Movement since 1970*. Philadelphia: University of Pennsylvania Press.

Doyle, Sady. 2014. "Taylor Swift Twerks while the World Burns." *In These Times* (August 22). http://inthesetimes.com/article/17117/taylor_swift_cant_shake_it_off.

Dries, Kate. 2013. "Miley's Need to Shock Was the Least Shocking Thing about It." *Jezebel* (August 26). http://jezebel.com/mileys-need-to-shock-was-the-least-shocking-thing-abou-1200886682.

Driscoll, Catherine. 2005. "Girl-Doll: Barbie as Puberty Material." In *Seven Going on Seventeen: Tween Studies in the Culture of Girlhood*, edited by Claudia Mitchell and Jacqueline Reid-Walsh, pp. 224–41. New York: Peter Lang.

Drotner, Kirsten. 2002. "Domesticating Disney: On Danish Children's Reception of a Global Media Giant." In *Children, Young People, and Media Globalisation*, edited by Cecilia von Feiletzen and Ulla Carlsson, pp. 111–23. Göteborg: NORDICOM.

Duane, Anna Mae. 2010. *Suffering Childhood in Early America: Violence, Race, and the Making of the Child Victim*. Athens: University of Georgia Press.

Dubrofsky, Rachel E. 2016. "A Vernacular of Surveillance: Taylor Swift and Miley Cyrus Perform White Authenticity." *Surveillance and Society* 14 (2): 184–96.

Dueck, Byron. 2013. *Musical Intimacies and Indigenous Imaginaries: Aboriginal Music and Dance in Public Performance*. New York: Oxford University Press.

Eckert, Penelope. 1996. "Vowels and Nail Polish: The Emergence of Linguistic Style in the Preadolescent Heterosexual Marketplace." In *Gender and Belief Systems: Proceedings of the Fourth Berkeley Women and Language Conference*, edited by Natasha Warner, pp. 183–90. Berkeley, CA: Berkeley Women and Language Group.

Edelman, Lee. 2004. *No Future: Queer Theory and the Death Drive*. Durham, NC: Duke University Press.

Eells, Josh. 2013. "Good Golly Miss Miley!" *Rolling Stone* (October 10), pp. 40–46.

Egan, R. Danielle, and Gail Hawkes. 2008. "Endangered Girls and Incendiary Objects: Unpacking the Discourse on Sexualization." *Sexuality and Culture* 12 (4): 291–311.

Ehrenreich, Barbara, Elizabeth Hess, and Gloria Jacobs. 1986. *Re-making Love: The Feminization of Sex*. Garden City, NY: Anchor Press/Doubleday.

Epstein, Joseph. 2004. "The Perpetual Adolescent and the Triumph of the Youth Culture." *Weekly Standard* (March 15). http://www.weeklystandard.com/Content/Public/Articles/000/000/003/825grtdi.asp.

Epstein, Rebecca, Jamilia J. Blake, and Thalia González. 2017. "Girlhood Interrupted: The Erasure of Black Girls' Childhood." Report. Washington, DC: Georgetown Law Center on Poverty and Inequality (June 27). https://www.law.georgetown.edu/news/black-girls-viewed-as-less-innocent-than-white-girls-georgetown-law-research-finds-2/.

Erlewine, Stephen Thomas. 2007. Review of *The Naked Brothers Band* by the Naked Brothers Band. *AllMusic*. Accessed August 7, 2019. http://www.allmusic.com/album/naked-brothers-band-mw0000488683.

Faderman, Lillian. 1981. *Surpassing the Love of Men: Romantic Friendship and Love between Women from the Renaissance to the Present*. New York: Morrow.

Farmer, Blake. 2007. "'Hannah Montana' Star Kicks Off Concert Tour." NPR (October 17). http://www.npr.org/templates/transcript/transcript.php?storyId=15391837.

Farrow, Ronan. 2014. "My Oh Miley!" *W Magazine* 42 (March), p. 308.

Fass, Paula S. 2012. "The Child-Centered Family? New Rules in Postwar America." In *Reinventing the Child after World War II*, edited by Paula S. Fass and

Michael Grossberg, pp. 1–18. Philadelphia: University of Pennsylvania Press.

Feilitzen, Cecilia von, and Keith Roe. 1990. "Children and Music: An Exploratory Study." In *Popular Music Research: An Anthology from NORDICOM-Sweden*, edited by Keith Roe and Ulla Carlsson, pp. 53–70. Göteborg: Department of Political Science, University of Göteborg.

Feld, Steven. 1984. "Sound Structure as Social Structure." *Ethnomusicology* 28 (3): 383–409.

Feldman, David Henry, and Martha J. Morelock. 2011. "Prodigies and Savants." In *The Cambridge Handbook of Intelligence*, pp. 210–34. New York: Cambridge University Press.

Field, Corinne. 2014. *The Struggle for Equal Adulthood: Gender, Race, Age, and the Fight for Citizenship in Antebellum America*. Chapel Hill: University of North Carolina Press.

Firestone, Shulamith. 1970. *The Dialectic of Sex: The Case for Feminist Revolution*. New York: Bantam Books.

Fleeger, Jennifer. 2014. "*Frozen* and the Disney Princess Song." *OUPblog* (December 11). http://blog.oup.com/2014/12/frozen-disney-princess-song/.

Fox, Aaron. 2004. "White Trash Alchemies of the Abject Sublime: Country as 'Bad' Music." In *Bad Music: The Music We Love to Hate*, edited by Christopher Washburne and Maiken Derno, pp. 29–46. New York: Routledge.

France, Lisa Respers. 2009. "Anger over West's Disruption at MTV Awards." CNN (September 14). http://www.cnn.com/2009/SHOWBIZ/09/14/kanye.west.reaction/index.html.

Frank, Thomas. 2004. *What's the Matter with Kansas? How Conservatives Won the Heart of America*. New York: Metropolitan Books.

Fraser, Nancy. 1998. *Social Justice in the Age of Identity Politics: Redistribution, Recognition, and Participation*. Salt Lake City, UT: Tanner Lectures on Human Values.

Fraser, Nancy. 2000. "Rethinking Recognition." *New Left Review* 3: 107–20.

Fraser, Nancy. 2009. "Feminism, Capitalism and the Cunning of History." *New Left Review* 56: 97–117.

Frere-Jones, Sasha. 2008. "Prodigy: The Rise of Taylor Swift." *New Yorker* 84 (November 10), p. 88.

Friedan, Betty. 1963. *The Feminine Mystique*. New York: Norton.

Friedman, Megan. 2010. "Kanye vs. Taylor: Who Won at the VMAS?" *Time* (September 13). http://newsfeed.time.com/2010/09/13/kanye-vs-taylor-who-won-at-the-vmas/.

Frith, Simon. 1987. "Towards an Aesthetic of Popular Music." In *Music and Society: The Politics of Composition, Performance, and Reception*, edited by Richard Lepperty and Susan McClary, pp. 133–49. New York: Cambridge University Press.

Frith, Simon. 1988. "Why Do Songs Have Words?" In *Music for Pleasure: Essays in the Sociology of Pop*, pp. 105–28. Cambridge: Polity Press.

Frith, Simon. 1998. *Performing Rites: On the Value of Popular Music*. Cambridge, MA: Harvard University Press.

Frith, Simon, and Angela McRobbie. 1978/79. "Rock and Sexuality." *Screen Education* 29: 3–19.

Gagné, Françoys. 2009. "Building Gifts into Talents: Detailed Overview of the DMGT 2.0." In *Leading Change in Gifted Education: The Festschrift of Dr. Joyce Vantassel-Baska*, edited by Bronwyn MacFarlane and Tamra Stambaugh, pp. 61–80. Waco, TX: Prufrock.

Gamson, Joshua. 2011. "The Unwatched Life Is Not Worth Living: The Elevation of the Ordinary in Celebrity Culture." *PMLA* 126 (4): 1061–69.

Gaunt, Kyra D. 2015. "YouTube, Twerking and You: Context Collapse and the Handheld Co-presence of Black Girls and Miley Cyrus." *Journal of Popular Music Studies* 27 (3): 244–73.

Genz, Stéphanie. 2010. "Singled Out: Postfeminism's 'New Woman' and the Dilemma of Having It All." *Journal of Popular Culture* 43 (1): 97–119.

Gerhard, Jane. 2005. "Sex and the City: Carrie Bradshaw's Queer Postfeminism." *Feminist Media Studies* 5 (1): 37–49.

Gevinson, Tavi. 2014. "Not a Girl, Not Yet a Woman: The Two Sides of Miley Cyrus." *Elle* (May). http://www.elle.com/pop-culture/cover-shoots/miley-cyrus-may-cover-story.

Gill, Rosalind. 2007. "Postfeminist Media Culture: Elements of a Sensibility." *European Journal of Cultural Studies* 10 (2): 147–66.

Gillis, John R. 2008. "The Islanding of Children—Reshaping the Mythical Landscapes of Children." In *Designing Modern Childhoods: History, Space, and the Material Culture of Children*, edited by Marta Gutman and Ning de Coninck-Smith, pp. 316–30. New Brunswick, NJ: Rutgers University Press.

Giroux, Henry A. 1999. *The Mouse That Roared: Disney and the End of Innocence*. Lanham, MD: Rowman and Littlefield.

Goff, Phillip Atiba, Matthew Christian Jackson, Brooke Allison Lewis Di Leone, Carmen Culotta, and Natalie Ann DiTomasso. 2014. "The Essence of Innocence: Consequences of Dehumanizing Black Children." *Journal of Personality and Social Psychology* 106 (4): 526–45.

Goldberg, Lesley. 2013. "Parents Television Council Blasts MTV's VMAs as Serving Sex to Teens." *Hollywood Reporter* (August 26). http://www.hollywoodreporter.com/live-feed/parents-television-council-blasts-mtvs-614448.

Götz, Maya, Dafna Lemish, Amy Aidman, and Hyesung Moon. 2005. *Media and the Make-Believe Worlds of Children: When Harry Potter Meets Pokémon in Disneyland*. Mahwah, NJ: Lawrence Erlbaum.

Gould, Philip. 1999. "Introduction: Revisiting the 'Feminization' of American Culture." *differences* 11 (3): i–xii.

Graham, Jefferson. 1997. "Disney Channel Reaches Out to Families." *USA Today* (July 2), p. 3D.

Graham, Stephen. 2015. "Justin Timberlake's Two-Part Complementary Forms: Groove, Extension, and Maturity in Twenty-First-Century Popular Music." *American Music* 32 (4): 448–74.

Graser, Marc. 2009. "A New World Re-order: Exec Shake-ups Offer Clues to Studio Goals." *Variety* (October 9), p. 6.

Green, Lucy. 1997. *Music, Gender, Education*. New York: Cambridge University Press.

Greenblatt, Leah. 2010a. "Demi Lovato: Read the EW Story That Hinted at the Disney Star's Troubles." *Entertainment Weekly* (November 3). http://www.ew.com/article/2010/11/03/demi-lovato-rehab-interview.

Greenblatt, Leah. 2010b. Review of *Can't Be Tamed* by Miley Cyrus. *Entertainment Weekly* (June 16). http://ew.com/article/2010/06/16/cant-be-tamed/.

Greenfeld, Karl Taro. 2008. "How Mickey Got His Groove Back." *Condé Nast Portfolio* (May), pp. 126–31, 150.

Griffin, Hollis. 2011. "Never, Sometimes, Always: The Multiple Temporalities of 'Post-Race' Discourse in Convergence Television Narrative." *Popular Communication* 9 (4): 235–50.

Gubar, Marah. 2001. "'Where Is the Boy?' The Pleasures of Postponement in the *Anne of Green Gables* Series." *Lion and the Unicorn* 25 (1): 47–69.

Gubar, Marah. 2003. "Species Trouble: The Abjection of Adolescence in E. B. White's *Stuart Little*." *Lion and the Unicorn* 27 (1): 98–119.

Gubar, Marah. 2013. "Risky Business: Talking about Children in Children's Literature Criticism." *Children's Literature Association Quarterly* 38 (4): 450–57.

Habermas, Jürgen. [1962] 1989. *The Structural Transformation of the Public Sphere: An Inquiry into a Category of Bourgeois Society*. Translated by Thomas Burger and Frederick Lawrence. Cambridge, MA: MIT Press.

Halberstam, Judith [Jack]. 2011. *The Queer Art of Failure*. Durham, NC: Duke University Press.

Harrison, Robert Pogue. 2014. *Juvenescence: A Cultural History of Our Age*. Chicago: University of Chicago Press.

Harrison, Shane. 2006. "Toned-Down Tunes for Kids." *Atlanta Journal-Constitution* (May 29), p. 3C.

Hasty, Katie. 2007. "Swift's Un-swift Climb: After 39 Weeks, Teenage Artist Finally Tops Country Chart." *Billboard* 119 (August 4), p. 9.

Heffley, Lynne. 1990. "'Minnie 'n Me' to Help Merchandise a Mouse." *Los Angeles Times* (August 22), p. 1.

Hendershot, Heather. 2004. "Nickelodeon's Nautical Nonsense: The Intergenerational Appeal of *SpongeBob SquarePants*." In *Nickelodeon Nation: The History, Politics, and Economics of America's Only TV Channel for Kids*, edited by Heather Hendershot, pp. 182–208. New York: New York University Press.

Hendrick, Harry. 1997. "Constructions and Reconstructions of British Childhood: An Interpretative Survey, 1800 to the Present." In *Constructing and Reconstructing Childhood: Contemporary Issues in the Sociological Study of Childhood*, 2nd ed., edited by Allison James and Alan Prout, pp. 33–60. New York: Falmer Press.

Henley, Nancy. 1977. *Body Politics: Power, Sex and Nonverbal Communication*. Englewood Cliffs, NJ: Prentice Hall.

Hentges, Beth, and Kim Case. 2013. "Gender Representations on Disney Channel, Cartoon Network, and Nickelodeon Broadcasts in the United States." *Journal of Children and Media* 7 (3): 319–33.

Hey, Valerie. 2002. "Horizontal Solidarities and Molten Capitalism: The Subject, Intersubjectivity, Self and the Other in Late Modernity." *Discourse: Studies in the Cultural Politics of Education* 23 (2): 227–41.

Hill, Logan. 2010. "The Evolution of an Apology." *New York Magazine* (November 21). http://nymag.com/arts/popmusic/features/69683/.

Hine, Thomas. 1999. *The Rise and Fall of the American Teenager*. New York: Perennial.

Hochschild, Arlie Russell. 2003. *The Commercialization of Intimate Life: Notes from Home and Work*. Berkeley: University of California Press.

Hochschild, Arlie Russell, with Anne Machung. [1989] 2003. *The Second Shift*, 2nd ed. New York: Penguin.

Hoffman, Jan. 2010. "Justin Bieber Is Living the Dream." *New York Times* (January 3), p. ST1.

Hogan, Lindsay. 2013. "The Mouse House of Cards: Disney Tween Stars and Questions of Institutional Authorship." In *A Companion to Media Authorship*, edited by Jonathan Gray and Derek Johnson, pp. 298–313. Malden, MA: Wiley Blackwell.

Holson, Laura M. 2010. "Fans of Miley Cyrus Question Her New Path." *New York Times* (July 11), p. ST1.

hooks, bell. 1992. *Black Looks: Race and Representation*. Boston: South End Press.

Hubbs, Nadine. 2014. *Rednecks, Queers, and Country Music*. Berkeley: University of California Press.

Hubler, Angela. 1998. "Can Anne Shirley Help 'Revive Ophelia'? Listening to Girl Readers." In *Delinquents and Debutantes: Twentieth-Century American Girls' Cultures*, edited by Sherrie A. Innes, pp. 266–84. New York: New York University Press.

Hunt, Pauline, and Ronald Frankenberg. 1990. "It's a Small World: Disneyland, the Family and the Multiple Re-representations of American Childhood." In *Constructing and Reconstructing Childhood: Contemporary Issues in the Sociological Study of Childhood*, edited by Allison James and Alan Prout, pp. 99–117. New York: Falmer Press.

Huyssen, Andreas. 1986. "Mass Culture as Woman: Modernism's Other." In *After the Great Divide: Modernism, Mass Culture, Postmodernism*, pp. 44–62. Bloomington: Indiana University Press.

Idelson, Karen. 2010. "Music-Filled Shows Gain Momentum Worldwide." *Variety* (September 26). http://variety.com/2010/film/news/music-filled-shows-gain-momentum-worldwide-1118024444/.

Ito, Mizuko. 2006. "Japanese Media Mixes and Amateur Cultural Exchange." In *Digital Generations: Children, Young People, and New Media*, edited by David Buckingham and Rebekah Willett, pp. 49–65. Mahwah, NJ: Lawrence Erlbaum.

Ito, Mizuko. 2007. "Technologies of the Childhood Imagination: *Yu-Gi-Oh!*, Media Mixes, and Everyday Cultural Production." In *Structures of Participation in Digital Culture*, edited by Joe Karaganis, pp. 88–110. New York: Social Science Research Council.

Ito, Mizuko. 2008a. "Introduction." In *Networked Publics*, edited by Kazys Varnelis, pp. 1–14. Cambridge, MA: MIT Press.

Ito, Mizuko. 2008b. "Mobilizing the Imagination in Everyday Play: The Case of Japanese Media Mixes." In *The International Handbook of Children, Media, and Culture*, edited by Kirsten Drotner and Sonia Livingstone, pp. 397–412. Thousand Oaks, CA: Sage.

Ivy, Marilyn. 1995. "Have You Seen Me? Recovering the Inner Child in Late Twentieth-Century America." In *Children and the Politics of Culture*, edited by Sharon Stephens, pp. 79–104. Princeton, NJ: Princeton University Press.

James, Robin. 2017. "Is the Post- in Post-identity the Post- in Post-genre?" *Popular Music* 36 (1): 21–32.

Jenison, David. 2007. "High School Rules '06 Album Sales." *E! Online* (January 4). http://www.eonline.com/news/54100/high-school-rules-06-album-sales.

Jenkins, Henry. 1998. "'Complete Freedom of Movement': Video Games as Gendered Play Spaces." In *From Barbie to Mortal Kombat: Gender and Computer Games*, edited by Justine Cassell and Henry Jenkins, pp. 262–97. Cambridge, MA: MIT Press.

Johnston, Janice. 2011. "Demi Lovato Interview: Teen Star Opens Up on Bulimia, Cutting Issues." *ABC News* (April 19). http://abcnews.go.com/Entertainment/demi-lovato-interview-teen-star-opens-bulimia-cutting/story?id=13405090.

Jones, Abigail. 2014. "Sex and the Single Tween." *Newsweek* 162 (January 24), pp. 7–44.

Kahn, Robert. 2009. "Cyrus Makes Some Britney Moves: Watchers Say 'Hannah' Star's Dance a Career Step: Bad Message, Some Say, but She's Used to Scandal." *Newsday* (August 11), p. 17.

Kaufman, Gil. 2007. "Hannah Montana Ticket Bonanza Spurs Officials to Investigate Resellers." *MTV News* (October 5). http://www.mtv.com/news/1571314/hannah-montana-ticket-bonanza-spurs-officials-to-investigate-resellers/.

Kearney, Mary Celeste. 2007. "Productive Spaces: Girls' Bedrooms as Sites of Cultural Production." *Journal of Children and Media* 1 (2): 126–41.

Keating, Gina, and Sue Zeidler. 2007. "Disney Backs Star after Her Apology for Nude Photo." *Reuters* (September 7). http://www.reuters.com/article/us-hudgens-nude-idUSN0746838620070908.

Keefe, Jonathan. 2008. Review of *Fearless* by Taylor Swift. *Slant Magazine* (November 16). http://www.slantmagazine.com/music/review/taylor-swift-fearless.

Keightley, Keir. 2001. "You Keep Coming Back Like a Song: Adult Audiences, Taste Panics, and the Idea of the Standard." *Journal of Popular Music Studies* 13: 7–40.

Kelland, Regina. 2001. "There's a Gap between Kids' and Teens' Music." *Los Angeles Times* (December 10). http://articles.latimes.com/2001/dec/10/entertainment/et-kelland10.

Kendall, Lori. 2011. "'White and Nerdy': Computers, Race, and the Nerd Stereotype." *Journal of Popular Culture* 44 (3): 505–24.

Kennedy, Melanie. 2014. "Hannah Montana and Miley Cyrus: 'Becoming' a Woman, 'Becoming' a Star." *Celebrity Studies* 5 (3): 225–41.

Keveney, Bill. 2007. "Can *High School Musical* Do It Again? The 2006 TV Movie Is Still a Marketing and Pop Culture Sensation. And Now: The Sequel." *USA Today* (August 10), p. 1A.

Kidd, Kenneth. 2011. *Freud in Oz: At the Intersections of Psychoanalysis and Children's Literature*. Minneapolis: University of Minnesota Press.

Kiley, Dan. 1983. *The Peter Pan Syndrome: Men Who Have Never Grown Up*. New York: Dodd Mead.

Kincaid, James R. 1998. *Erotic Innocence: The Culture of Child Molesting*. Durham, NC: Duke University Press.

Kincaid, James R. 2004. "Producing Erotic Children." In *Curiouser: On the Queerness of Children*, edited by Steven Bruhm and Natasha Hurley, pp. 3–16. Minneapolis: University of Minnesota Press.

Klein, Bethany. 2008. "'The New Radio': Music Licensing as a Response to Industry Woe." *Media, Culture & Society* 30 (4): 463–78.

Knopper, Steve. 2009. *Appetite for Self-Destruction: The Spectacular Crash of the Record Industry in the Digital Age*. New York: Free Press.

Knopper, Steve. 2014. "How 'Frozen' Went from Small Soundtrack to Worldwide Phenomenon." *Rolling Stone* (March 11). http://www.rollingstone.com/movies/news/how-frozen-went-from-small-soundtrack-to-worldwide-phenomenon-20140311.

Kulynych, Jessica. 2001. "No Playing in the Public Sphere: Democratic Theory and the Exclusion of Children." *Social Theory and Practice* 27 (2): 232–64.

Lai, Amy T. Y. 2005. "Consuming *Hello Kitty*: Tween Icon, Sexy Cute, and the Changing Meaning of 'Girlhood.'" In *Seven Going on Seventeen: Tween Studies in the Culture of Girlhood*, edited by Claudia Mitchell and Jacqueline Reid-Walsh, pp. 242–56. New York: Peter Lang.

Lange, Patricia G. 2007. "Publicly Private and Privately Public: Social Networking on YouTube." *Journal of Computer-Mediated Communication* 13 (1): 361–80.

Lange, Patricia G. 2009. "Videos of Affinity on YouTube." In *The YouTube Reader*, edited by Pelle Snickars and Patrick Vonderau, pp. 70–88. Stockholm: National Library of Sweden / Wallflower Press.

Langer, Beryl. 2004. "The Business of Branded Enchantment: Ambivalence and Disjuncture in the Global Children's Culture Industry." *Journal of Consumer Culture* 4 (2): 251–77.

Leeds, Jeff. 2001. "That Awkward Phase." *Los Angeles Times* (December 2). http://articles.latimes.com/2001/dec/02/entertainment/ca-10567.

Lenz, Elinor. 1985. *The Feminization of America: How Women's Values Are Changing Our Public and Private Lives*. New York: St. Martin's Press.

Levine, Robert. 2006. "The Top-Selling Tunes on *Billboard*, Sung by Children for Children." *New York Times* (March 6), p. C1.

Levine, Stuart. 2003. "Now That Duff's Had Enough . . . Is It Time for Disney Channel to Rethink No-Ads Strategy?" *Variety* (June 5). http://variety.com/2003/tv/features/now-that-duff-s-had-enough-1117887469.

Lewis, C. S. 1950. *The Lion, the Witch, and the Wardrobe*. London: Geoffrey Bles.

Lipsitz, George. 2006. *The Possessive Investment in Whiteness: How White People Benefit from Identity Politics*, rev. ed. Philadelphia: Temple University Press.

Lott, Eric. 1993. *Love and Theft: Blackface Minstrelsy and the American Working Class*. New York: Oxford University Press.

MacDonald, George. 1872. *The Princess and the Goblin*. London: Strahan.

MacLeod, Anne Scott. 1984. "The *Caddie Woodlawn* Syndrome: American Girlhood in the Nineteenth Century." In *A Century of Childhood, 1820–1920*, edited by Mary Lynn Stevens, pp. 97–117. Rochester, NY: Margaret Woodbury Strong Museum.

MacPherson, Alex. 2012. "Taylor Swift: 'I Want to Believe in Pretty Lies.'" *Guardian* (October 18). http://www.guardian.co.uk/music/2012/oct/18/taylor-swift-want-believe-pretty-lies.

Marsh, Kathryn. 2008. *The Musical Playground: Global Tradition and Change in Children's Songs and Games*. New York: Oxford University Press.

Martens, Todd, and Yvonne Villareal. 2009. "Kanye West Expresses Swift Regret on Blog and 'Jay Leno Show.'" *Los Angeles Times* (September 15), p. D1.

Martin, Denise. 2004. "In Search of Tweens: Disney Signs with Creators of 'Lizzie,' 'Raven.'" *Variety* (November 3). http://variety.com/2004/scene/news/in-search-of-tweens-1117912986/.

Mason, Anthony. 2007. "'High School Musical' Popular among Teens, Is a Lucrative Phenomenon." *CBS Evening News* (August 16).

Mayo, Jenny. 2007. "Tween Pop Rules Seriously; Marketing Industry Is Responding to Youth Subgroup's Taste in Music." *Washington Times* (January 19), p. D01.

McCarthy, Sean L. 2006. "Children of the (Music) Revolution: Think Top 40 Is 'Crazy' Now? Hear the Voice of the New Generation." *Boston Herald* (September 1), p. E04.

McClary, Susan. 1991. "Sexual Politics in Classical Music." In *Feminine Endings: Music, Gender, and Sexuality*, pp. 53–79. Minneapolis: University of Minnesota Press.

McCormick, Moira. 1994. "The ABCs of Audio: The Sound Market Retrenches and Gets Real after the Hype Settles." *Billboard* 106 (February 19), p. 68.

McCormick, Moira. 2000. "Child's Play: Disney's Back on Top of the Year-End Audio Chart with a Set of 'Jams.'" *Billboard* 112 (December 30), p. 69.

McCormick, Moira. 2001. "Child's Play: Disney Responds to Changing Industry—Best-Selling 'Jams' Set Features Top 40 That Appeals to All Ages." *Billboard* (February 24), p. 63.

McCormick, Moira, Matthew LaFollette, and Jackie Stasi. 1991. "The Major Labels Are Signing Children's Artists—A Sure Sign of Progress and Promise for the Hyperactive Kids Audio and Video Market." *Billboard* 103 (August 3), p. C1.

McGillis, Roderick. 2003. "Coprophilia for Kids: The Culture of Grossness." In *Youth Cultures: Texts, Images, and Identities*, edited by Kerry Mallan and Sharyn Pearce, pp. 183–96. Westport, CT: Praeger.

McKeon, Michael. 2005. *The Secret History of Domesticity: Public, Private, and the Division of Knowledge*. Baltimore, MD: Johns Hopkins University Press.

McMullen, Tracy. 2006. "Corpo-Realities: Keepin' It Real in 'Music and Embodiment' Scholarship." *Current Musicology* 82: 61–80.

McNamara, Tara. 2007a. "Mitchell Gossett: Director of Youth at Cunningham Eyes Multitalents." *Variety* (October 4). http://www.variety.com/article/VR1117973379?refCatId=2721.

McNamara, Tara. 2007b. "Youth Impact Report 2007: Up Next: Taylor Swift." *Variety* (October 4). http://www.variety.com/article/VR1117973337.

McNutt, Myles. 2015. "The Kidz Are All Right." *Slate* (November 8). http://www.slate.com/articles/arts/culturebox/2015/11/kidz_bop_30_and_the_growing_conservativism_of_children_s_music_why_are_kidz.html.

McPherson, Gary, and Aaron Williamon. 2016. "Building Gifts into Musical Talents." In *The Child as Musician: A Handbook of Musical Development*, 2nd ed., edited by Gary McPherson, pp. 340–60. New York: Oxford University Press.

McRobbie, Angela. 2009. *The Aftermath of Feminism: Gender, Culture, and Social Change*. Thousand Oaks, CA: Sage.

McRobbie, Angela, and Jenny Garber. 1976. "Girls and Subcultures." In *Resistance through Rituals: Youth Subcultures in Post-war Britain*, edited by Stuart Hall and Tony Jefferson, pp. 209–22. London: HarperCollins Academic.

Merritt, Russell. 1990. "D. W. Griffith's *The Birth of a Nation*: Going after Little Sister." In *Close Viewings: An Anthology of New Film Criticism*, edited by Peter Lehman, pp. 215–37. Tallahassee: Florida State University Press.

Meyrowitz, Joshua. 1985. *No Sense of Place: The Impact of Electronic Media on Social Behavior*. New York: Oxford University Press.

Michaels, Walter Benn. 2006. *The Trouble with Diversity: How We Learned to Love Identity and Ignore Inequality*. New York: Metropolitan Books.

Miers, Jeff. 2014. "Taylor Swift Leaves Country for Pop on '1989.'" *Buffalo News* (October 28). http://buffalo.com/2014/10/27/featured/taylor-swift-leaves-country-for-pop-on-1989/.

Mifflin, Lawrie. 1999. "A Growth Spurt Is Transforming TV for Children." *New York Times* (April 19), p. A1.

Miller, Veronica. 2010. "The Best Week Ever for Black Girls." NPR (October 21). https://www.npr.org/sections/tellmemore/2010/10/21/130729009/the-best-week-ever-for-black-girls.

Minks, Amanda. 1999. "Growing and Grooving to a Steady Beat: Pop Music in Fifth-Graders' Social Lives." *Yearbook for Traditional Music* 31: 77–101.

Mitroff, Donna, and Rebecca Herr Stephenson. 2007. "The Television Tug-of-War: A Brief History of Children's Television Programming in the United States." In *The Children's Television Community*, edited by J. Alison Bryant, pp. 3–34. New York: Routledge.

Mjøs, Ole J. 2010. "The Symbiosis of Children's Television and Merchandising: Comparative Perspectives on the Norwegian Children's Television Channel NRK Super and the Global Disney Channel." *Media, Culture & Society* 32 (6): 1031–42.

Montgomery, James. 2012. "Taylor Swift's *Red*: Let the Golden Age Begin." *MTV News* (October 17). http://www.mtv.com/news/1695777/taylor-swift-red-album-career-evolution/.

Montgomery, Kathryn C. 1989. *Target: Prime Time: Advocacy Groups and the Struggle over Entertainment Television*. New York: Oxford University Press.

Montgomery, Kathryn C. 2007a. "Advocating Children's Television." In *The Children's Television Community*, edited by J. Alison Bryant, pp. 229–57. New York: Routledge.

Montgomery, Kathryn C. 2007b. *Generation Digital: Politics, Commerce, and Childhood in the Age of the Internet*. Cambridge, MA: MIT Press.

Moody, Nekesa Mumbi. 2009. "Kanye Calls Taylor Swift after 'View' Appearance." *Billboard* (September 15). http://www.billboard.com/articles/news/267390/kanye-west-calls-taylor-swift-at-the-view.

Morris, Monique W. 2016. *Pushout: The Criminalization of Black Girls in Schools*. New York: New Press.

Moseley, Rachel, and Jacinda Read. 2002. "'Having It Ally': Popular Television (Post-)Feminism." *Feminist Media Studies* 2 (2): 231–49.

Mulvey, Laura. 1975. "Visual Pleasure and Narrative Cinema." *Screen* 16 (3): 6–18.

Muñoz, José Esteban. 2009. *Cruising Utopia: The Then and There of Queer Futurity*. New York: New York University Press.

Nash, Ilana. 2003. "Hysterical Scream or Rebel Yell? The Politics of Teen-Idol Fandom." In *Disco Divas: Women and Popular Culture in the 1970s*, edited by Sherrie A. Innes. Philadelphia: University of Pennsylvania Press.

Neal, Mark Anthony. 2005. "White Chocolate Soul: Teena Marie and Lewis Taylor." *Popular Music* 24 (3): 369–80.

Newman, Michael Z. 2009. "Tween Comedies and the Evolution of a Genre." *In Media Res* (October 19). http://mediacommons.futureofthebook.org/imr/2009/10/18/tween-comedies-and-evolution-genre.

Ngai, Sianne. 2005. "The Cuteness of the Avant-Garde." *Critical Inquiry* 31 (4): 811–47.

Nielsen Holdings N.V. 2012. "Music Discovery Still Dominated by Radio, Says Nielsen Music 360 Report." Press release (August 14). http://www.nielsen.com/us/en/press-room/2012/music-discovery-still-dominated-by-radio-says-nielsen-music-360.html.

Noxon, Christopher. 2006. *Rejuvenile: Kickball, Cartoons, Cupcakes, and the Reinvention of the American Grown-Up*. New York: Three Rivers Press.

Oakley, Ann. 1993. "Women and Children First and Last: Parallels and Differences between Children's and Women's Studies." In *Childhood as a Social Phenomenon: Lessons from an International Project*, edited by Jens Qvortrup, pp. 51–69. Vienna: European Centre for Social Welfare Policy and Research.

O'Connor, Jane. 2008. *The Cultural Significance of the Child Star*. New York: Routledge.
Orenstein, Peggy. 2011. *Cinderella Ate My Daughter: Dispatches from the Front Lines of the New Girlie-Girl Culture*. New York: HarperCollins.
Ortner, Sherry B. 1972. "Is Female to Male as Nature Is to Culture?" *Feminist Studies* 1 (2): 5–31.
Pang, Kevin. 2006. "'Kidz Bop 10' Bopping Its Way to the Top of the Charts. 'Wooooh!'" *Chicago Tribune* (August 11). http://articles.chicagotribune.com/2006-08-11/features/0608100349_1_kidz-bop-new-york-city-label-sing-a-longs-and-lullabies.
Pecknold, Diane. 2011. "The Jonas Brothers Are Dorky and Miley Cyrus Is a Slut: Gender, Power, and Money in the Disney Ghetto." Paper presented at the EMP Pop Conference, New York, February 25.
Pecknold, Diane, ed. 2013. *Hidden in the Mix: The African American Presence in Country Music*. Durham, NC: Duke University Press.
Pecknold, Diane. 2016. "'Those Stupid Little Sounds in Her Voice': Valuing and Vilifying the New Girl Voice." In *Voicing Girlhood in Popular Music: Performance, Authority, Authenticity*, edited by Jacqueline Warwick and Allison Adrian, pp. 77–98. New York: Routledge.
Pecknold, Diane. 2017. "The Politics of Voice in Tween Girls' Music Criticism." *Jeunesse: Young People, Texts, Cultures* 9 (2): 69–90.
Pecora, Norma. 1998. *The Business of Children's Entertainment*. New York: Guilford Press.
Pederson, Erik. 2010. "How Teen Anger Turned to 'Love': Swift's Tantrum Led to Her Becoming Youngest BMI Song of Year Winner." *Hollywood Reporter* 414 (May 20), p. 7.
Pesce, Nicole Lyn. 2007. "Bite Me, Barbie! Disney's Hannah Montana Takes Over as Most Wanted Toy." *NY Daily News* (November 19). http://www.nydailynews.com/life-style/bite-barbie-disney-hannah-montana-takes-wanted-toy-article-1.256616.
Petridis, Alexis. 2010. Review of *Can't Be Tamed* by Miley Cyrus. *Guardian* (June 24). https://www.theguardian.com/culture/2010/jun/24/miley-cyrus-cant-be-tamed-review.
Petrusich, Amanda. 2015. "Free to Be Miley." *Paper* (June 9). http://www.papermag.com/free-to-be-miley-1427581961.html.
Pietroluongo, Swift. 2009. "Swift Swipes Audience Mark." *Billboard* 121 (August 15), p. 42.
Pittman, Frank. 1999. *Grow Up! How Taking Responsibility Can Make You a Happy Adult*. New York: St. Martin's Griffin.
Platon, Adelle. 2013. "Miley Cyrus Asked for a 'Black' Sound for Single, Says Songwriters Rock City." *Vibe* (June 12). http://www.vibe.com/article/miley-cyrus-asked-black-sound-single-says-songwriters-rock-city.
Plourde, Lorraine. 2018. "Babymetal and the Ambivalence of Cuteness." *International Journal of Cultural Studies* 21 (3): 293–307.

Pollock, Valerie. 2014. "Forever Adolescence: Taylor Swift, Eroticized Innocence, and Performing Normativity." MA thesis, Georgia State University.

Porterfield, Sally, Keith Polette, and Tita French Baumlin. 2009. *Perpetual Adolescence: Jungian Analyses of American Media, Literature, and Pop Culture*. Albany: State University of New York Press.

Postman, Neil. 1982. *The Disappearance of Childhood*. New York: Delacorte.

Powers, Ann. 2009. "Swift Reaction at MTV Video Music Awards." *Los Angeles Times* (September 14). https://web.archive.org/web/20090923184302/http://theenvelope.latimes.com/la-et-vma14-2009sep14,0,2035661.story.

Powers, Ann. 2014. "Taylor Swift Aims for Pop's Throne." NPR (August 20). http://www.npr.org/sections/therecord/2014/08/20/341702579/taylor-swift-aims-for-pops-throne.

Price, Deborah Evans. 2006. "Big Machine Gets Bigger: Taylor Swift Is Ambitious Nashville Upstart Label's Latest Success Story." *Billboard* 118 (October 28), p. 16.

Projansky, Sarah. 2007. "Mass Magazine Cover Girls: Some Reflections on Postfeminist Girls and Postfeminism's Daughters." In *Interrogating Postfeminism: Gender and the Politics of Popular Culture*, edited by Yvonne Tasker and Diane Negra, pp. 40–72. Durham, NC: Duke University Press.

Prout, Alan, and Allison James. 1997. "A New Paradigm for the Sociology of Childhood? Provenance, Promise, and Problems." In *Constructing and Reconstructing Childhood: Contemporary Issues in the Sociological Study of Childhood*, 2nd ed., edited by Allison James and Alan Prout, pp. 7–32. New York: Falmer Press.

Pugh, Allison J. 2009. *Longing and Belonging: Parents, Children, and Consumer Culture*. Berkeley: University of California Press.

Quemener, Tangi. 2008. "Miley Cyrus, America's Billion-Dollar Girl Sensation." *Agence France Presse* (April 27).

Qvortrup, Jens. 1994. "Childhood Matters: An Introduction." In *Childhood Matters: Social Theory, Practice, and Politics*, edited by Jens Qvortrup, Marjatta Bardy, Giovanni Sgritta, and Helmut Wintersberger, pp. 1–24. Aldershot, UK: Avebury.

Rackl, Lori. 2011. "Mother's Sacrifice Not Forgotten by Former Child Star." *Chicago Sun-Times* (October 17). http://www.suntimes.com/entertainment/television/8268770-421/mothers-sacrifice-not-forgotten-by-former-child-star.html.

Radway, Janice A. 1984. *Reading the Romance: Women, Patriarchy, and Popular Literature*. Chapel Hill: University of North Carolina Press.

Rayner, Ben. 2013. "The Prodigy vs. the Newbie: It's Justin Bieber against Carly Rae Jepsen, Who He Tweeted to Fame, at Sunday's Junos." *Toronto Star* (April 20), p. E1.

Razor & Tie Media. 2008. "Information for Parents." *KidzBop.com*. Accessed July 13, 2018. https://web.archive.org/web/20081207080648/http://www.kidzbop.com:80/parents/faq.

Razor & Tie Media. 2010. "Advertise with Us." *KidzBop.com*. Accessed May 27, 2010. https://web.archive.org/web/20130922120428/http://www.kidzbop.com/advertise-with-us.

Razor & Tie Media. 2012. "KIDZBOP 22 DEBUTS AT #3 ON BILLBOARD TOP 200 ALBUM CHART." *KidzBop.com* (July 25). https://web.archive.org/web/20121006053246/http://kidzbop.mediaroom.com/index.php?s=2429&item=122485.

Reed, Adolph, Jr. 2013a. "*Django Unchained*, or, *The Help*: How 'Cultural Politics' Is Worse Than No Politics at All, and Why." *Nonsite* 9 (Spring). http://nonsite.org/feature/django-unchained-or-the-help-how-cultural-politics-is-worse-than-no-politics-at-all-and-why.

Reed, Adolph, Jr. 2013b. "Marx, Race, and Neoliberalism." *New Labor Forum* 22 (1): 49–57.

Rhodes, Joe. 1990. "A Little Minnie Music. Christa Larson: Future Star—In the Studio with Walt Disney Records First Artist." *Entertainment Weekly* (August 31). http://www.ew.com/article/1990/08/31/christa-larson-future-star.

Richmond, Ray. 1996. "Disney Channel Surfs for Niche, Not Nick." *Variety* (June 24), p. 21.

Richmond, Ray. 1997. "Mouse Builds Basics." *Variety* (February 3), p. 23.

Rosen, Jody. 2008. "Country's Most Precocious Teen Princess Lets the World Read Her Diary." *Rolling Stone* 1065 (November 13), pp. 89–90.

Rosen, Jody. 2013. "Platinum Underdog: Why Taylor Swift Is the Biggest Pop Star in the World." *Vulture* (November 17). http://www.vulture.com/2013/11/taylor-swift-reigning-queen-of-pop.html.

Rosenfeld, Michael J. 2007. *The Age of Independence: Interracial Unions, Same-Sex Unions, and the Changing American Family*. Cambridge, MA: Harvard University Press.

Rossie, Amanda. 2014. "New Media, New Maternities: Representations of Maternal Femininity in Postfeminist Popular Culture." PhD dissertation, Ohio State University.

Rousseau, Jean-Jacques. [1762] 1979. *Emile: or, On Education*. Translated by Allan Bloom. New York: Basic Books.

Rowe, Kathleen. 2011. *The Unruly Woman: Gender and the Genres of Laughter*. Austin: University of Texas Press.

Ryan, Patrick, and Brian Mansfield. 2014. "Taylor Swift Shakes Off Country with First Pop Album." *USA Today* (August 18). http://www.usatoday.com/story/life/music/2014/08/18/taylor-swift-shakes-off-country-with-first-pop-album-1989/14256849/.

Rys, Richard. 2008. "Exit Interview: Taylor Swift." *Philadelphia Magazine* (October 21). http://www.phillymag.com/articles/exit-interview-taylor-swift/.

Ryzik, Melena. 2014. "The Nominees Are Blockbusters: Oscar-Nominated Songs with Familiar Composers." *New York Times* (February 19). http://www.nytimes.com/2014/02/20/movies/awardsseason/oscar-nominated-songs-with-familiar-composers.html.

Sales, Nancy Jo. 2013. "Taylor Swift's Telltale Heart." *Vanity Fair* 55 (April). https://www.vanityfair.com/hollywood/2013/04/taylor-swift-cover-story.

Salvato, Nick. 2009. "Out of Hand: YouTube Amateurs and Professionals." *TDR/The Drama Review* 53 (3): 67–83.

Sammond, Nicholas. 2005. *Babes in Tomorrowland: Walt Disney and the Making of the American Child, 1930–1960*. Durham, NC: Duke University Press.

Sammond, Nicholas. 2015. *Birth of an Industry: Blackface Minstrelsy and the Rise of American Animation*. Durham, NC: Duke University Press.

Samuelson, Robert J. 2003. "Adventures in Agelessness." *Newsweek* (November 3), p. 47.

Sawdey, Evan. 2010. Review of *Can't Be Tamed* by Miley Cyrus. *Pop Matters* (July 15). http://www.popmatters.com/review/128152-miley-cyrus-cant-be-tamed/.

Schor, Juliet B. 2004. *Born to Buy: The Commercialized Child and the New Consumer Culture*. New York: Scribner.

Scott, A. O. 2002. "It's a Joy Ride, and the Kids Are Driving." *New York Times* (August 11), p. AR11.

Scott, A. O. 2014. "The Post-Man: Charting the Final, Exhausted Collapse of the Adult White Male, from Huck Finn to 'Mad Men.'" *New York Times Magazine* (September 11), pp. 38–41, 60.

Seiter, Ellen. 1993. *Sold Separately: Children and Parents in Consumer Culture*. New Brunswick, NJ: Rutgers University Press.

Sheffield, Rob. 2010. "America's Sweetheart Edges toward Adulthood on Her Best Disc Yet." *Rolling Stone* 1117 (November 11), pp. 69–70.

Sicha, Choire. 2009. "Leave Kanye Alone." *Daily Beast* (September 14). http://www.thedailybeast.com/articles/2009/09/14/team-kanye.html.

Silverman, Linda Kreger, and Nancy B. Miller. 2009. "A Feminine Perspective of Giftedness." In *International Handbook on Giftedness*, edited by Larisa V. Shavinina, pp. 99–128. New York: Springer.

Sisario, Ben. 2006. "A Musical for Tweens Captures Its Audience." *New York Times* (February 8), pp. E1, E3.

Slaughter, Anne-Marie. 2012. "Why Women Still Can't Have It All." *Atlantic Monthly* 310 (July/August): 84–102.

Smith, Brian Bowen. 2010. "Miley Cyrus's Stylist Dishes on Her Racy 'Can't Be Tamed' Album Cover." *People* (June 22). http://people.com/style/miley-cyruss-stylist-dishes-on-her-racy-cant-be-tamed-album-cover/.

Smith, Darron T. 2014. "The Transformation of Justin Bieber from a White Youth to a Black Man." *Huffington Post* (October 2). http://www.huffingtonpost.com/darron-t-smith-phd/the-transformation-of-jus_b_5900958.html.

Smolko, Joanna R. 2012. "Southern Fried Foster: Representing Race and Place through Music in Looney Tunes Cartoons." *American Music* 30 (3): 344–72.

Sørenssen, Ingvild Kvale. 2014. "Domesticating the Disney Tween Machine: Norwegian Tweens Enacting Age and Everyday Life." PhD dissertation, Norwegian University of Science and Technology.

Sørenssen, Ingvild Kvale. 2016. "Consuming Disney Channel: An Actor-Network Perspective." *Young Consumers* 17 (4): 363–75.

Spigel, Lynn. 1992. *Make Room for TV: Television and the Family Ideal in Postwar America*. Chicago: University of Chicago Press.

Spigel, Lynn. 1993. "Seducing the Innocent: Childhood and Television in Postwar America." In *Ruthless Criticism: New Perspectives in U.S. Communication History*, edited by William S. Solomon and Robert W. McChesney, pp. 259–83. Minneapolis: University of Minnesota Press.

Stedman, Alex. 2014. "'Frozen' Becomes the Highest-Grossing Animated Film Ever." *Variety* (March 30). http://variety.com/2014/film/news/frozen-becomes-the-highest-grossing-animated-film-ever-1201150128/.

Stephens, Sharon. 1995. "Children and the Politics of Culture in 'Late Capitalism.'" In *Children and the Politics of Culture*, edited by Sharon Stephens, pp. 3–48. Princeton, NJ: Princeton University Press.

Stern, Mike. 2013. "The Kids Are All Right: Why Former Disney and Nickelodeon Stars Are Winning at Radio, Charts." *Billboard* 125 (June 22), p. 25.

Sterngold, James. 1997. "After 14 Years, One Network for Children Refocuses . . ." *New York Times* (July 27), p. H28.

Stewart, Andrew. 2014. "'Frozen' Reaches $1.219 Bil to Become Fifth-Highest Grossing Film Globally." *Variety* (May 25). http://variety.com/2014/film/news/frozen-reaches-1-219-bil-to-become-fifth-highest-grossing-film-globally-1201192156/.

Stimeling, Travis. 2016. "Taylor Swift's 'Pitch Problem' and the Place of Adolescent Girls in Country Music." In *Country Boys and Redneck Girls: New Essays in Gender and Country Music*, edited by Diane Pecknold and Kristine M. McCusker, pp. 84–101. Jackson: University Press of Mississippi.

Strangelove, Michael. 2011. *Watching YouTube: Extraordinary Videos by Ordinary People*. Toronto: University of Toronto Press.

Sutton, Lisa. 2001. "Snap, Crackle, Rock & Roll: Cereal Box Records." In *Bubblegum Music Is the Naked Truth*, edited by Kim Cooper and David Smay, pp. 289–90. Los Angeles: Feral House.

Sutton-Smith, Brian. 1997. *The Ambiguity of Play*. Cambridge, MA: Harvard University Press.

Telotte, J. P. 2004. *Disney TV*. Detroit, MI: Wayne State University Press.

Thompson, Helen. 2009. "The Personal Is Political: Domesticity's Domestic Contents." *Eighteenth Century* 50 (4): 355–70.

Thorne, Barrie, and Zella Luria. 1986. "Sexuality and Gender in Children's Daily Worlds." *Social Problems* 33 (3): 176–90.

Tillson, Diana R. 1995. "The Golden Age of Children's Records." *Antique Phonograph News* (March–April): 3–6, 12.

Tirella, Joseph V. 2008. "Miley Cyrus: The Billion Dollar Girl." *Condé Nast Portfolio* (February 7). http://upstart.bizjournals.com/culture-lifestyle/culture-inc/arts/2008/02/07/Hannah-Montanas-Earning-Potential.html.

Tobin, Joseph J., ed. 2004. *Pikachu's Global Adventure: The Rise and Fall of Pokémon*. Durham, NC: Duke University Press.

Tolentino, Jia. 2015. "The Kidz Bop Is All Right: A Night Alone with America's Shrillest Pop Franchise." *Jezebel* (October 21). http://jezebel.com/the-kidz-bop-is-all-right-a-night-alone-with-americas-1737540112.

Tongson, Karen. 2015. "Empty Orchestra: The Karaoke Standard and Pop Celebrity." *Public Culture* 27 (1): 85–108.

Tucker, Ken. 2008a. "Taylor Swift Goes Global: With the Release of 'Fearless,' Swift Unveils a Plan to Introduce the World to Country Music." *Billboard* 120 (October 25), p. 22.

Tucker, Ken. 2008b. "Taylor Swift's 'Fearless' Follow-Up Album." NPR (December 4). http://www.npr.org/2008/12/04/97800838/taylor-swifts-fearless-follow-up-album.

Tucker, Ken. 2012. "Taylor Swift Leaps into Pop with 'Red.'" NPR (November 5). http://www.npr.org/2012/11/05/164340690/taylor-swift-leaps-into-pop-with-red.

Turner, Sarah E. 2014. "BBFFs: Interracial Friendships in a Post-Racial World." In *The Colorblind Screen: Television in Post-Racial America*, edited by Sarah Nilsen and Sarah E. Turner, pp. 237–57. New York: New York University Press.

Umstead, R. Thomas. 2001. "Disney Bounces Videos, Concerts from Schedule." *Multichannel News* (June 24). http://www.multichannel.com/news/orphan-articles/disney-bounces-videos-concerts-schedule/131915.

Underhill, Paco. 2009. *Why We Buy: The Science of Shopping—Updated and Revised for the Internet, the Global Consumer, and Beyond*. New York: Simon and Schuster.

Unterberger, Andrew. 2013. "Miley Cyrus' 'Can't Be Tamed' Revisited: Why Her First Rebellion Didn't Work." *Billboard* (October 3). http://www.billboard.com/articles/columns/pop-shop/5747935/miley-cyrus-cant-be-tamed-revisited-why-her-first-rebellion-didnt.

Valdivia, Angharad N. 2008. "Mixed Race on the Disney Channel: From Johnny Tsunami through Lizzie McGuire and Ending with the Cheetah Girls." In *Mixed Race Hollywood*, edited by Mary Beltrán and Camilla Fojas, pp. 269–89. New York: New York University Press.

Varenne, Hervé, and Ray McDermott. 1998. *Successful Failure: The School America Builds*. Boulder, CO: Westview Press.

Vena, Jocelyn. 2010a. "Justin Bieber Is a 'Prodigy,' Usher Says." MTV News (March 26). http://www.mtv.com/news/articles/1634785/justin-bieber-prodigy-usher.jhtml.

Vena, Jocelyn. 2010b. "Justin Bieber 3-D Movie Is 'a Story for Our Time,' Director Says." MTV News (August 19). http://www.mtv.com/news/articles/1646083/justin-bieber-3-d-movie-story-our-time-director.jhtml.

Vena, Jocelyn. 2010c. "Justin Bieber's 'Never Say Never' Director Explains Movie's Plot." MTV News (October 26). http://www.mtv.com/news/articles/1650810/justin-biebers-never-never-director-explains-movies-plot.jhtml.

Vena, Jocelyn. 2010d. "Taylor Swift Lashes Out at Her Critics on 'Mean.'" MTV News (October 19). http://www.mtv.com/news/1650286/taylor-swift-lashes-out-at-her-critics-on-mean/.

Vena, Jocelyn. 2013. "Miley Cyrus Added 'Swag' to 'We Can't Stop' after Rihanna Passed." *MTV News* (June 10). http://www.mtv.com/news/1708756/miley-cyrus-we-cant-stop-rihanna-mike-will-made-it/.
Vozick-Levinson, Simon. 2009. "Kanye West and Taylor Swift: Why Do People Care So Much about This Story?" *Entertainment Weekly* (September 15). http://ew.com/article/2009/09/15/kanye-west-taylor-swift-why/.
Warner, Kara. 2010. "Justin Bieber Gives Fans a Chance to Be in His 3-D Movie." *MTV News* (August 24). http://www.mtv.com/news/articles/1646427/justin-bieber-gives-fans-chance-be-his-3-d-movie.jhtml.
Warner, Michael. 2002. *Publics and Counterpublics*. New York: Zone Books.
Wartella, Ellen, and Sharon Mazzarella. 1990. "A Historical Comparison of Children's Use of Leisure Time." In *For Fun and Profit: The Transformation of Leisure into Consumption*, edited by Richard Butsch, pp. 173-94. Philadelphia: Temple University Press.
Warwick, Jacqueline. 2007. *Girl Groups, Girl Culture: Popular Music and Identity in the 1960s*. New York: Routledge.
Wasko, Janet, Mark Phillips, and Eileen R. Meehan, eds. 2001. *Dazzled by Disney? The Global Disney Audiences Project*. London: Leicester University Press.
Weikle-Mills, Courtney A. 2008. "'Learn to Love Your Book': The Child Reader and Affectionate Citizenship." *Early American Literature* 43 (1): 35-61.
Weikle-Mills, Courtney A. 2013. *Imaginary Citizens: Child Readers and the Limits of American Independence, 1640-1868*. Baltimore, MD: Johns Hopkins University Press.
Weisbard, Eric. 2014. *Top 40 Democracy: The Rival Mainstreams of American Music*. Chicago: University of Chicago Press. Kindle edition.
Werde, Bill. 2006. "Lessons Learned: Disney's 'High School Musical' Mega-Phenomenon." *Billboard* 118 (December 23), p. 12.
West, Diana. 2008. *The Death of the Grown-Up: How America's Arrested Development Is Bringing Down Western Civilization*. New York: St. Martin's Griffin.
Whiteley, Sheila. 2005. *Too Much Too Young: Popular Music, Age, and Gender*. New York: Routledge.
Widdicombe, Lizzie. 2012. "Teen Titan: The Man Who Made Justin Bieber." *New Yorker* 88 (September 3), p. 48.
Wiegman, Robyn. 1993. "The Anatomy of Lynching." *Journal of the History of Sexuality* 3 (3): 445-67.
Willett, Rebekah. 2011. "An Ethnographic Study of Preteen Girls' Play with Popular Music on a School Playground." *Journal of Children and Media* 5 (4): 341-57.
Williams, Chris. 2009. Review of "You Belong with Me" by Taylor Swift. *Billboard* 121 (May 2), p. 30.
Willis, Ellen. 2006. "Escape from Freedom: What's the Matter with Tom Frank (and the Lefties Who Love Him)?" *Situations: Project of the Radical Imagination* 1 (2): 5-20.
Willis, Ellen. [1970] 2014. "Women and the Myth of Consumerism." In *The Essential Ellen Willis*, edited by Nona Willis Aronowitz. Minneapolis: University of Minnesota Press. Kindle edition.

Willman, Chris. 2006. "Surprise! Albums for Kids Dominate the Chart." *Entertainment Weekly* (March 4). http://www.ew.com/article/2006/03/04/surprise-albums-kids-dominate-chart.

Willman, Chris. 2010. Review of *Speak Now* by Taylor Swift. *Hollywood Reporter* (October 19). http://www.hollywoodreporter.com/review/taylor-swift-speak-album-31396.

Wood, Mikael. 2009. Review of *Music from the 3D Concert Experience* by the Jonas Brothers. *Billboard* 121 (February 28), p. 33.

Wordsworth, William. [1807] 1992. "Ode: Intimations of Immortality from Recollections of Early Childhood." In *Wordsworth: Selected Poetry*, edited by Nicholas Roe, pp. 207–13. New York: Penguin.

Wullschläger, Jackie. 2001. *Inventing Wonderland: The Lives of Lewis Carroll, Edward Lear, J. M. Barrie, Kenneth Grahame, and A. A. Milne*, rev. ed. London: Methuen.

Yano, Christine R. 2013. *Pink Globalization: Hello Kitty's Trek across the Pacific*. Durham, NC: Duke University Press.

Youth Liberation of Ann Arbor. 1972. *Youth Liberation: News, Politics and Survival Information*. Washington, NY: Times Change Press.

Zelizer, Viviana A. 1985. *Pricing the Priceless Child: The Changing Social Value of Children*. Princeton, NJ: Princeton University Press.

Zelizer, Viviana A. 2009. *The Purchase of Intimacy*. Princeton, NJ: Princeton University Press.

Zimmerman, Kevin. 1992. "Baby Boomers Nurture Growth in Kiddie Labels." *Variety* (July 27), p. 64.

Zimmerman, Kevin. 1994. "Special Report: PBS 25th Anniversary: Making Room for Quality Time." *Variety* (March 14), p. 31.

Zuckerman, Esther. 2013. "Explaining Five Songs from 'Frozen.'" *Wire* (November 26). http://www.thewire.com/entertainment/2013/11/explaining-five-songs-frozen/355512/.

INDEX

Adorno, Theodor, 10
adulthood, infantilization of, 10–14, 188n9
adultification, 27–28
affectionate citizenship, 188n7
age compression, 15–18; causes of, 189n12; as discourse of precocity, 149; and Disney's early tween music, 63; and *High School Musical* audience, 16, 188n11; implications for Black girls, 27–28; and Top 40 on kids' media outlets, 66, 68
Aguilera, Christina, 169
Allen, Harry, 126
All-New Mickey Mouse Club, The (MMC), 63–65, 82
Ally McBeal, 93, 94, 192n4
Anderson, Benedict, 28–29
Anderson, Kurt, 12
Angelou, Maya, 12
Anne of Green Gables series (Montgomery), 104, 193n8 (chap. 3)
anti-adult themes, 31, 68, 86

B5, 195n6
Baker, Sarah, 44
Banet-Weiser, Sarah, 23, 79, 106, 165
Bangerz (Cyrus), 110, 112, 113, 116, 117–18, 139
Barber, Benjamin, 12–13, 22

Beatlemania, 20–21, 32, 47, 48
bedroom culture, 164, 165
Bell, Drake, 76, 84
Berlant, Lauren: on gender and identity politics, 33; on infantilization of public culture, 11–12, 14; on intimate public, 28, 122; production of intimate public femininity, 92; on race and women's genres, 135, 136
Bernstein, Robin, 27, 120, 138
Bessolo, Mike, 66
Beyoncé, 125
Bieber, Justin: adult career of, 108; discovery of, 140, 194n1 (chap. 5); infantilization of, 137, 153–56; Mindless Behavior as contrast to, 181–82; portrayal of, as child celebrity, 140–41; portrayed as prodigy, 144, 147–49, 156–59, 164, 166; radio airplay for, 54, 82, 190n9; tween solidarity, display of, 168–69, 171–72. See also *Never Say Never*
Big Time Rush, 76
Birth of a Nation, 134–35
Black artists, emergence of, in tween music, 179–83
Black children, innocence as not historically granted to, 27, 110, 118, 138
Black girls, adultification of, 27–28
Blacking, John, 146

Blackness: Bieber's puerility and embracing of tropes of, 142–44; and Cyrus's rejection of childhood innocence, 88, 109–18, 138–39; representations of, in Swift's work, 118–19, 123–24, 132–33, 139, 193n5; and sexuality, 110–13, 116–17, 118–19, 132, 184–85, 193n2
Blake, Jamilia, 27–28
Bleu, Corbin, 180
Blue, Morgan, 91, 101, 104, 109, 115
Bly, Robert, 12
bodily functions, and gross-out humor, 25–26
"book-and-tape" read-alongs, 59
Borchetta, Scott, 120
boyd, danah, 165
Bradby, Barbara, 122
Brand, Russell, 169–72
Braun, Scooter, 152, 154, 155, 157, 158, 159–60
Breihan, Tom, 123
Bridget Jones's Diary, 93
Brown, Robert, 17, 189n12
Brown, Ruth Nicole, 27
Brownlee, Sophia Grace, 183–85
Buckingham, David, 16, 18
buffoon archetype, 102
Bunch, Ryan, 178
Butler, Judith, 34

Caddie Woodlawn syndrome, 24
Cahn, Alice, 56
Camp Rock, 70
"Can't Be Tamed" (Cyrus), 109
Can't Be Tamed (Cyrus), 109–10, 117–18
Caramanica, Jon, 132
cartoons, and merchandising, 71–73
Cavallo, Bob, 70, 83
Cecire, Natalia, 25, 142, 188n10
Chasez, JC, 63
Cheetah Girls, The, 23, 78–79, 81, 180
childhood: co-construction of femininity and, 24–25; as cultural identity, 5–6, 188n7; digital media adapted to cultural norms of, 18; gender and innocence in, 142–44; and identity politics, 32–35; privatization and sacralization of, 30, 91–92; as public entity, 30–31, 172; race as key factor in cultural constructions of, 27–28, 118–34
childishness, 25–27; elements of, in Swift and Bieber, 137; mainstreaming of, 183–85; markers of, removed from tween music, 52–53. *See also* infantilization; puerility
child labor, 6–7
children: and age compression, 15; commercials and participation of, in public culture, 46–52; Cyrus on, 193n9; disempowerment of eighteenth- and nineteenth-century, 187n3; and identity politics, 32–35; Kidz Bop and participation of, in public culture, 45–46; live pop-oriented shows for, 190n6; marginalization of, 46; shift in relationship between pop music and, 183–85; as singers in Kidz Bop recordings, 53–55, 174–77, 190n7; status of, in twentieth-century public culture, 6–9; as wage laborers, 6–7
children's media and music: and age compression, 15–18; as central part of children's cultural life, 2–3; and children's relationship to mainstream public culture, 5–6; Disney as key figure in, 56–57; history of, 2–4; and infantilization of public culture, 10; markers of childishness removed from, 52–53; multiculturalism in, 179–83; music integrated into, 80–81; as pop music format, 4; popularity and visibility of, 4; tension between "mainstream" music and, 86, 87. *See also* Disney Channel; Nickelodeon; tween pop / music industry
Chu, John, 159, 163
Ciara, 42
Clarkson, Kelly: Kidz Bop video for "Since U Been Gone," 36–37, 42–46, 50, 53
Coates, Norma, 20
Coleman, Monique, 180
commercials, and children's participation in public culture, 46–52
consumer culture and industries: children in twentieth-century, 7–8, 9; tweens in, 21–28, 47–48

222 ☆ Index

consumption: of children as familial problem, 100; and "having it all" in *Hannah Montana*, 95–97; and intimate friendship in *Hannah Montana*, 100, 101
Cook, Daniel Thomas, 4–5, 7, 22, 23–24, 47, 87
Cooper, Wilbert, 117
Cosgrove, Miranda, 76, 168–69, 171–72
Cottom, Tressie McMillan, 112, 117
Coulter, Natalie, 20, 47–48
counterpublic, 31, 68, 86
Country Music Television (CMT) Awards (2009), 123–24
Crawford, Chace, 169
Cross, Gary, 188n9
crossing over, 85
Cyrus, Miley: adult career of, 108; Bieber's portrayal as child celebrity versus, 140–41, 142; breaks from past with Disney, 109–10, 116, 117; on children, 193n9; Disney records released by, 70; mainstream success of, 83–84, 88; music of, coded as "children's music," 79–80; poses racial Blackness in rejection of childhood innocence, 88, 109–18, 138–39; race made visible in transitional moments of, 107; radio airplay for, 54, 82; scandalous behavior of, 87–89, 108. See also *Hannah Montana*

Danesi, Marcel, 12
Davis, Rich, 79–80
Dean, Josh, 176, 177
DeGeneres, Ellen, 183–84
Differentiated Model of Giftedness and Talent (DMGT), 144–46
Disney: and age compression, 15–16; Cyrus breaks from past with, 109–10, 116, 117; *Frozen*, 177–79; history of changing relationship to pop music, 58–70; Hollywood Records, 65, 70, 191n5; as key figure in children's music, 56–57; Music Box Artists Series, 60–62; pop music developed by, 77–86; and tween pop in mainstream, 19; Walt Disney Records, 59–65, 70, 191n5

Disney Channel: aspirational business plan of, 87; and childhood as intimate public, 31–32; gendering of, 84, 85–86; integrates pop music into programming, 70–71, 75–76, 87; and original pop music for kids, 68–70; pop musical programming on Nickelodeon versus, 191n6; pop music and success of, 56–57; pop music developed by, 77–86; and racialization and gendering of tween category, 22–23; racially diverse casting on, 106, 180–81, 194n5 (conc.); rebranding of, 190n1; Top 40 pop on, 66–68. See also *Hannah Montana*; *High School Musical*
Disney XD, 84
diversity: in Disney Channel casting, 106, 180–81, 194n5 (conc.); and racialization of tween category, 22–23; in tween media, 179–83. See also Blackness; race; whiteness
Dole, Carol, 105
Dorrell, Torrie, 59, 60, 62, 63–65, 191n2
double address, 19
double-coding, 69
double motion, 58
Dow, Bonnie J., 93
Doyle, Sady, 119
Driscoll, Catherine, 24
Duane, Anna Mae, 138
Dubrofsky, Rachel, 132–33
Duff, Hilary, 4, 54, 68, 70, 82. See also *Lizzie McGuire*
Duggan, Ervin, 73

Eells, Josh, 113
Efron, Zac, 83, 169
Ehrenreich, Barbara, 20–21, 32
Ellen DeGeneres Show, The, 183–84
embodiment, in popular music performance, 148
Epstein, Joseph, 12
Epstein, Rebecca, 27–28

Fearless (Swift), 121, 122, 123, 125, 139
Feld, Steven, 146–47

femininity, co-construction of childhood and, 24–25

feminism: and gendering of tween category, 23; and "having it all," 90–91; and infantilization of public culture, 13–14. *See also* postfeminism

Field, Corinne, 10

"Fifteen" (Swift), 121–23

Fleeger, Jennifer, 178

Foote, Norman, 60–61

formats, radio, 84–86

Foster, Stephen, 138

Fox, Aaron, 116

Frank, Betsy, 15

Fraser, Nancy, 34

Frere-Jones, Sasha, 144

friendship: and "having it all" in *Hannah Montana*, 97–103; implications of emphasis on, in TV shows, 192n3

Frith, Simon, 29–30, 48, 53, 148

Frozen, 177–79

"Fuego" (Cheetah Girls), 78

Gagné, Françoys, 144–46

Gaunt, Kyra, 28, 112

gender: and bedroom culture, 164, 165; and Bieber's portrayal as child celebrity, 140–41, 142–44; and Disney Channel audience, 84, 85–86; and "having it all," 90–91; and identity politics, 33; and performative femininity of Lilly in *Hannah Montana*, 101–2; and popular music production and consumption, 44–45, 48–49; and social and cultural markers of tweens, 21–27

genres, 84–85

Genz, Stéphanie, 93–94, 104

Gerhard, Jane, 94

giftedness, 144–47, 158

Gill, Rosalind, 101

Girls, 192n4

Goff, Phillip, 27

Gomez, Selena, 70, 76, 180, 181

González, Thalia, 27–28

Good, Ryan, 152

Graham, Stephen, 143

Grande, Ariana, 76

Green, Lucy, 44

gross-out humor, 25–26

Gubar, Marah, 96, 104

Halberstam, Jack, 104–5, 163

Hamilton, Kenny, 152, 160–61

Hannah Montana: and age compression, 16; "having it all" formula in, 90–93, 95, 96–97, 103–5; and integration of pop music into television, 74–75; intimate friendship in, 97–103; investments in whiteness in, 115–16, 139; issues of childhood and public participation in, 80; nonwhite characters in, 106; success and impact of, 89–90; success of soundtrack, 57, 89; tension between public and private life in, 89, 90–93, 95, 96–97; and trope of children's fantastical public music consumption, 51–52

Harrison, Robert Pogue, 188n9

"having it all": in *Hannah Montana*, 90–93, 97–105; tweens and, 96–97; in women's media, 93–95, 192n4

Henley, Nancy, 26

Hess, Elizabeth, 20–21

Hey, Valerie, 99

High School Musical: and age compression, 16, 188n11; contextualized musical performances in, 81; and explosion of tween music industry, 167; issues of childhood and public participation in, 80; mainstream success of stars of, 83; and multiculturalism in tween media, 23, 180, 195n6; music of, coded as "children's music," 79–80; success of soundtrack, 4, 57

High School Musical 2, 1, 4

Hollywood Records, 65, 70, 191n5

hooks, bell, 112–13

Hudgens, Vanessa, 83, 108, 180

identity politics, 32–35

If the Shoe Fits (Foote), 60–61

infantile citizenship, 188n7

infantilization: emergence of, 187n5; of Justin Bieber, 137, 153–56; of pop music, 24; of public culture, 9–14, 188n9. *See also* childishness; puerility

innocence: appropriation of Blackness in Cyrus's rejection of, 88, 109–18, 138–39; Black popular culture, compatibility with, 184–85; construction of, as emptiness, 137–38; eroticization of, 137; gender and race and childhood, 142–44; Swift's entangled investments in whiteness and, 118–34, 193n5; valorization of, 137; whiteness and construction of, 27–28, 106–8, 134–39, 180; withheld from Black children, 27, 110, 118

"Innocent" (Swift), 127, 128–29

internet: adapted to cultural norms of childhood, 18; as key figure in *Never Say Never*, 159. *See also* YouTube

intimate public, 28–32, 122–23, 172

Jacobs, Gloria, 20–21
Jaffe, Mark, 59, 63
James, Robin, 133
Japanese popular culture, 18, 184, 195n9
Jem and the Holograms, 72, 74
Jenkins, Henry, 8, 165
John, Elton, 178
Jonas Brothers: and age compression, 16; contextualized musical performances of, 81; Disney records released by, 70; introduction of, 57; mainstream success of, 83; music of, coded as "children's music," 79–80; tween solidarity in support of, 169–72
Jones, Abigail, 189n13
Jones, Coco, 181

Kaiser, Susan, 4–5, 22, 23–24, 47, 87
Kaluli, 145–47
Kaye, Allison, 152, 161
Kearney, Mary Celeste, 46, 165
Kelland, Regina, 82
Kennedy, Melanie, 192n2

"kids getting older younger" (KGOY). *See* age compression

kids' pop format, 85

Kidz Bop: changes model, 174–77, 190n7; child voices, use of, 53–55, 174–77, 190n7; inauguration of series, 189n1; lyrics of, 42, 189n2, 194n4 (conc.); markers of childishness removed from, 52–53; *More Kidz Bop*, 189n1; and popularity and visibility of children's music, 4; quality of songs produced by, 53, 190n7; success of, 41–42; video for Clarkson's "Since U Been Gone," 36–37, 42–46, 50, 53

KidzBop.com, 46, 174–75, 176
Kiley, Dan, 188n8
Kincaid, James, 137, 138
Korean popular culture, 184, 195n9

Lambert, Miranda, 114–15, 120
Langer, Beryl, 22
Larson, Christa, 61–63
Laybourne, Geraldine, 71–72
Lee, Carol, 66
"Let It Go," 178
Let It Shine, 181
Lion King, The, 178
Lizzie McGuire, 70, 74
Lohan, Lindsay, 107–8
Lovato, Demi, 70, 108, 178, 180, 181, 190n9
"Love Story" (Swift), 129

MacLeod, Anne Scott, 24
Madison Square Garden, 156–59
Madonna, 113, 156
Marsh, Kathryn, 146
McClain, China, 181
McClelland, Rosie, 183–85
McCormick, Moira, 191n2
McDermott, Ray, 146
McGillis, Roderick, 25
McNutt, Myles, 194n4 (conc.)
McPherson, Gary, 146
McRobbie, Angela, 23, 48
"Mean" (Swift), 127–29

Menzel, Idina, 178
merchandising, 71–75, 191n6
Miller, Cymphonique, 181
Miller, Nancy B., 146
Minaj, Nicki, 183–84, 193n5
Mindless Behavior, 181–82
Minks, Amanda, 44
Minnie 'n Me (Larson), 62–63
MMC, 63–65, 82
Montgomery, Kathryn, 18
More Kidz Bop, 189n1
Morris, Carin, 152
Morris, Monique, 27
Moseley, Rachel, 93
"Mrs. Right" (Mindless Behavior), 182
MTV Video Music Awards (2008), 169–72
MTV Video Music Awards (2009), 125–27, 134–35, 168–69, 171–72
MTV Video Music Awards (2013), 110–17, 139
Murphy Brown, 93
Music Box Artists Series, 60–62

Naked Brothers Band, 76, 84
Nash, Ilana, 21, 25, 32
Neal, Mark Anthony, 143
"Never Grow Up" (Swift), 127
Never Say Never: Bieber's commercial achievement framed in terms of prodigy in, 141–42, 156–59; domestication of commercial and public spaces in, 151–53, 164–66; infantilization of Bieber in, 153–56; narrative strands in, 149–51; puerility of Bieber in, 142; and trope of children's fantastical public music consumption, 51; YouTube as mediator between public and private in, 159–64
New Kids on the Block, 72, 74
Nickelodeon: and age compression, 17–18; and childhood as intimate public, 31–32; and commercial pressure to produce cartoons, 72–73; pop musical programming on, 191n6; and racialization and gendering of tween category, 23; strategy of Disney Channel versus, 58, 68, 86; and trope of children's fantastical public music consumption, 49–50, 52; turns to musical programming, 76
Nickelodeon Nation, 49–50, 52
1989 (Swift), 131–32
Noxon, Christopher, 12

"One Time" (Bieber), 160, 161
"1, 2 Step" (Ciara), 42
ordinariness, performative, 54–55
"Our Song" (Swift), 121

Palin, Sarah, 170
Parton, Dolly, 115, 190n9
paternalism, in *Never Say Never*, 153–56
PBS, 73
Pecknold, Diane, 46, 54
Pecora, Norma, 71–72
performative ordinariness, 54–55
Perry, Katy, 184
Phillips, Randy, 156–57
Pierce, David, 191n3
Pittman, Frank, 12
Pokémon, 18
pop music: and age compression, 15–16; children as audience of, 3–4; developed by Disney, 77–86; Disney Channel and original, for kids, 68–70; on Disney Channel versus Nickelodeon, 191n6; feminization and infantilization of, 24; gendered roles in production and consumption of, 44–45; history of Disney's changing relationship to, 58–70; integrated into kids' television, 70–77; made "safe" by Kidz Bop, 41–42; preadolescent girls, as audience of, 20–21; and public intimacy, 29–30; shift in children's relationship to, 183–85; and success of Disney Channel, 56–57; tween pop in mainstream of, 19–20. *See also* children's media and music; Top 40 pop; tween pop / music industry
postfeminism, 23, 91, 93–95, 97, 99, 101, 103. *See also* feminism
Postman, Neil, 11–12, 13, 14, 188n6
Pritchard, Steven, 56

prodigy, 144-49, 156-59, 164, 166
Projansky, Sarah, 192n4
promise rings, 169-71, 194n3 (conc.)
public culture and spaces: children's music and children's relationship to mainstream, 5-6; commercials and children's participation in, 46-52; domestication of, 164-66; infantilization of, 9-14, 188n9; Kidz Bop and children's participation in, 45-46; status of children in twentieth-century, 6-9; tween pop staged as social and political provocation within, 168-72
public intimacy, 28-32, 122-23, 172
publics, 28-29
puerility, 25-27, 142-43, 188nn9-10. *See also* childishness; infantilization
Pugh, Allison, 9, 100
Pussycat Dolls, The, 78-79

race: and Cyrus's rejection of childhood innocence, 88, 109-18, 138-39; and Disney Channel casting, 79, 106, 180-81, 194n5 (conc.); and gendered childhood innocence, 142-44; as key factor in cultural constructions of childhood, 27-28; and multiculturalism in tween media, 179-83; and sexuality, 110-13, 116-17, 118-19, 132, 184-85, 193n2; and Swift's entangled investments in innocence and whiteness, 118-34; and transitional moments of tween stars, 107; and tween solidarity, 168-69, 171-72; and voicing of women's genres as children's genres, 135-36. *See also* Blackness; diversity; whiteness
radio airplay: for children, tweens, and teens, 54, 60, 64-67, 82-83, 190n9; for Justin Bieber, 149, 160-61
Radio Disney, 65-66, 85
Radio Disney Jams, 65-66
Radio Disney Jams 2, 66
radio formats, 84-86
Raffi, 59, 63, 82
Raven-Symoné, 78, 180, 195n5
Read, Jacinda, 93

read-alongs, "book-and-tape," 59
Red (Swift), 129-31
Reid, LA, 157, 161
Rosenfeld, Michael J., 192n4
Ross, Rich, 56, 57, 68, 69
Rousseau, Jean-Jacques, 8
Rowe, Kathleen, 25-26
Russell, Keri, 63

safety: and marketing of Kidz Bop, 41-42; and pop music developed by Disney, 77, 78-79, 81-83; and Top 40 content on Disney Channel, 67-68
Sales, Nancy Jo, 122
Samuelson, Robert, 12
Schor, Juliet, 17
Scott, A. O., 13, 19, 26, 192n3
Sefton-Green, Julian, 16, 18
Seiter, Ellen, 47, 193n7 (chap. 3)
self-alienation, 92-93
self-objectification, 101
Sex and the City, 93, 94, 192n4
sexuality, and gendered border of childhood, 24-25
"Shake It Off" (Swift), 118-19, 132-33
Shrek, 19
Sicha, Choire, 126
Silverman, Linda Kreger, 146
"Since U Been Gone" (Clarkson), 36-37, 42-46, 50, 53
Slaughter, Anne-Marie, 90
Smith, Darron, 143
Smith, Mama Jan, 152, 153, 154, 155-56
Smith, Willow, 181
social media, 46, 160-61, 165, 174-75, 176. *See also* YouTube
Sonny with a Chance, 70, 106, 180
Sophia Grace and Rosie, 183-85
Sørenssen, Ingvild, 16
Sparks, Jordin, 170-72
Speak Now (Swift), 127-29
Spears, Britney, 68, 77, 81, 88, 107-8, 122
Stuart Little (White), 96
"Super Bass" (Minaj), 183-84, 193n5

Surf's Up Fruit Snacks commercials, 47
Sutton-Smith, Brian, 25
Sweeney, Anne, 66, 69
Swift, Taylor: adult career of, 108; and Bieber's description as prodigy, 144; Bieber's portrayal as child celebrity versus, 140; elements of childishness of, 137; entangled investments in innocence and whiteness, 118-34, 193n5; on promise rings, 194n3 (conc.); race made visible in transitional moments of, 107; radio airplay for, 54, 82, 190n9; tween solidarity in support of, 168-69, 171-72; and voicing of women's genres as children's genres, 135-36

talent, 144-47, 158
Teddy Grahams commercials, 47, 48-49
teenyboppers, 20-21, 32
television: children's media industry and expansion of, 7-8; commercials and children's participation in public culture, 46-52; Disney's reorientation toward, 58-70; and infantilization of public culture, 11, 13; integration of pop music into kids', 70-86. *See also* Disney Channel; Nickelodeon
That's So Raven, 23, 106, 180, 194n5 (conc.)
Thicke, Robin, 111
Tolentino, Jia, 176, 190n7
Tongson, Karen, 53
Top 40 pop: as defined by female audiences, 84; gendered critiques of authenticity of, 19-20; on kids' radio and TV, 65-68; Kidz Bop and, 44. *See also* pop music; tween pop / music industry
T-Pain, 124
Turner, Sarah, 23, 106
"tween moment," 2, 21, 28, 34, 149, 167-68, 172-73
tween pop / music industry: Disney's cultivation of, 84-85; explosion of, 167; in mainstream of popular music, 19-20; staged as social and political provocation within public culture, 168-72; after tween moment, 172-74. *See also* children's media and music; pop music; Top 40 pop
tween(s): and age compression, 15-18; in consumer culture and industries, 21-28, 47-48; as demographic label, 4-6; in-betweenness of, 95-97; intimate public of, 28-32; marginalization of, 46; media aimed at, 19; social and cultural markers of, 21-28; solidarity among, 168-72; versus teenager, 96; versus teenybopper, 20-21
twerking, 112-13, 118-19

Umstead, R. Thomas, 68
Uncle Tom's Cabin (Stowe), 136
Underhill, Paco, 35
Unterberger, Andrew, 117-18
Usher, 143, 158

Valdivia, Angharad, 22-23
Varenne, Hervé, 146
Victorious, 76
VMAs (2008), 169-72
VMAs (2009), 125-27, 134-35, 168-69, 171-72
VMAs (2013), 110-17, 139

wage labor, 6-7, 8-9
Walt Disney Records, 59-65, 70, 191n5
Warner, Michael, 31, 92
Washton, Ruth, 17, 189n12
"We Are Never Ever Getting Back Together" (Swift), 129-30
"We Can't Stop" (Cyrus), 111, 112
Weikle-Mills, Courtney, 10, 187n3, 187n5, 188n7
Weisbard, Eric, 84, 85, 190n9
West, Diana, 188n9
West, Kanye, 125-27, 134-35, 168-69, 171-72
"Whip My Hair" (Smith), 181
White, E. B., 96
whiteness: children's television's investment in, 179; and construction of tween innocence, 27-28, 106-8, 134-39, 180; and gendered childhood innocence, 142-44; innocence as unmarked, 138; investments

in, in *Hannah Montana*, 115-16, 139; Swift's entangled investments in innocence and, 118-34, 193n5
Whiteside, Damon, 77, 188n11
Williamon, Aaron, 146
Williamson, Marianne, 12
Willis, Ellen, 34
Wizards of Waverly Place, 106, 180
women: marginalization of children and, 46; and puerility, 25-26; as wage laborers, 8-9
women's genres, voiced as children's genres, 135-36

women's media, "having it all" in, 93-95, 192n4
Wordsworth, William, 137
working-class buffoon archetype, 102

Yankovic, "Weird Al," 193n5
"You Belong with Me" (Swift), 123, 125-27, 128
YouTube, 140, 141, 148, 150-51, 159-64, 165-66, 183, 194n1 (chap. 5)

Zelizer, Viviana, 6-7
Zendaya, 181

www.ingramcontent.com/pod-product-compliance
Lightning Source LLC
Chambersburg PA
CBHW031355230426
43670CB00006B/549